High School Equivalency Test Preparation

SCIENCE

Student Edition

PAXEN

PAXEN

Melbourne, Florida

www.paxen.com

Acknowledgments

For each of the selections and images listed below, grateful acknowledgment is made for permission to excerpt and/or reprint original or copyrighted material, as follows:

Text

36 From *The New York Times,* December 23, 2006 © The New York Times All rights reserved. Used by permission and protected by the Copyright Laws of the United States. The printing, copying, redistribution, or retransmission of the Material without express written permission is prohibited. **181** From *The New York Times,* August 24, 2006 © The New York Times All rights reserved. Used by permission and protected by the Copyright Laws of the United States. The printing, copying, redistribution, or retransmission of the Material without express written permission is prohibited. **182** Used with the permission of the International Astronomical Union at www.iau.org/public_press/themes/pluto. **183** Used with the permission of *Scientific American.*

Images

(cover) Daniel Aguilera/Getty Images.
v iStockphoto. **vi** iStockphoto. **x** Jamie Carroll/iStockphoto.

ISBN: 978-1-934350-60-7

1 2 3 4 5 6 7 8 9 10   1689   20 19 18 17 16 15 14   Printed in the U.S.A.

4500508872

High School Equivalency Test Preparation

Science Student Book

Table of Contents

About High School Equivalency Tests

Simply by turning to this page, you've made a decision that will change your life for the better. Each year, thousands of people just like you decide to pursue a high school equivalency certificate. Like you, they left school for one reason or another. And now, just like them, you've decided to continue your education by studying for and taking the high school equivalency tests.

However, these tests are no easy task. The tests, five in all, are spread across the subject areas of Language Arts/Reading, Language Arts/Writing, Mathematics, Science, and Social Studies. Preparation for the tests can involve extensive study and review. The payoff, however, is significant: more and better career options, higher earnings, and the sense of achievement that comes with a high school equivalency certificate. Employers and colleges and universities accept the certificate as they would a high school diploma. On average, certificate recipients earn $10,000 more per year than do employees without a high school diploma or an equivalency certificate.

High school equivalency tests are designed to mirror a high school curriculum. Although you will not need to know all of the information typically taught in high school, you will need to answer a variety of questions in specific subject areas. In Language Arts/Writing, you will need to write an essay.

In all cases, you will need to effectively read and follow directions, correctly interpret questions, and critically examine answer options. The table below details the five subject areas. Since different states have different requirements for the number of tests you may take in a single day, you will need to check with your local adult education center for requirements in your state or territory.

SUBJECT AREA TEST	CONTENT AREAS
Language Arts/Reading	Literary Texts Informational Texts
Language Arts/Writing (Editing)	Organization of Ideas Language Facility Writing Conventions
Language Arts/Writing (Essay)	Development and Organization of Ideas Language Facility Writing Conventions
Mathematics	Numbers and Operations on Numbers Data Analysis/Probability/Statistics Measurement/Geometry Algebraic Concepts
Science	Life Science Earth/Space Science Physical Science
Social Studies	History Civics/Government Economics Geography

Three of the subject-area tests—Language Arts/Reading, Science, and Social Studies—will require you to answer questions by interpreting passages. The Science and Social Studies tests also require you to interpret tables, charts, graphs, diagrams, timelines, political cartoons, and other visuals. In Language Arts/Reading, you also will need to answer questions based on workplace and consumer texts. The Mathematics Test will require you to use basic computation, analysis, and reasoning skills to solve a variety of word problems, many of them involving graphics. On most tests, questions will be multiple-choice with four answer options. An example follows:

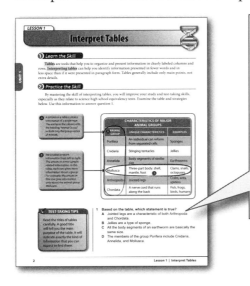

Based on the table, which statement is true?

A Jointed legs are a characteristic of both Arthropoda and Chordata.

B Jellies are a type of sponge.

C All the body segments of an earthworm are basically the same size.

D The members of the group Porifera include Cnidaria, Annelida, and Mollusca.

On the Mathematics Test, you will have four or five answer options for each multiple-choice question.

As the table on page iv indicates, the Language Arts/Writing Test contains two parts, one for editing and the other for essay. In the editing portion of Language Arts/Writing, you will be asked to identify and correct common errors in various passages and texts while also deciding

on the most effective organization of a text. In the essay portion, you will write an essay that analyzes texts or provides an explanation or an opinion on a single topic of general knowledge.

So now that you understand the task at hand—and the benefits of a high school equivalency certificate—you must prepare for the tests. In the pages that follow, you will find a recipe of sorts that, if followed, will help guide you toward successful completion of your certificate. So turn the page. The next chapter of your life begins right now.

About *High School Equivalency Test Preparation*

Along with choosing to pursue your high school equivalency certificate, you've made another smart decision by selecting this program as your main study and preparation tool. Simply by purchasing *High School Equivalency Test Preparation,* you've joined an elite club with thousands of members, all with a common goal—earning their high school equivalency certificates. In this case, membership most definitely has its privileges.

For more than 70 years, high school equivalency tests have offered a second chance to people who need it most. To date, more than 17 million Americans like you have studied for and earned high school equivalency certificates and, in so doing, jump-started their lives and careers. Benefits abound for certificate holders. Recent studies have shown that people with certificates earn more money, enjoy better health, and exhibit greater interest in and understanding of the world around them than do those without.

In addition, many certificate recipients plan to further their educations, which will provide them with more and better options. As if to underscore the point, the U.S. government's Division of Occupational Employment Projections estimates that through 2022, about 3.1 million new jobs will require a bachelor's degree for entry.

Your pathway to the future—a *brighter* future—begins now, on this page, with *High School Equivalency Test Preparation.* Unlike other programs, which take months to teach through a content-based approach, *High School Equivalency Test Preparation* gets to the heart of the tests—and quickly—by emphasizing *concepts.* At their core, the majority of the tests are reading-comprehension exams. Test-takers must be able to read and interpret excerpts, passages, and various visuals—tables, charts, graphs, timelines, and so on—and then answer questions based upon them.

High School Equivalency Test Preparation shows you the way. By emphasizing key reading and thinking concepts, *High School Equivalency Test Preparation* equips learners like you with the skills and strategies you'll need to correctly interpret and answer questions on the tests. Five-page lessons in each student book provide focused and efficient instruction, while callout boxes, sample exercises, and test-taking and other thinking strategies aid in understanding complex concepts.

Unlike other high school equivalency test preparation materials, which were designed *for* the classroom, these materials were designed *from* the classroom, using proven educational theory and cutting-edge classroom philosophy. For learners who have long had the deck stacked against them, the odds are finally in their favor. And yours.

HIGH SCHOOL EQUIVALENCY TESTS— FAST FACTS

- About 800,000 people take high school equivalency exams each year.
- Workers with a high school equivalency certificate earn an average of $10,000 a year more than people without a high school diploma or its equivalent.
- Over 3,000,000 students drop out of high school each year.
- Over 85% of Americans have a high school diploma or its equivalent.
- High school dropouts are not eligible for 90% of U.S. jobs.

About *High School Equivalency Test Preparation: Science*

For those who think science high school equivalency tests are a breeze, think again. The science test is a rigorous exam that will assess your ability to understand and interpret subject-specific text or graphics. You will answer questions organized across three main content areas: Life Science, Earth/Space Science, and Physical Science. Material in *High School Equivalency Test Preparation: Science* has been organized with these content areas in mind.

High School Equivalency Test Preparation: Science helps deconstruct the different elements of the test by helping learners like you build and develop key reading and thinking skills. A combination of targeted strategies, informational callouts and sample questions, tips and hints (Test-Taking Tips, Using Logic, and Making Assumptions), and ample assessment help to clearly focus study efforts in needed areas, all with an eye toward the end goal: success on high school equivalency tests.

As on the social studies test, the science test uses the thinking skills of *comprehension*, *application*, *analysis*, and *evaluation*. In addition, items on the science test assess understanding of science processes, including experimental design.

The **Learn the Skill** section defines and provides additional information about the skill to be studied.

Callouts provide strategies and information that you may use to understand and interpret various passages or graphics.

Test-Taking Tips offer broad or specific support for answering multiple-choice questions.

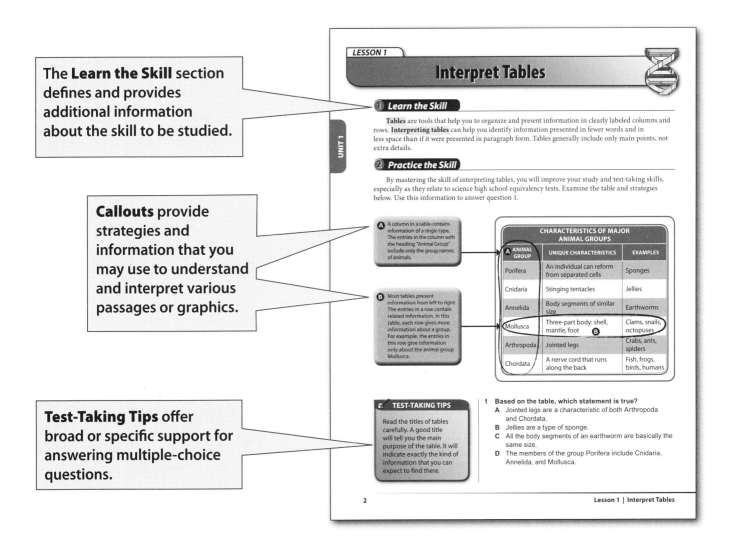

LESSON 1

Interpret Tables

UNIT 1

① Learn the Skill

Tables are tools that help you to organize and present information in clearly labeled columns and rows. **Interpreting tables** can help you identify information presented in fewer words and in less space than if it were presented in paragraph form. Tables generally include only main points, not extra details.

② Practice the Skill

By mastering the skill of interpreting tables, you will improve your study and test-taking skills, especially as they relate to science high school equivalency tests. Examine the table and strategies below. Use this information to answer question 1.

Ⓐ A column in a table contains information of a single type. The entries in the column with the heading "Animal Group" include only the group names of animals.

Ⓑ Most tables present information from left to right. The entries in a row contain related information. In this table, each row gives more information about a group. For example, the entries in this row give information only about the animal group Mollusca.

CHARACTERISTICS OF MAJOR ANIMAL GROUPS

Ⓐ ANIMAL GROUP	UNIQUE CHARACTERISTICS	EXAMPLES
Porifera	An individual can reform from separated cells	Sponges
Cnidaria	Stinging tentacles	Jellies
Annelida	Body segments of similar size	Earthworms
Mollusca	Three-part body: shell, mantle, foot Ⓑ	Clams, snails, octopuses
Arthropoda	Jointed legs	Crabs, ants, spiders
Chordata	A nerve cord that runs along the back	Fish, frogs, birds, humans

TEST-TAKING TIPS

Read the titles of tables carefully. A good title will tell you the main purpose of the table. It will indicate exactly the kind of information that you can expect to find there.

1 Based on the table, which statement is true?
   A Jointed legs are a characteristic of both Arthropoda and Chordata.
   B Jellies are a type of sponge.
   C All the body segments of an earthworm are basically the same size.
   D The members of the group Porifera include Cnidaria, Annelida, and Mollusca.

2

Lesson 1 | Interpret Tables

Test-Taking Tips

High school equivalency tests include questions across the five subject-area exams of Language Arts/Reading, Language Arts/Writing, Mathematics, Science, and Social Studies. In each test, you will need to apply some amount of subject-area knowledge. However, because all of the questions are multiple-choice items largely based on text or visuals (such as tables, charts, or graphs), the emphasis in *High School Equivalency Test Preparation* is on helping learners like you build and develop core reading and thinking skills. As part of the overall strategy, various test-taking tips are included below and throughout the book to help you improve your performance on the tests. For example:

◆ *Always thoroughly read the directions so that you know exactly what to do.* For example, on many tests direction lines explicitly state which questions are to be answered using information in a passage, visual, map, or chart. Pay attention to these directions in order to make sure you are correctly matching up these test elements.

◆ *Read each question carefully so that you fully understand what it is asking.* Some questions, for example, may present more information than you need to correctly answer them.

◆ *Manage your time with each question.* Because the tests are timed exams, you'll want to spend enough time with each question, but not *too* much time. You can save time by first reading each question and its answer options before reading the passage or examining the graphic. Once you understand what the question is asking, review the passage or visual for the appropriate information.

◆ *Note any unfamiliar words in questions.* First, attempt to reread the question by omitting the unfamiliar word(s). Next, try to substitute another word in its place.

◆ *Answer all questions, regardless of whether you know the answer or are guessing at it.* There is no benefit in leaving questions unanswered. Keep in mind the time that you have for each test and manage it accordingly. For time purposes, you may decide to initially skip one or more questions. However, note them with a light mark beside the question and try to return to and answer it before the end of the test.

◆ *Narrow answer options by rereading each question and the text or graphic that goes with it.* Although all answer choices are *possible*, keep in mind that only one of them is *correct*. You may be able to eliminate one or two answers immediately; others may take more time and involve the use of either logic or assumptions. In some cases, you may need to make your best guess between two options. If so, keep in mind that test makers often avoid answer patterns; that is, if you know the previous answer is **B** and are unsure of the answer to the next question but have narrowed it to options **B** and **D**, you may want to choose **D**.

◆ *Read all answer choices.* Even though the first or second answer choice may appear to be correct, be sure to thoroughly read all answer choices. Then go with your instinct when answering questions. For example, if your first instinct is to mark **A** in response to a question, it's best to stick with that answer unless you later determine that answer to be incorrect. Usually, the first answer you choose is the correct one.

◆ *Correctly complete your answer sheet by marking one lettered space on the answer sheet beside the number that corresponds to it.* Mark only one answer for each item; multiple answers will be scored as incorrect. If time permits, double-check your answer sheet after completing the test to ensure that you have made as many marks—no more, no less—as there are questions.

Study Skills

You've already made two very smart decisions in trying to earn your high school equivalency certificate and in purchasing *High School Equivalency Test Preparation* to help you to do so. The following are additional strategies to help you optimize your success on the tests.

3 weeks out ...

◆ Set a study schedule. Choose times in which you are most alert, and places, such as a library, that provide the best study environment.

◆ Thoroughly review all material in *High School Equivalency Test Preparation*.

◆ Make sure that you have the necessary tools for the job: sharpened pencils, pens, paper, and, for mathematics, a calculator.

◆ Keep notebooks for each of the subject areas that you are studying. Folders with pockets are useful for storing loose papers.

◆ When taking notes, restate thoughts or ideas in your own words rather than copying them directly from a book. You can phrase these notes as complete sentences, as questions (with answers), or as fragments, provided you understand them.

1 week out ...

◆ Take the pretests, noting any troublesome subject areas. Focus your remaining study around those subject areas.

◆ Prepare the items you will need for the test day: admission ticket (if necessary), acceptable form of identification, some sharpened No. 2 pencils (with erasers), a watch, eyeglasses (if necessary), a sweater or jacket, and a high-protein snack to eat during breaks.

◆ Map out the course to the test center, and visit it a day or two before your scheduled exam. If you drive, find a place to park at the center.

◆ Get a good night's sleep the night before the tests. Studies have shown that learners with sufficient rest perform better in testing situations.

The day of ...

◆ Eat a hearty breakfast high in protein. As with the rest of your body, your brain needs ample energy to perform well.

◆ Arrive 30 minutes early to the testing center. This will allow sufficient time in the event of a change to a different testing classroom.

◆ Pack a sizeable lunch, especially if you plan to be at the testing center most of the day.

◆ Focus and relax. You've come this far, spending weeks preparing and studying for the tests. It's your time to shine.

Before You Begin: Using Logic and Making Assumptions

At several hours in length, the high school equivalency tests are to testing what marathons are to running. Just like marathons, though, you may train for success on the tests. As you know, the exams test your ability to interpret and answer questions about various passages and visual elements. Your ability to answer such questions involves the development and use of core reading and thinking skills. Chief among these are the skills of reasoning, logic, and assumptions.

Reasoning involves the ability to explain and describe ideas. **Logic** is the science of correct reasoning. Together, reasoning and logic guide our ability to make and understand assumptions. An **assumption** is an idea that we know to be true and which we use to understand the world around us.

You use logic and make assumptions every day, sometimes without even knowing that you're doing so. For example, you might go to bed one night knowing that your car outside is dry; you might awaken the next morning to discover that your car is wet. In that example, it would be *reasonable* for you to *assume* that your car is wet because it rained overnight. Even though you did not see it rain, it is the most *logical* explanation for the change in the car's appearance.

When thinking logically about items on the tests, you identify the consequences, or answers, from text or visuals. Next, you determine whether the text or visuals logically and correctly support the consequences. If so, they are considered valid. If not, they are considered invalid. For example, read the following passages and determine whether each is valid or invalid:

Passage A

High school equivalency tests assess a person's reading comprehension skills. Ellen enjoys reading. Therefore, Ellen will do well on the tests.

Passage B

High school equivalency tests cover material in five different subject areas. Aaron has geared his studies toward the tests, and he has done well on practice tests. Therefore, Aaron may do well on the actual tests.

Each of the above situations has a consequence: *Ellen will* or *Aaron may* do well on the tests. By using reasoning and logic, you can make an assumption about which consequence is valid. In the example above, it is *un*reasonable to assume that Ellen *will* do well on the tests simply because she likes to read. However, it *is* reasonable to assume that Aaron *may* do well on the tests because he has studied for the tests and has done well on the practice tests in each of the five subject areas.

Use the same basic principles of reasoning, logic, and assumptions to determine which answer option logically and correctly supports a question on the science test. You may find occasions in which you have narrowed the field of possible correct answers to two, from which you must make a best, educated guess. In such cases, weigh both options and determine the one that, reasonably, makes the most sense.

Directions: Following are a series of questions to use in practicing the skills of reasoning, logic, and assumptions. The first one has been done for you.

CHARACTERISTICS OF MAJOR ANIMAL GROUPS		
ANIMAL GROUP	**UNIQUE CHARACTERISTICS**	**EXAMPLES**
Porifera	An individual can reform from separated cells	Sponges
Cnidaria	Stinging tentacles	Jellies
Annelida	Body segments of similar size	Earthworms
Mollusca	Three-part body: shell, mantle, foot	Clams, snails, octopuses
Arthropoda	Jointed legs	Crabs, ants, spiders
Chordata	A nerve cord that runs along the back	Fish, frogs, birds, humans

1 Which conclusion can you come to based only on the information in the table?

A Because scorpions have jointed legs, they belong to the group Porifera.

B A dog has four feet, so it belongs to group Mollusca.

C Animals that can reform from single cells are the most sophisticated forms of life.

D Sea anemones have stinging tentacles, so they belong to group Cnidaria.

A You can eliminate option **A**, simply by thoroughly reading the table.

B In some cases, answer options use more general statements. You must review the information, consider it logically, make comparisons, and construct an assumption from it. In the case of option **C**, even though the table does not directly prove or disprove the answer choice, you must use the information here and your own knowledge to assume that other forms of life are more sophisticated.

C Some answer options require you to use logic and reasoning, such as **B** and **D**. You must determine whether these statements are logical.

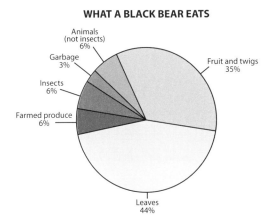

WHAT A BLACK BEAR EATS

Animals (not insects) 6%
Garbage 3%
Insects 6%
Farmed produce 6%
Fruit and twigs 35%
Leaves 44%

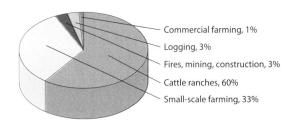

CAUSES OF DEFORESTATION IN THE AMAZON

Commercial farming, 1%
Logging, 3%
Fires, mining, construction, 3%
Cattle ranches, 60%
Small-scale farming, 33%

2 Which of the following statements is best supported by the data above?

A Black bears often eat mice, chickens, and rabbits.

B Berries are a black bear's favorite food.

C Black bears might have a hard time finding food in the winter.

D No other animals eat black bears.

3 What is the leading cause of deforestation in the Amazon?

A cattle ranches

B small-scale farming

C commercial farming

D logging

Answers: **2.** C; **3.** A

Unit 1

Unit Overview

Whenever you eat lunch, go to the gym, or even take a nap, you are using information from the life sciences to guide and enrich your well-being. On a much larger scale, life science enables us to understand ourselves and our environment.

Similarly, life science plays an important part in science high school equivalency tests, comprising about 50 percent of all questions. As with other areas of the science test, life science questions will test your ability to interpret text or graphics and to answer questions about them by using thinking skills such as comprehension, application, analysis, and evaluation. In Unit 1, the introduction of core reading skills and graphics, combined with essential science concepts, will help you prepare for high school equivalency tests in science.

Table of Contents

Key Life Science Terms

abiotic factors: nonliving physical features of the environment

adaptation: any characteristic of an organism that makes it better able to survive in its environment

antibiotics: drugs that kill bacteria, as well as fungi and some parasites; they do not work against viruses

biomes: large geographic areas that have similar climates and ecosystems

biotic factors: living organisms in the environment

carrying capacity: the largest number of individuals that an environment can support and maintain over time

cell: basic unit of all forms of life

chromosome: threadlike strands of DNA and protein in a cell nucleus that carry the code for the cell characteristics of an organism

commensalism: a symbiotic relationship that benefits one partner, but not the other

community: all the populations of different species that live in the same place at the same time and interact with each other

consumer: an organism that relies on other organisms for its energy and food supply

DNA: *deoxyribonucleic acid*; a chemical in the nuclei of cells that codes and stores genetic information

dominant: the form of a genetic trait that appears to mask another form of the same trait

ecosystem: a community interacting with the nonliving parts of its environment

evolution: changes that occur over time in the hereditary features of a species of organisms

food chain: a model used to show how energy from food passes from one organism to another

food web: a model used to describe a series of overlapping food chains

gene: the segment of DNA of a chromosome that directs the making of a specific protein, thus controlling traits that are passed to offspring

invasive species: plants and animals that have migrated to places where they are not native

life cycle: all the stages an organism goes through from the beginning of one generation to the next

metamorphosis: the change in body form during the life cycle—for example: egg, larva, pupa, adult

mutualism: a symbiotic relationship that benefits both partners

nitrogen cycle: the continuous movement of nitrogen from the atmosphere, to plants, and back to the atmosphere again

nonvascular plant: a plant lacking vascular tissue; a plant that absorbs water directly through its cell membranes

nucleus: the structure that contains a cell's genetic material and controls the cell's activities

nutrient: a substance in food that produces energy and materials for life activities

parasitism: a symbiotic relationship that benefits the parasite but harms the parasite's partner

population: organisms of one species that live in the same place at the same time and that can produce offspring

predator: an organism that feeds on another organism

prey: an organism that is eaten by another organism

producer: an organism that can capture energy from sunlight or chemicals and use it to produce food from inorganic compounds

recessive: the form of a genetic trait that seems to disappear in a population but can reappear depending on how the alleles combine

symbiosis: a close relationship between two organisms from different species that live closely together

theory: a description of nature, based on many observations; subject to change when evidence changes

trophic level: a step in a food chain or food web

vaccine: a solution made from damaged virus or bacteria particles or from killed or weakened viruses or bacteria; can prevent, but not cure, many viral and bacterial diseases

vascular plant: a plant containing vascular tissue made up of tubelike cells that transport food and water throughout the plant

watershed: the area drained by a river or river system

wetland: ecosystem in which water either covers the soil or is present at or near the surface of the soil for at least part of the year

Interpret Tables

① Learn the Skill

Tables are tools that help you to organize and present information in clearly labeled columns and rows. **Interpreting tables** can help you identify information presented in fewer words and in less space than if it were presented in paragraph form. Tables generally include only main points, not extra details.

② Practice the Skill

By mastering the skill of interpreting tables, you will improve your study and test-taking skills, especially as they relate to science high school equivalency tests. Examine the table and strategies below. Use this information to answer question 1.

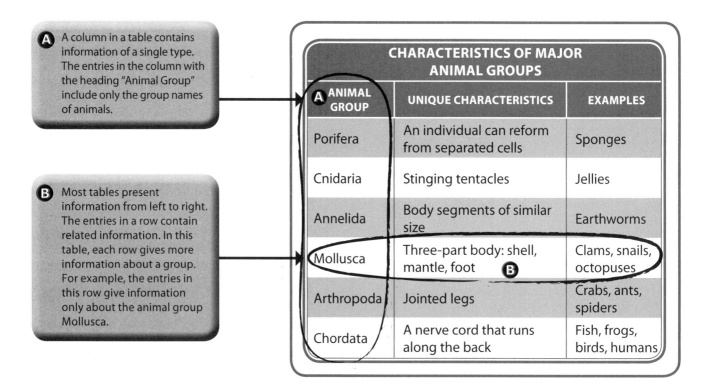

A A column in a table contains information of a single type. The entries in the column with the heading "Animal Group" include only the group names of animals.

B Most tables present information from left to right. The entries in a row contain related information. In this table, each row gives more information about a group. For example, the entries in this row give information only about the animal group Mollusca.

CHARACTERISTICS OF MAJOR ANIMAL GROUPS

A ANIMAL GROUP	UNIQUE CHARACTERISTICS	EXAMPLES
Porifera	An individual can reform from separated cells	Sponges
Cnidaria	Stinging tentacles	Jellies
Annelida	Body segments of similar size	Earthworms
Mollusca	Three-part body: shell, mantle, foot B	Clams, snails, octopuses
Arthropoda	Jointed legs	Crabs, ants, spiders
Chordata	A nerve cord that runs along the back	Fish, frogs, birds, humans

✓ TEST-TAKING TIPS

Read the titles of tables carefully. A good title will tell you the main purpose of the table. It will indicate exactly the kind of information that you can expect to find there.

1 Based on the table, which statement is true? ✓

   A Jointed legs are a characteristic of both Arthropoda and Chordata.

   B Jellies are a type of sponge.

   C All the body segments of an earthworm are basically the same size.

   D The members of the group Porifera include Cnidaria, Annelida, and Mollusca.

③ Apply the Skill

Directions: Questions 2 through 6 are based on the information below.

Chordates are animals with nerve cords that run along their backs. Most chordates have backbones that protect the nerve cords and provide the body with support. The main groups of chordates are fish, amphibians, reptiles, birds, and mammals.

Fish generally spend their entire lives in water. Amphibians generally begin life in water but spend their adult lives on land. Most reptiles spend their entire lives on land. Some groups of birds and mammals live in water, but the majority live on land.

GROUP	BODY COVER	BREATHING STRUCTURES	REPRODUCTION
Fish	Scales	Gills	Some lay eggs; some give birth to live young
Amphibians	Thin skin	Gills early in life; lungs as adults	Lay eggs with no shells
Reptiles	Scaly skin	Lungs	Lay eggs with leathery shells
Birds	Feathers	Lungs	Lay eggs with brittle shells
Mammals	Hair or fur	Lungs	Give birth to live young (most)

2 Which of the following is the best title for the table?
A Examples of Chordates
B Animals with Backbones
C Characteristics of Animals
Ⓓ Characteristics of Chordate Groups

3 Which of the following would be an appropriate heading for a fifth column of the table?
A Non-Chordate Groups
B Fur Color
C Kind of Eggs They Lay
Ⓓ Types of Limbs

4 Which animal groups are most alike?
A amphibians and fish
B birds and fish
C mammals and birds
Ⓓ reptiles and birds

5 Which statement supports the information in the paragraph and the table?
A Chordates are the only animals that lay eggs.
B Fish are the only chordates that live in water.
C Hair is a defining characteristic of chordates.
Ⓓ The majority of chordates rely on lungs at some point in their life cycles.

6 Which statement describes the best way to change the table to include all the information in the paragraph?
A Add a new row to the bottom of the table entitled "Animals That Live in Water."
B Add more detailed information to the column "Breathing Structures."
Ⓒ Add a column with the heading "Main Habitat."
Ⓓ Replace the last column of the table with a column called "Structures for Movement."

Directions: Questions 7 through 11 are based on the information below.

One of the activities of the International Union for Conservation of Nature (IUCN) is to help find solutions to the problem of decreasing biodiversity. The IUCN maintains the Red List, a document that identifies the status of thousands of species around the world. The table below gives only a tiny portion of the information found in the IUCN Red List.

VERTEBRATE GROUP	NUMBER OF THREATENED SPECIES IN 2006	NUMBER OF THREATENED SPECIES IN 2013
Mammals	1,093	1,140
Birds	1,206	1,313
Reptiles	341	847
Amphibians	1,770	1,948
Fishes	800	2,110

Source: Data from 2013 IUCN Red List

7 Which of the following statements can be derived from the table?
  A Earth has more amphibians than fishes.
  B Between 2006 and 2013, 107 new species of birds were discovered.
  C There were many more species of fishes in 2013 than in 2006.
  D Mammals had the fewest additional species listed as threatened from 2006 to 2013.

8 Which of the following would be the best title for the table?
  A Characteristics of Vertebrate Groups
  B New Animal Species Discovered in 2013
  C Numbers of Threatened Vertebrate Species by Group
  D Increases in Vertebrate Population Sizes from 2006 to 2013

9 Bill examined the data in the table. Based on all the data, which of the following is the most valid conclusion Bill can make?
  A The number of threatened species in all groups increased between 2006 and 2013.
  B Among the groups listed, number of threatened fish species shows the sharpest decline between 2006 and 2013.
  C The number of threatened species in all groups decreased between 2006 and 2013.
  D Overall, there was little change in the number of threatened species between 2006 and 2013.

10 Based on the data in the table, what would be a reasonable assumption to make about threatened species in 2015?
  A The number of threatened species in all groups will decrease.
  B The number of threatened species in all groups will continue to increase.
  C The number of threatened fish species will increase, but the number of threatened amphibian species will decrease.
  D The number of threatened species in all groups will stay the same.

11 For which study would information from this table be most useful?
  A a study comparing the number of species in each animal group
  B a study comparing the characteristics of fish and reptiles
  C a study comparing how the number of threatened species changes over time
  D a study comparing how quickly a given species will go extinct

Directions: Questions 12 and 13 are based on the information below.

Scientists think that reptiles share a common amphibian ancestor. This ancestor species probably lived more than 300 million years ago. Adaptations that arose in ancestors of reptiles, such as scaly skin and leathery egg shells, allowed reptiles to move into drier environments in which amphibians could not survive.

GROUP	CHARACTERISTICS
Amphibians	Moist skin
	Toes lack claws
	Eggs lack shells
	Young use gills, but adults use lungs (most)
	Young go through a metamorphosis
Reptiles	Scaly skin
	Toes have claws
	Eggs have leathery shells
	Use lungs their entire lives
	Young do not go through a metamorphosis

12 The main purpose of the table is to
A identify general characteristics of animals.
B prove that amphibians and reptiles are closely related.
C show ways in which amphibians and reptiles differ.
D describe the habitats of reptiles and amphibians.

13 Which of the following ideas is supported by the paragraph and table?
A Reptiles are not as well adapted to the environment as amphibians are.
B Reptiles and amphibians have adaptations that allow them to survive in different environments.
C Reptiles evolved much earlier than amphibians did.
D Reptiles and amphibians have no characteristics in common.

Directions: Questions 14 and 15 are based on the information below.

The chromosome number for a species is the total number of chromosomes in each body cell of an individual of that species.

SPECIES	ANIMAL GROUP	CHROMOSOME NUMBER
Human	Mammal	46
King crab	Arthropod	208
Mosquito	Arthropod	6
Housefly	Arthropod	12

14 For which study would information from this table be most useful?
A a study comparing major arthropod groups
B a study examining differences between the chromosome numbers of mammals
C a study examining characteristics of arthropods
D a study comparing arthropod chromosome numbers

15 After compiling the data in the table, a researcher decided to eliminate the "Human" row. Which of the following explanations most likely reflects the researchers's thinking?
A Humans do not have chromosomes.
B Humans are mammals; the other organisms listed are arthropods.
C Humans have only two legs; all the other organisms listed in the table have six or more legs.
D The number of chromosomes in human body cells cannot be determined.

Directions: Questions 16 through 19 are based on the information below.

Primates are one major group of mammals. Perhaps the most distinctive trait of primates involves the presence of the opposable thumb, which allows them to grasp and manipulate objects with strength and dexterity. Scientists further divide primates into groups by their posture and by the nature of the digits on their hands and feet. The three main groups of primates are prosimians (pre-monkeys), monkeys, and apes (which include humans). Primates vary in size. For example, a mouse lemur weighs only a few ounces, while a gorilla can weigh more than 400 pounds. Primates eat mostly vegetation, because that food source is more readily available than others.

CHARACTERISTICS OF PRIMATE GROUPS

GROUP	EXAMPLES	TRAITS
Prosimians	Lemurs Lorises Tarsiers	Long snouts Long tails Five digits, each hand and foot Hair

Monkeys (New World)	Marmosets
	Tamarins
	Squirrel monkeys
	Capuchin monkeys
	Howler monkeys
	Spider monkeys
		Shorter noses
		Prehensile
		  (grasping) tails
		Five digits, each
		  hand and foot
		  (except spider
		  monkey)
		Hair

Monkeys (Old World)	Baboons
	Macaques
	Colobuses
	Langurs
	Proboscis monkeys
		Shorter noses
		No prehensile
		  (grasping) tails
		Five digits, each
		  hand and foot
		Hair

Apes	Gibbons Orangutans Gorillas Chimpanzees Bonobos Humans	Short noses No tails Five digits, each hand and foot Hair

16 Which statement describes the main difference between New World monkeys and Old World monkeys?
   A New World monkeys have shorter noses than Old World monkeys.
   B New World monkeys have prehensile tails, whereas Old World monkeys do not.
   C New World monkeys have five digits on each hand and foot, whereas Old World monkeys do not.
   D New World monkeys have hair, whereas Old World monkeys do not.

17 One piece of information is presented in the paragraph but not in the table. Which statement presents this information?
   A Lemurs and lorises are prosimians.
   B Primates can be grouped by the nature of the digits on their hands and feet.
   C Primates have opposable thumbs.
   D Gorillas, orangutans, and chimpanzees are part of the ape family.

18 Based on information in the paragraph and the table, which of these traits do all primates share?
   A similar size and posture
   B prehensile tails
   C long snouts
   D hair

19 Where in the table would be the best place to add information about the diets of primate groups?
   A the top row
   B the bottom row
   C the middle column
   D a new column

LESSON 2

Interpret Charts and Graphs

① Learn the Skill

Charts and graphs are visual ways to show data. **Interpreting charts and graphs** can help you answer questions about data. Unlike tables, which are generally used to show data as text, graphs and charts visually depict parts of a whole or changes over time.

② Practice the Skill

By mastering the skill of interpreting charts and graphs, you will improve your study and test-taking skills, especially as they relate to science high school equivalency tests. Study the paragraph and circle graph below. Use this information to answer question 1.

A Circle graphs show parts of a whole. The sum of the percentages of the sections in a circle graph is always 100%. Sometimes, the sections are color-coded and correspond to a legend or key. In this example, the sections are individually labeled.

B The relative sizes of the sections of a circle graph provide visual clues about the relationships among the sections. In this graph, the largest sections represent the foods that black bears eat most often. The smallest sections represent the foods that black bears eat least often.

Black bears live in many parts of the United States. Many people think that black bears eat mainly meat and berries. However, their diets can vary greatly. The circle graph shows the different kinds of foods a typical black bear may eat.

WHAT A BLACK BEAR EATS

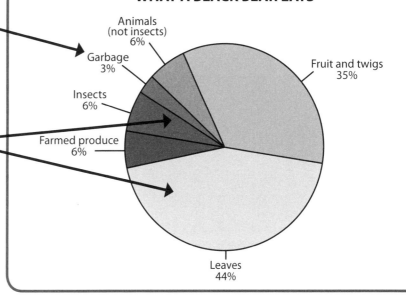

☑ TEST-TAKING TIPS

When interpreting a graph, always read the title and labels on the graph carefully. The title and labels give important information about the data in the graph. If the graph has a legend, or key, study it carefully, too.

1 Based on the information, which of the following statements about a black bear's diet is true?

  A It contains more meat than plants.
  B It is mainly insects and animals.
  C It consists of equal amounts of garbage and insects.
  D It consists mainly of fruit and other plants.

Directions: Questions 2 through 5 are based on the information below.

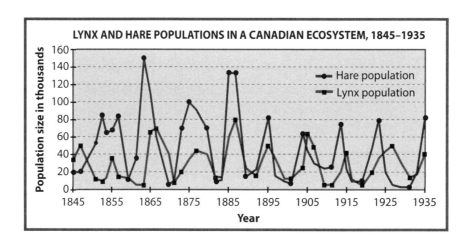

LYNX AND HARE POPULATIONS IN A CANADIAN ECOSYSTEM, 1845–1935

Lynxes are large cats. They eat many smaller animals, including hares. In most cases, there are many more hares than lynxes in an ecosystem. The graph shows the number of hares and the number of lynxes in a Canadian ecosystem from 1845 to 1935.

2 Based on the information, about how many hares lived in this ecosystem in 1875?
A about 40,000
B about 100,000
C about 40
D about 100

3 Which generalization is supported by the data?
A Hare populations always exceed lynx populations.
B Hare populations increase at the same time as lynx populations.
C Lynx populations increase after hare populations increase.
D Hare populations decrease as lynx populations decrease.

4 Based on the information in the graph, what was a likely research question for scientists collecting and organizing this data?
A Are lynx and hare populations interrelated in a Canadian ecosystem?
B Do hares live in a Canadian ecosystem?
C Are Canadian ecosystems different from those found in the United States?
D Are lynxes carnivores?

5 Which statement best summarizes the hare and lynx populations in 1935?
A The two populations are the same size.
B The hare population is larger than the lynx population.
C The lynx population is larger than the hare population.
D The lynx population is decreasing.

Directions: Questions 6 through 8 are based on the information below.

St. Matthew Island is a small island—about 125 square miles—located in the Bering Sea. In 1944, the U.S. Coast Guard stocked St. Matthew Island with 29 reindeer. The island had a lot of vegetation, but no large predators. Experts estimated that the island could support about 15 reindeer per square mile. So they estimated that the island's carrying capacity (the maximum reindeer population the island could support for a long period of time) was about 2,000 reindeer. The graph shows the population of reindeer on St. Matthew Island from 1944 to 1966.

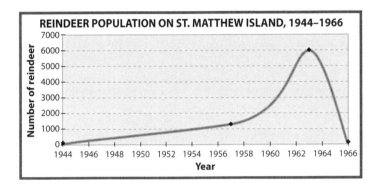

REINDEER POPULATION ON ST. MATTHEW ISLAND, 1944–1966

6 **During which time period did the reindeer population change the most?**
   A between 1950 and 1955
   B between 1955 and 1960
   C between 1960 and 1963
   D between 1963 and 1966

7 **The data support the generalization that reindeer population on St. Matthew Island**
   A increased and then decreased suddenly.
   B did not change from 1944 to 1955.
   C decreased and then increased slowly.
   D grew more between 1944 and 1950 than between 1955 and 1960.

8 **Which of the following is a conclusion that can be drawn from the information in the paragraph and the graph?**
   A The reindeer population on St. Matthew Island was largest during the 1950s.
   B Fewer reindeer lived on St. Matthew Island in 1960 than in 1950.
   C Predators kept the reindeer population under control in the 1940s and 1950s.
   D In the early 1960s, the reindeer population on St. Matthew Island was greater than the island's carrying capacity.

Directions: Questions 9 and 10 are based on the circle graph below.

CAUSES OF DEFORESTATION IN THE AMAZON

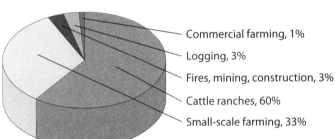

Commercial farming, 1%
Logging, 3%
Fires, mining, construction, 3%
Cattle ranches, 60%
Small-scale farming, 33%

9 **What is the leading cause of deforestation in the Amazon?**
   A cattle ranches
   B small-scale farming
   C commercial farming
   D logging

10 **The data support which of the following generalizations?**
   A Small-scale farming, logging, and commercial farming have combined to cause more than half of the deforestation in the Amazon.
   B Logging is a bigger cause of deforestation in the Amazon than fires, mining, and construction.
   C Small-scale farming and commercial farming have caused the same amount of deforestation in the Amazon.
   D Cattle ranches account for more deforestation in the Amazon than all of the other causes combined.

Directions: Questions 11 and 12 are based on the two graphs below.

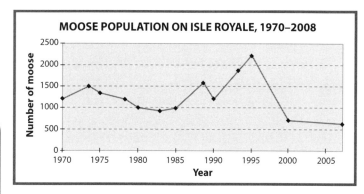

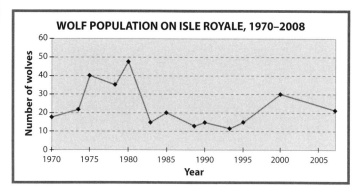

Directions: Questions 13 and 14 are based on the information below.

Farmers try to get rid of weeds because weeds can prevent crops from growing well. The weeds and the crops compete for nutrients in the soil. However, crops also can keep weeds from growing if the crops are planted correctly. The graph shows how the number of wheat plants in a field affects the weeds that grow in that field.

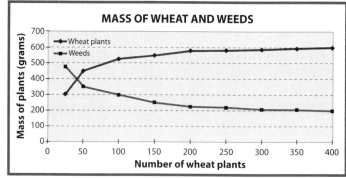

11 Which statement below most accurately reflects the change in the wolf population between 1980 and 1983?
   A The wolf population gradually decreased.
   B The wolf population rapidly decreased.
   C The wolf population rapidly increased.
   D The wolf population gradually increased.

12 When were moose populations on Isle Royale the largest?
   A during even-numbered years
   B in the mid-1970s
   C when wolf populations were large
   D when wolf populations were small

13 Which of the following statements is supported by the information in the paragraph and the graph?
   A To produce the greatest mass of wheat, a farmer should plant about 100 seeds.
   B Weeds and wheat plants are always present in equal masses.
   C The greatest mass of wheat plants grows when few seeds are planted.
   D As the number of wheat plants increases, the mass of weeds decreases.

14 What would you expect to happen if the number of wheat plants suddenly decreased?
   A The number of weeds would remain the same.
   B A farmer would begin planting another crop, such as corn.
   C The amount of weeds would increase.
   D The amount of weeds would decrease.

Directions: Questions 15 through 17 are based on the graph below.

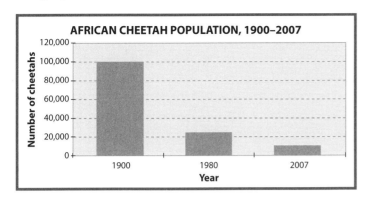

15 About how many cheetahs lived in Africa in 1980?
A about 100,000
B about 50,000
C about 25,000
D about 12,000

16 Which of the following statements best summarizes the information in the graph?
A The cheetah population in Africa has decreased significantly since 1900.
B There are more cheetahs living in Africa today than there were in 1980.
C The African cheetah population has begun to recover from a sharp decrease in 1980.
D There were fewer cheetahs in Africa in 1900 than there are today.

17 Which of the following would best show the reasons for the change in the cheetah population?
A a line graph
B a bar graph
C a circle graph
D a line graph and bar graph

Directions: Questions 18 through 20 are based on the information below.

Bacteria are tiny, single-celled organisms. They reproduce by dividing in half. Scientists often grow bacteria in small glass dishes that contain a nutrient broth. The bacteria population continues to grow as long as there are enough nutrients left in the broth. When the nutrients run out, the bacteria starve and begin to die. The graph shows how the population of bacteria in a sample of broth changed over time.

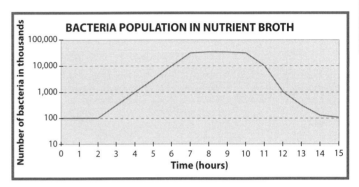

18 When was the bacteria population largest?
A at about 1 hour
B at about 3 hours
C at about 5 hours
D at about 8 hours

19 Based on the information in the paragraph and graph, when did the food for the bacteria most likely run out?
A after about 1 hour
B after about 4 hours
C after about 7 hours
D after about 12 hours

20 What must happen for the bacteria population to again grow at a high level?
A decrease the amount of broth
B place the bacteria in a larger container
C increase the number of bacteria
D add more nutrients to the broth

Interpret Diagrams

① Learn the Skill

Diagrams show the relationships between ideas, objects, or events in a visual way. Diagrams also can be used to show the order in which events occur. When you **interpret diagrams**, you see how objects or events relate to one another.

② Practice the Skill

By mastering the skill of interpreting diagrams, you will improve your study and test-taking skills, especially as they relate to science high school equivalency tests. Examine the diagram and strategy below. Use this information to answer question 1.

> An ecosystem includes all of the living things in an area, along with their nonliving environment. The living things in an ecosystem interact with one another and with the nonliving parts of the same ecosystem. A food chain shows the feeding relationships among the living things in an ecosystem.
>
> **GRASSLAND FOOD CHAIN**
>
> Sparrow
>
> Grasshopper
>
> Grass

A When studying a diagram, pay attention to the way that the parts are arranged. The parts of this food chain are arranged in a line, with arrows pointing from one to the next. Arrangements like this one are often used to indicate that things occur in a certain order.

☑ TEST-TAKING TIPS

Read and compare the answer choices to the diagram. Think about what the diagram would have to look like in order for each answer choice to be true. Then compare that possible diagram with the actual diagram to determine the correct answer.

1 **Based on the information, which of the following is a true statement about feeding relationships in a grassland ecosystem?**
   A   sparrows eat grass
   B   grass eats grasshoppers
   C   grasshoppers eat sparrows
   D   sparrows eat grasshoppers

Directions: Questions 2 through 4 are based on the Venn diagram below.

DIETS OF TWO DESERT ANIMALS

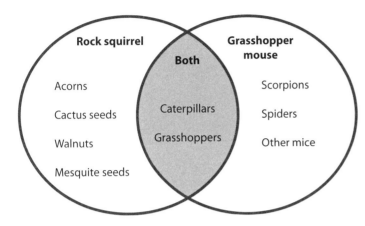

Directions: Questions 5 and 6 are based on the information below.

A food web is a more complete way to show the feeding relationships in an ecosystem. Unlike a food chain, which shows only one set of feeding relationships, a food web shows many different feeding relationships. Food webs show how many different living things are related.

GRASSLAND FOOD WEB

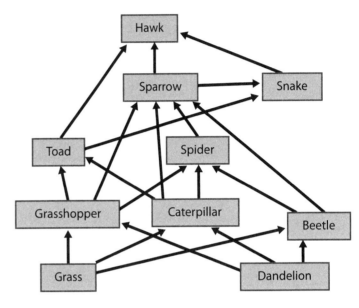

2 **Which of these living things do both rock squirrels and grasshopper mice eat?**
A cactus seeds
B scorpions
C spiders
D caterpillars

3 **What can you learn from this diagram?**
A the foods eaten by some animals in a desert
B which animals eat rock squirrels
C the names of all the animals that live in the desert
D which foods are most plentiful in the desert

4 **Which of the following statements is supported by the diagram?**
A Scorpions are prey for both rock squirrels and caterpillar mice.
B Grasshopper mice eat other types of mice.
C Only rock squirrels eat grasshoppers.
D Acorns are higher in a food chain than walnuts.

5 **Based on the information in the diagram, what do sparrows eat?**
A grass
B plants and hawks
C insects
D hawks and snakes

6 **Which of the following statements is supported by the diagram?**
A Grass is food for many living things in a grassland.
B Each kind of animal eats only one other kind of animal or plant.
C Hawks eat both plants and animals.
D Food chains show more complex relationships than food webs.

UNIT 1

Directions: Questions 7 and 8 are based on the information below.

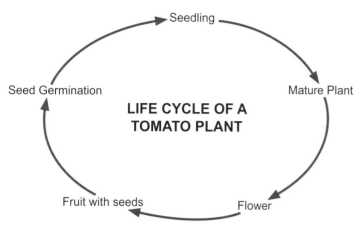

LIFE CYCLE OF A TOMATO PLANT

Seedling — Mature Plant — Flower — Fruit with seeds — Seed Germination

A life cycle is all of the stages an organism goes through from the beginning of one generation to the next. These stages vary, depending on the organism. Flowering plants grow from seeds. A seed forms when an egg, which forms at the base of the flower, is fertilized by the male sex cells, called pollen. A pollinated flower grows into a fruit that surrounds the seeds. Each seed holds an embryo. When conditions are right, the seeds germinate and the life cycle begins again.

7   What can you learn from this life cycle diagram?
  A the number of seeds in a tomato plant's fruit
  B the number of flowers that form on the average tomato plant
  C the stages in the life cycle of a tomato plant
  D the varieties of tomato plants that grow in the Midwest

8   What stage in a tomato plant's life cycle occurs after flowers are pollinated?
  A germination
  B fruit formation
  C growth of seedling
  D egg production

Directions: Questions 9 and 10 are based on the information below.

Animals also experience life cycles. Most mammals experience simple life cycles. For example, a dog's life cycle includes fertilization of an egg, the birth of a puppy, growth, and then maturity. The adult dog can the reproduce and begin the cycle again.

Other animals have life cycle stages that are less familiar. Amphibians and most insects go through changes known as metamorphosis. The stages of a butterfly's life cycle include fertilized egg, larva (caterpillar), chrysalis (cocoon or pupa), and adult. The stages in a frog's life cycle are shown below.

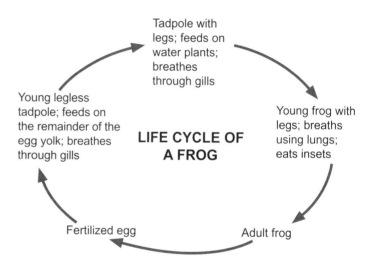

LIFE CYCLE OF A FROG

Tadpole with legs; feeds on water plants; breathes through gills — Young frog with legs; breaths using lungs; eats insets — Adult frog — Fertilized egg — Young legless tadpole; feeds on the remainder of the egg yolk; breathes through gills

9   How are the life cycles of frogs, flowering plants, dogs, and butterflies the same?
  A They all include pollination.
  B They all include tadpoles.
  C They all include fertilized eggs.
  D They all live part of their life in water, and part on land.

10 Starting with a fertilized egg, what are the second stages in the life cycles of a frog and butterfly?
  A emerging adult and legless tadpole
  B tadpole and chrysalis
  C adult frog and butterfly
  D tadpole and larva

Directions: Questions 11 through 14 are based on the information below.

In the 1970s, scientists traveled to the ocean floor to study the rocks and minerals there. They did not expect to find any life that deep in the ocean. Surprisingly, they discovered an entire ecosystem deep below the ocean's surface. Tiny bacteria form the base of the ecosystem. These bacteria use chemicals from within Earth to make food. The diagram below shows some of the relationships between the living things in that ecosystem.

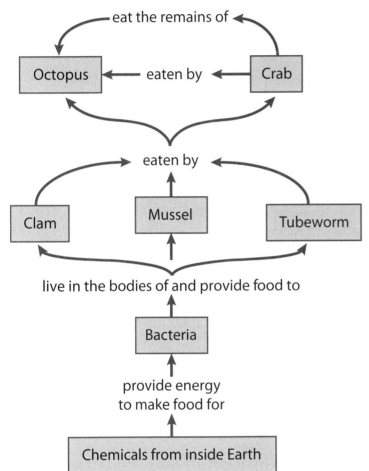

11 **Based on the information in the paragraph and diagram, what is the ultimate source of energy for all of the living things in the ecosystem?**
  A octopuses
  B light from scientists' diving ships
  C bacteria
  D chemicals from within Earth

12 **Based on the information in the diagram, how do tubeworms get food?**
  A by eating crabs, clams, and mussels
  B from bacteria that live inside their tissues
  C by filtering ocean water
  D from the remains of other living things

13 **A type of large fish also lives in this ecosystem. It eats tubeworms, clams, mussels, and crabs. Its position in the food web is most similar to which of the following animals?**
  A crabs
  B clams
  C mussels
  D octopuses

14 **Based on the information in the diagram, which of the following animals eats the remains of other animals?**
  A clams
  B mussels
  C tubeworms
  D crabs

Directions: Questions 15 through 18 are based on the information below.

Scientists often group the living things in an ecosystem based on how they get food. These different groups are also called trophic levels. Living things that make their own food from nonliving materials, such as carbon dioxide and water, are called producers. Plants are producers in almost all land-based ecosystems. Producers make up the first trophic level. Living things that get food by eating producers are called primary consumers. Primary consumers make up the second trophic level. Living things that eat primary consumers are called secondary consumers. Living things that eat secondary consumers are called tertiary consumers. The diagram below shows examples of these groupings for a desert ecosystem.

Tertiary consumers

Hawks   Foxes

Fourth trophic level

Secondary consumers
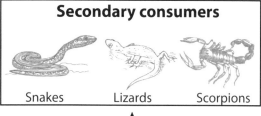
Snakes   Lizards   Scorpions

Third trophic level

Primary consumers
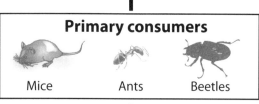
Mice   Ants   Beetles

Second trophic level

Producers

Cactuses   Shrubs   Flowers

First trophic level

15 Based on the information in the paragraph and the diagram, which of the following living things are tertiary consumers in a desert ecosystem?
A   foxes and hawks
B   snakes and lizards
C   ants and scorpions
D   hawks and cactuses

16 Based on the information in the paragraph and diagram, in which trophic level do hawks belong?
A   first trophic level
B   second trophic level
C   third trophic level
D   fourth trophic level

17 Based on the information in the paragraph and diagram, which of the following statements about this ecosystem is true?
A   Scorpions, lizards, and snakes are secondary consumers.
B   Cactuses, shrubs, and flowers are primary consumers.
C   Mice and ants are in the first trophic level.
D   Hawks and foxes are in the third trophic level.

18 Which of the following statements can be derived from the paragraph and the diagram?
A   Hawks eat only producers.
B   Plants get food from small animals.
C   Scorpions eat other animals.
D   Ants eat both plants and animals.

Interpret Illustrations

① Learn the Skill

Illustrations are often used to show many parts that make up a whole. For example, if an engineer is assembling an aircraft engine, he or she will look at several illustrations to see how the parts fit together. When you **interpret illustrations**, you look at the labels and figures within an illustration to understand how the parts of a whole fit together.

② Practice the Skill

By mastering the skill of interpreting illustrations, you will improve your study and test-taking skills, especially as they relate to science high school equivalency tests. Examine the illustration and read the strategies below. Use this information to answer question 1.

A This is a cutaway diagram of a bacterium. In cutaway diagrams, part of an object or organism is cut away so that you can see what is inside. In this case, you can see the tiny structures inside the bacterium cell.

B Lines point from structures inside the cell to labels that explain the structures. To interpret the illustration, begin by reading one label, such as "cell wall." Then look at the shape of this structure in the illustration. To help you remember the label, think of ways that the name "cell wall" helps describe this structure in the cell.

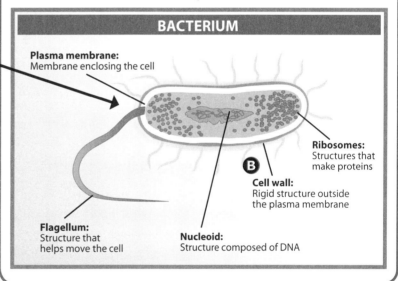

Bacteria are one-celled organisms. *Bacteria* is the plural of the word. *Bacterium* is singular.

BACTERIUM

Plasma membrane: Membrane enclosing the cell

Ribosomes: Structures that make proteins

Cell wall: Rigid structure outside the plasma membrane

Flagellum: Structure that helps move the cell

Nucleoid: Structure composed of DNA

☑ **TEST-TAKING TIPS**

Test questions may ask you to identify part of an illustration or how parts of an illustration relate to one another. Look at the labels to determine these answers.

1 **Which structure inside the bacterium cell makes proteins?**
   A cell wall
   B flagellum
   C nucleoid
   D ribosome

Directions: Questions 2 through 4 are based on the information below.

Animal cells all contain the same basic structures for making energy, digesting food, and reproducing. Mitochondria make energy, lysosomes digest food, and the beginning stages of reproduction occur in the nucleus. Some early light microscopes allowed scientists to see cells. But the electron microscope, invented in the 1950s, finally allowed scientists to see the internal structures of cells.

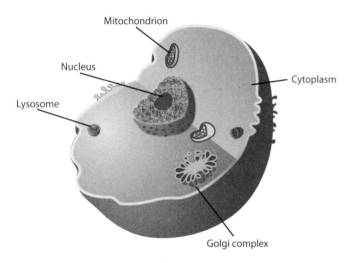

2 Where are lysosomes located?
A outside the cell
B in the nucleus
C in the Golgi complex
D in the cytoplasm

3 What would happen to this cell if something destroyed its nucleus?
A It would not be able to reproduce properly.
B It would have no energy for its processes.
C It would store more energy.
D It would become a plant cell.

4 Before the 1950s, scientists did not know
A the shape of cells.
B the size of cells.
C that living things are made of cells.
D the location of ribosomes or lysosomes in cells.

Directions: Questions 5 through 7 are based on the information below.

Your body's many types of cells are organized into different systems, such as the circulatory system and the nervous system. Your nervous system is composed of about 100 billion nerve cells, or neurons. Neurons carry signals through your body that allow you to move, sense things, think, and learn. The illustration below shows a neuron.

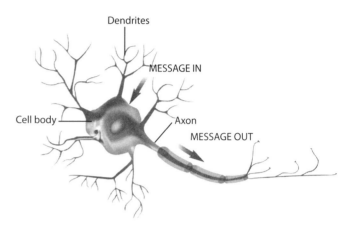

5 Based on the information and illustration, axons
A are in the cell's nucleus.
B receive information.
C send information.
D are part of the cell body.

6 What function do dendrites serve?
A They control growth.
B They provide protection.
C They produce energy.
D They receive information.

7 Which of the following statements best summarizes the structure of the neuron?
A Dendrites branch far from the cell body, axons branch close to the cell body.
B The cell body is located at the branching end of the dendrites.
C The neuron has many dendrites, but only one axon.
D The neuron has many axons, but only one dendrite.

Directions: Questions 8 and 9 are based on the information below.

A cell's nucleus controls the activities of the cell. The nucleus also contains the cell's genetic material—the DNA that makes each cell the same as its parents.

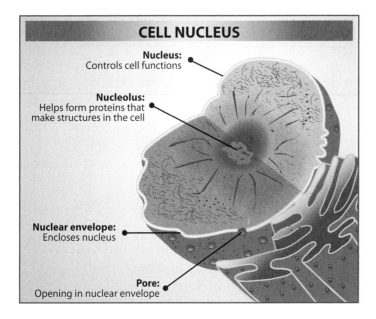

CELL NUCLEUS

Nucleus:
Controls cell functions

Nucleolus:
Helps form proteins that make structures in the cell

Nuclear envelope:
Encloses nucleus

Pore:
Opening in nuclear envelope

8 **What is the most likely function of the pore?**
A   to enclose the genetic material
B   to contain the nuclear envelope
C   to let materials in and out of the nucleus
D   to form proteins

9 **What information can an illustration such as this provide?**
A   the structures found in the nucleus
B   the size of a cell nucleus
C   the location of the nucleus in relation to other parts of a cell
D   the way the nucleus helps a cell reproduce

Directions: Questions 10 through 12 are based on the information below.

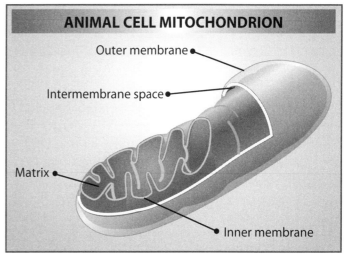

ANIMAL CELL MITOCHONDRION

Outer membrane

Intermembrane space

Matrix

Inner membrane

Mitochondria release energy stored in foods such as sugar.

10 **The illustration above shows the mitochondrion of an animal cell. The purpose of this illustration is to show**
A   the comparative size of different mitochondria.
B   the parts of a whole mitochondrion.
C   how a mitochondrion changes over time.
D   the process of making energy in the outer membrane.

11 **Based on the illustration, which is true of the mitochondrion?**
A   It is the largest structure inside a cell.
B   It has two membranes.
C   It is part of the nucleolus.
D   It can move easily in and out of blood cells.

12 **Along with an illustration, which of the following also would best show the process of energy production in a mitochondrion?**
A   a circle graph
B   a bar graph
C   a line graph
D   a diagram

Directions: Questions 13 through 15 are based on the information below.

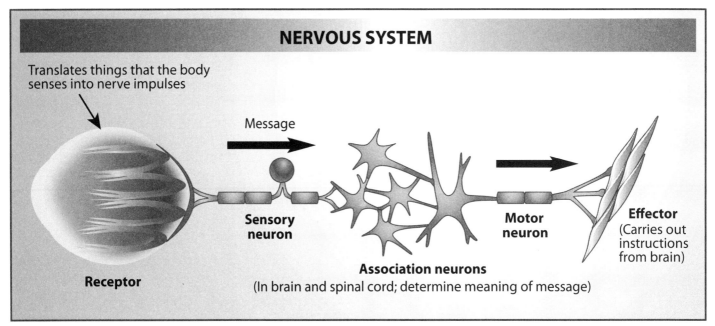

NERVOUS SYSTEM

Translates things that the body senses into nerve impulses

Message

Receptor

Sensory neuron

Association neurons
(In brain and spinal cord; determine meaning of message)

Motor neuron

Effector
(Carries out instructions from brain)

There are many types of nerve cells, or neurons, in the nervous system. They all have different functions. When you see a delicious-looking piece of chocolate cake, receptor neurons in your eyes receive the image of the cake. They send the image of the chocolate cake along sensory neurons to the association neurons in your brain and spinal cord. In a fraction of a second, your brain decides what the information means and what your body should do about it. Your brain decides that the correct response is to reach for the cake. As a result, your brain sends this signal through your motor neurons to the effector neurons in your hand. The muscles in your hand move, and you grasp the plate that holds the cake.

13 **What function do the association neurons perform?**
   A   carry out instructions from brain
   B   recognize and translate initial sensations
   C   send signals back to the receptor
   D   determine the meaning of the message

14 **Which best describes the relationship between the text and the illustration?**
   A   The text describes a change over time, and the illustration shows that change using arrows.
   B   The text explains a part of a process, and the illustration shows the whole process.
   C   The text describes nerve cells only by using words, and the illustration shows nerve cells only by using images.
   D   The text describes a process, and the illustration shows the same process.

15 **Music is playing at a party, and you want to dance. If you did not have motor neurons, you would not be able to**
   A   move your feet to dance.
   B   hear the music.
   C   decide that you want to dance.
   D   recognize the sound as music.

Directions: Questions 16 through 19 are based on the information below.

Plants use energy from sunlight to make their own food through the process of photosynthesis. During photosynthesis, a plant turns a gas from the air (carbon dioxide, or CO_2) and water from the soil into glucose. Glucose is a simple sugar stored in the plant's tissues. Another gas (oxygen, or O_2) is released during the process. Photosynthesis occurs in tiny structures called chloroplasts. Chloroplasts contain chlorophyll, a material that absorbs sunlight and is necessary for changing light energy into the chemical energy the plant uses for life processes.

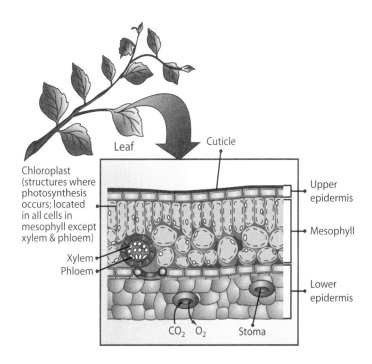

16 What happens at a stoma?
   A Carbon dioxide enters the chloroplasts.
   B Gases are exchanged.
   C Photosynthesis occurs.
   D Oxygen is stored as starch.

17 Where does photosynthesis happen?
   A in the xylem and phloem
   B in the cuticle
   C in the mesophyll
   D in the stoma

18 Janelle wants to observe the gases released from a leaf during photosynthesis. Which of the following procedures should she follow?
   A Submerge the leaf in a beaker of water, and place the beaker in bright sunlight so that she can see bubbles of gas released from the leaf.
   B Examine the leaf with a hand lens so that she can see the gases released from the leaf.
   C Stand in bright sunlight while holding the leaf close to her face so that she can feel the gases released from the leaf.
   D Peel back the leaf's cuticle so that she can more easily see the gases as they are released from the leaf.

19 What would be the best title for this illustration?
   A How Photosynthesis Works
   B Leaf Structure
   C Understanding Chloroplasts
   D How Leaf Cells Function

Directions: Question 20 is based on the illustration below.

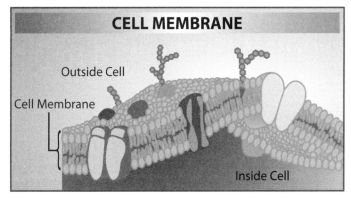

20 What does this illustration show?
   A the contents of a typical cell
   B the barrier that surrounds a cell
   C the nucleus of a cell
   D the way that cells reproduce

Main Idea and Details

① Learn the Skill

The **main idea** is the most important point of a passage, story, table, or graphic. **Supporting details** provide additional information about the main idea. Such details include facts, statistics, explanations, and descriptions. A main idea may be clearly stated or it may be implied. If it is implied, you must use supporting details to determine the main idea.

② Practice the Skill

By mastering the skill of determining the main idea and supporting details, you will improve your study and test-taking skills, especially as they relate to science high school equivalency tests. Read the paragraph and strategies below. Use this information to answer question 1.

A The main idea usually is found near the beginning of a paragraph, but it is not always the first sentence. To tell the main idea and supporting details apart, examine each sentence or idea and ask yourself whether the rest of the passage gives more information about this particular point. If so, this is most likely the main idea. The title of a passage or a visual also can provide clues to the main idea.

B Supporting details generally follow the main idea. They give more information about the main idea. Here, the supporting details are examples of ways that many kinds of bacteria are helpful.

> **BACTERIA: NOT ALWAYS THE BAD GUY**
>
> We often think of bacteria in negative terms. Not all bacteria, however, cause disease. Soil may contain millions of bacteria. Many of these bacteria are decomposers, which break down and recycle nutrients in the bodies of dead plants and animals. Many helpful bacteria live inside the human body, where they aid digestion and produce vitamins the body needs. Bacteria play a role in the production of many popular foods such as cheeses. Scientists have even discovered how to put bacteria to work to clean up contaminated water and soil.

✓ TEST-TAKING TIPS

Read all the answer choices for a question carefully. Just because an answer choice is a true statement does not mean it is the correct answer to the question.

1 Which of the following is another detail that supports the main idea of this passage?
A Bacteria are single-celled organisms.
B Bacteria are used in the production of some medications.
C Bacteria are too small to see without a microscope.
D Bacteria can be killed with antibiotics.

Directions: Question 2 is based on the table below.

GROUPS OF BACTERIA BY SHAPE	
BACTERIA	**SHAPE**
Cocci	Sphere
Bacilli	Rod
Spirilla	Short, right corkscrew

2 **Which main idea do the details of this table support?**

  A Bacteria have many uses.

  B Rod-shaped bacteria are bacilli.

  C Bacteria can be grouped by shape.

  D Cocci are the most common bacteria shape.

Directions: Question 3 is based on the information below.

The bacteria streptococci contain a variety of species, each with its particular effect. For example, *Streptococcus pyogenes,* or Group A streptococcus bacteria, can cause diseases from tonsilitis to scarlet fever. Other forms of streptococci can result in tooth decay, sinus infections, meningitis, or pneumonia. However, some forms of streptococci aid in the production of butter, yogurt, and certain cheeses.

3 **Which detail supports the main idea that streptococci have both different species and effects?**

  A *Streptococcus pyogenes* can cause diseases ranging from tonsilitis to scarlet fever.

  B Streptococci can cause sinus infections.

  C Tooth decay can be a result of a streptococcus bacterium.

  D Some forms of streptococci can cause disease, while others help produce foods.

Directions: Questions 4 and 5 are based on the information below.

Plants need nitrogen to survive and grow. However, most of the nitrogen in the environment is in a form (gaseous nitrogen) plants cannot use. Gaseous nitrogen can become a form of nitrogen that plants *can* use through a process called nitrogen fixation. In this process, certain types of bacteria in the soil "fix" nitrogen, or turn it into a different form. Some of these bacteria live in small nodules on the roots of some plants. Legumes, which include soybeans and peanuts, live with these nitrogen-fixing bacteria on their roots. Legumes are a major source of usable nitrogen in the soil.

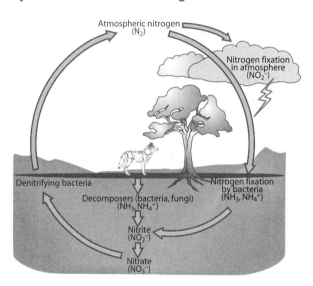

4 **Which statement identifies the main idea of the passage?**

  A Legumes include soybeans and peanuts.

  B Plants need nitrogen to survive.

  C Bacteria help provide nitrogen to plants.

  D Bacteria live in the root systems of legumes.

5 **Together, the details in the passage and diagram support which main idea?**

  A Nitrogen changes form as it is cycled through the environment.

  B Plants cannot survive without nitrogen-fixing bacteria.

  C Most nitrogen in the environment is in a form that plants cannot use.

  D Gaseous nitrogen is produced constantly in the atmosphere.

UNIT 1

Directions: Questions 6 and 7 are based on the table below.

BACTERIUM	DISEASE IT CAUSES
Salmonella typhi	Typhoid
Helicobacter pylori	Stomach ulcers
Streptococcus mutans	Tooth decay
Borrelia burgdorferi	Lyme disease

6 The title of a table usually tells you the main idea of the table. Which of the following is the best title for this table?

   A Types of Common Bacteria
   B Common Bacteria-Borne Diseases
   C Microorganisms Cause Disease
   D List of Common Diseases

7 What details does this table provide that directly support the main idea?

   A diseases each microorganism can cause
   B cures for various bacterial diseases
   C examples of the ways that different types of microorganisms can cause disease
   D the names of all the various microorganisms

Directions: Questions 8 and 9 are based on the following paragraph and diagram.

    During the 1300s, a plague called the Black Death killed one-third of the population of Europe. The plague, caused by the bacterium *Yersinia pestis,* began in the East. Rats that carried bacteria-infected fleas stowed away aboard ships, spreading the plague to distant ports. Neither the fleas nor the rats were affected by the bacterium, but when a flea bit a human, the result was deadly. The bacterium then could transfer from human to human. In some European towns, nearly every single person died, often within a day of infection.

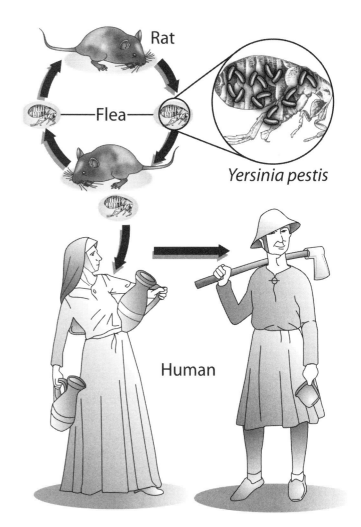

Rats and fleas could carry the bacterium without infection, but most infected humans died.

8 What is the main idea of the paragraph and diagram?

   A the effects of seafaring on early European villages
   B the ecological relationship between fleas and rats
   C the method of transmission of the Black Death in Europe
   D the fluctuation of rat populations in the 1300s

9 Which of the following is a detail that supports the main idea?

   A Bacteria-infected fleas spread the disease.
   B Flea-infected rats traveled on ships.
   C The plague killed one-third of Europe's population.
   D The bacterium is called *Yersinia pestis.*

Directions: Questions 10 through 12 are based on the information below.

Water treatment plants purify sewage. They remove debris and harmful substances so that the water can be released safely back into the environment. Primary treatment first filters debris using screens and other devices. Chemicals such as chlorine kill harmful bacteria. The remaining smelly sludge then moves to secondary treatment. In one process, liquid sludge is sprayed over beds of crushed stone. Other bacteria and protozoa break down harmful materials in the sludge, and some of this sludge can be used as fertilizer. The clean water trickles off, free of the bacteria and sludge from secondary treatment. The water purification plant then releases the purified water to nearby lakes and streams.

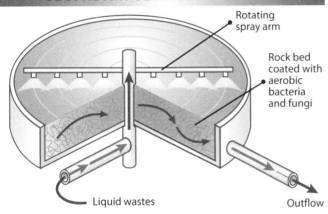

SECONDARY SEWAGE TREATMENT

Rotating spray arm

Rock bed coated with aerobic bacteria and fungi

Liquid wastes

Outflow

10 **Which statement best summarizes the main idea of this passage?**
  A Water purification plants need bacteria, protozoa, and crushed stone to function.
  B Although chlorine kills harmful bacteria, it helps save thousands of lives a year.
  C Purification of sludge provides fertilizer and fresh water to many Americans.
  D Water treatment includes primary treatment and secondary treatment to remove all harmful materials and bacteria.

11 **One detail this illustration of secondary sewage treatment shows is that bacteria**
  A live among the crushed rocks in the tank.
  B are sprayed onto the crushed rocks.
  C are in the air above the secondary treatment tank.
  D are part of a chemical that is sprayed over the tank.

12 **Which detail supports the main idea of the paragraph?**
  A The fresh water is free of bacteria.
  B The sludge is very smelly.
  C Some sludge can be used as fertilizer.
  D Secondary treatment always follows primary treatment.

Directions: Question 13 is based on the information below.

Microorganisms can cause diseases, but they also can help cure them. Researchers use some microorganisms to develop antibiotics, or drugs that kill harmful microorganisms. The first widely used antibiotic was penicillin. In 1928, scientist Alexander Fleming observed the microorganism *Penicillium notatum* growing in patches among bacterial colonies. It seemed to be killing the bacteria. In the 1940s, scientists identified the substance killing the bacteria as penicillin. Doctors now use penicillin and various antibiotics to fight bacterial infections. For example, the bacterium *Streptomyces griseus* yielded streptomycin, which treats tuberculosis. Many other antibiotics treat bacterial and fungal infections.

13 **Which statement best summarizes the main idea of this passage?**
  A Penicillin is a useful drug that treats many bacterial infections.
  B Streptomycin is more useful than penicillin.
  C Researchers began the development of antibiotics in the 1940s.
  D Microorganisms have helped produce many useful antibiotics.

Directions: Questions 14 and 15 are based on the information below.

Antibiotics are still very useful tools in fighting disease, but the more they are used, the less useful they become. Many bacteria that cause infections have become resistant to one or more antibiotics. In other words, the antibiotics no longer kill them. As a result, doctors find it increasingly difficult to find antibiotics that will successfully treat some bacterial infections.

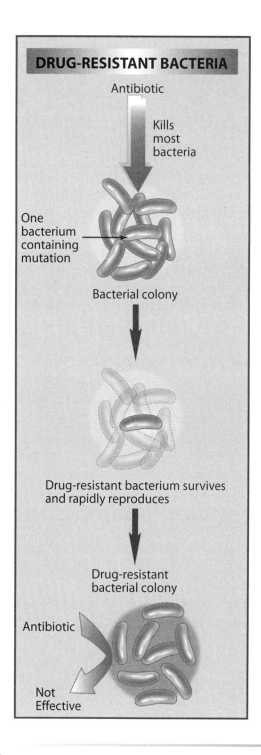

DRUG-RESISTANT BACTERIA

Antibiotic

Kills most bacteria

One bacterium containing mutation

Bacterial colony

Drug-resistant bacterium survives and rapidly reproduces

Drug-resistant bacterial colony

Antibiotic

Not Effective

14 Which statement best summarizes the main idea of this passage?
  A Antibiotics are the most valuable tools we have in fighting disease.
  B Most bacteria will become resistant to at least one antibiotic.
  C When a bacterium becomes resistant, it can infect other bacteria.
  D Overuse of antibiotics can make them less effective.

15 Which detail from the diagram supports the main idea of the passage?
  A The antibiotic will kill most of the bacteria.
  B Bacteria live in colonies.
  C A resistant bacterium can reproduce quickly.
  D Antibiotics are effective at killing bacteria.

Directions: Question 16 is based on the paragraph below.

Fresh air on a sunny day might look clean, but it's really full of microorganisms. The fact that these tiny invisible organisms are in the air isn't a surprise; it's the fact that there are so many! Scientists took air samples in two Texas cities over several weeks. They discovered 1,800 different kinds of bacteria in the air—both harmless bacteria and those that cause disease. The information could be useful in several ways. First, knowing the bacteria that are naturally in the air can help scientists determine when unnatural levels of harmful bacteria might mean a biological attack. Second, the information can show patterns of how climate change affects different amounts of bacteria in the air. Scientists will repeat the sampling over the next few years. This will help them determine how climate change might alter bacteria populations.

16 Which statement best summarizes the main idea of this passage?
  A Most bacteria in the air are not harmful.
  B Scientists are surprised to discover that the air contains bacteria.
  C Bacteria in the air indicate that climate change is underway.
  D Scientists find the air more crowded with bacteria than previously thought.

Lesson 5 | Main Idea and Details

Summarize

① Learn the Skill

When you **summarize** a passage or other feature such as a table, graph, or diagram, you briefly identify and describe its main points. A summary generally does not contain the exact words of the original passage, and it is almost always shorter.

② Practice the Skill

By mastering the skill of summarizing, you will improve your study and test-taking skills, especially as they relate to science high school equivalency tests. Read the paragraph and strategies below. Use this information to answer question 1.

A Summarizing involves separating the most relevant information (main idea and supporting details) from less relevant information (extra details). Here, the relative sizes of duckweed and sequoias is an interesting detail, but it does not belong in a summary. The data in the first sentence is also an extra, trivial detail.

B This paragraph does not state the main idea in a single sentence. Instead, there are two major points that form the main idea. A summary of this passage should identify these major points, but it should word them in a different, simpler way.

> There are at least 300,000 different types of plants on Earth. <u>Plants can be found in most types of environments</u>—from cold polar areas to the heat of the tropics. Most plants live on land, but plants also grow in water. Tiny water plants, such as duckweed, have leaves just a few millimeters wide. At the other end of the size scale, giant sequoias can reach a height of more than 90 meters. Regardless of their size or the environment in which they live, <u>plants play a critical role in the survival of many other organisms.</u> Plants form the base of most food chains on Earth, capturing sunlight and using the energy to produce food in a process called photosynthesis. Oxygen, which plants give off during photosynthesis, is essential for animal life on Earth.

USING LOGIC

Summarizing requires using and recognizing synonyms or the different ways that an idea can be stated. Here, the passage does not state specifically that other organisms rely on plants, but all the details of the second half of the passage describe ways organisms depend, or rely, on plants.

1 **Which sentence best summarizes the passage above?**
   A Plants are a diverse group of organisms on which other organisms rely.
   B Plants produce oxygen that animals need.
   C Plants range in size from smaller than an inch to hundreds of feet tall.
   D Plants produce food for themselves and other forms of life during photosynthesis.

Directions: Questions 2 through 4 are based on the information below.

Plants can be grouped according to whether they have vascular tissue. Vascular tissue is a system of tubes running through a plant's body. One kind of vascular tissue, called xylem, carries water and minerals from the soil up through the stems and leaves. Xylem is made up of stacks of dead cells. The other kind of vascular tissue, called phloem, moves sugars produced in the leaves throughout the plant's body. Phloem is made up of living cells.

Nonvascular plants lack vascular tissues. Without such tissues to move materials throughout the plant's body, nonvascular plants must be small. This small size allows water and sugars to move through the plant cell by cell. Most nonvascular plants grow close to the ground in wet areas. Many of the cells of a nonvascular plant can take water and other nutrients directly from the environment.

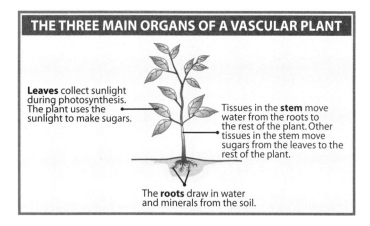

THE THREE MAIN ORGANS OF A VASCULAR PLANT

Leaves collect sunlight during photosynthesis. The plant uses the sunlight to make sugars.

Tissues in the **stem** move water from the roots to the rest of the plant. Other tissues in the stem move sugars from the leaves to the rest of the plant.

The **roots** draw in water and minerals from the soil.

2 **Which of the following summarizes the most important idea in the diagram?**
A The organs of a vascular plant have specific roles.
B Vascular plants have organs, whereas nonvascular plants do not.
C Phloem is found in roots, stems, and leaves.
D Vascular plants depend on roots to collect water.

3 **Which statement best summarizes the information in the passage?**
A Xylem carries water throughout a plant's body, and phloem carries sugars.
B Nonvascular plants grow in wet areas.
C Vascular plants are larger than nonvascular plants.
D Vascular plants and nonvascular plants move materials through their bodies in different ways.

4 **Which of the following points should be included in a summary of the passage and diagram?**
A Vascular plants have three basic organs: roots, stems, and leaves.
B The organs of vascular plants work together to move materials through the plant's body.
C Roots, stems, and leaves contain both xylem and phloem.
D Both vascular plans and nonvascular plants carry out photosynthesis to produce sugars.

Directions: Question 5 is based on the information below.

Cactuses are flowering plants that generally live in and have adapted to arid, or dry, regions. There are about 1,500 species of cactuses, the largest number of which grow in Mexico. The leaves of cactuses are much reduced, compared with the leaves of other plants. In the absence of significant leaves, the thick, woody stems of the cactuses carry out photosynthesis. The root systems of cactuses are thick and shallow, allowing for broad absorption of surface moisture.

5 **Which title best summarizes the passage?**
A Cactuses: Mexico's Underrated Flowers
B The Unique Features of Cactuses
C Life in Arid Regions
D Root Systems and Water

Directions: Questions 6 and 7 are based on the information below.

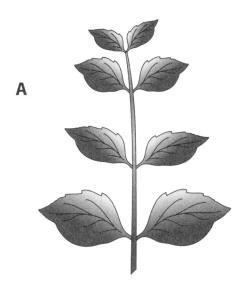

A

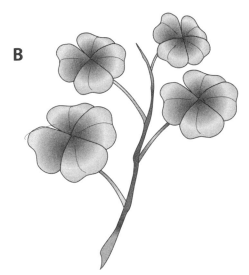

B

The shape and location of a plant's leaves can give important information about the identity of the plant. Most plant leaves grow in one of two different arrangements. In some plants, the leaves grow on opposite sides of the stem and line up with one another, as shown in Part A of the diagram. In other plants, the leaves grow on opposite sides of the stem but do not line up. This type of arrangement is shown in Part B of the diagram.

6   Which of the following statements best summarizes the information in the paragraph and diagram?
   A   All plants have leaves.
   B   A clover plant's leaves grow on opposite sides of its stem.
   C   Leaves generally grow in pairs.
   D   Most plant leaves grow in one of two different ways.

7   Which of the following parts of the diagram should you examine most closely as you attempt to summarize the information in the paragraph?
   A   the shapes of the leaves on each plant
   B   the examples of each type of plant
   C   where the leaves on each plant are located
   D   the sizes of the various leaves

Directions: Question 8 is based on the information below.

Mosses are common plants, but they are often overlooked because they are so small. In fact, mosses are different from many other plants. For one thing, mosses are nonvascular plants. In other words, a moss plant does not contain a system of tubes for transporting water and other nutrients. Instead, the moss's cells absorb water and nutrients directly from the environment. Another way mosses are different from most plants is that mosses are seedless plants. Instead of using seeds to reproduce, mosses produce tiny spores.

8   Which of the following titles best summarizes the paragraph?
   A   Transport of Nutrients in Plant Tissues
   B   How Mosses Reproduce
   C   The Transport System Inside Plants
   D   How Mosses Differ from Other Plants

Directions: Questions 9 and 10 are based on the information below.

People often appreciate flowers for their beauty. However, flowers do much more than just please us; they attract other organisms, such as bees, to the plants. Those organisms then help the plant reproduce. When a bee drinks nectar from a flower, pollen from the flower rubs onto the bee's body. When the bee flies to another flower, it carries the pollen with it. When the bee touches the new flower, it leaves pollen behind. The sperm cell in a pollen grain can then fertilize one of the egg cells in the second flower. The fertilized egg forms a seed. As the seed matures, a fruit grows around the seed to protect it. Eventually, the seed leaves the fruit, falls to the ground, and grows into a new plant.

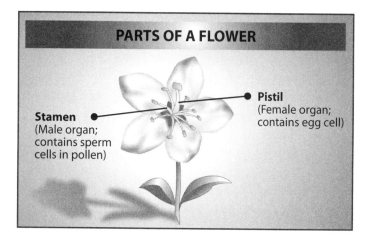

PARTS OF A FLOWER

Stamen
(Male organ;
contains sperm
cells in pollen)

Pistil
(Female organ;
contains egg cell)

9   **Read the following summary.**

Flowers are important structures for plant reproduction. Bees play an important role in pollinating flowers and producing fruit.

Which detail would fit best into the summary?
A   Bees are attracted to flowers.
B   Sperm cells in the pollen fertilize egg cells.
C   A fruit grows around the seed, and it falls to the ground.
D   Bees move pollen from one flower to another.

10 **Which of these statements best summarizes the information in the flower diagram?**
A   Flowers have both male and female parts.
B   Beautiful petals attract bees.
C   A flower's female organs are in its center.
D   Flower petals enclose the pollen.

Directions: Questions 11 and 12 are based on the information below.

Plants seeds are spread in several ways. Some seeds just drop to the ground and grow near to the parent plant. Some seeds are encased in fruits. Animals eat these fruits, but cannot digest the seeds. The seeds pass through the animals' bodies and are eliminated in the animals' wastes. New plants may grow wherever the animals drop the seeds. Some seeds cannot grow unless they pass through the digestive system of a specific animal!

Some seeds have little hooks on their surfaces. The hooks stick to the fur or feathers of animals, which can carry the seeds far from the parent plant. Other seeds are spread by wind, water, or fire. Wind can carry light seeds of certain shapes. Water can move seeds along rivers or streams. The dwarf pine requires fire to release its seeds! Only intense heat can melt the protective layer from the cone, and the seeds pop out, landing often at a great distance from the parent.

11 **Which of the following titles best summarizes the passage?**
A   How Wind Can Spread Seeds
B   How Animals Spread Seeds
C   Types of Seeds
D   Different Ways of Spreading Seeds

12 **Which of the following sentences could begin a summary of the passage?**
A   Many plants rely on other living things or on the physical environment to spread their seeds.
B   Some seeds are covered in tiny hooks, which stick to the fur or feathers of animals.
C   Animals can carry plant seeds long distances.
D   The wind helps spread some plant seeds.

Directions: Questions 13 through 15 are based on the information below.

YEAR	EVENT
1876	Kudzu is introduced at the Philadelphia Centennial Exposition.
1907	Kudzu hay is exhibited in Jamestown, Virginia.
1935	Government encourages U.S. farmers to plant kudzu to prevent soil erosion.
1950–1965	Kudzu increasingly recognized as a weed. Farmers no longer use kudzu to control erosion.
1998	Congress lists kudzu as a "federal noxious weed."
2008	Kudzu is listed as invasive in at least 22 states.

Sometimes, people introduce organisms from one ecosystem into another. The introduced species can become problematic in the new ecosystem. One example of such a problematic species is the kudzu vine. Kudzu is native to Japan. People first planted it in the southern United States to try to stop soil erosion. Although the vine did help reduce erosion, it had no controls on its growth in the new environment. It began to grow out of control. Kudzu can grow up to a foot in a single day, and it is hard to kill. In only a few weeks or months, it can completely cover buildings, other structures, and even trees. Although weed-killing chemicals can kill kudzu, these chemicals also harm other plants. Today, kudzu grows wild in every state in the southeastern United States. It has spread as far north as New York and Massachusetts, and as far west as Texas and Nebraska.

13 **Which of the following best summarizes the paragraph and table?**
A Species can be harmful if they are transported to a new ecosystem.
B Kudzu is a Japanese vine that is not native to the United States. Kudzu is very hard to kill.
C Introduced species can harm ecosystems. One example of a harmful introduced species is the kudzu vine.
D Kudzu was first planted in the United States to help stop soil erosion. It now grows throughout the country.

14 **A student wrote the following summary of the paragraph and table:**

"Sometimes, people introduce organisms from one ecosystem into another. The introduced species can become problematic in the new ecosystem. One example of such a problematic species is the kudzu vine."

What is the main problem with the student's summary?
A The summary is shorter than the paragraph.
B The summary uses the exact same wording as the paragraph.
C The summary does not give all the details about kudzu.
D The summary does not include the main idea of the paragraph.

15 **What would make the best combined title for the table and paragraph?**
A The History of Kudzu
B The Battle Against Soil Erosion
C Kudzu: An Invasive and Problematic Plant
D Southeastern U.S. Braces for Kudzu

Use Context Clues

① Learn the Skill

Context clues can help you to determine the meaning of a word or passage. With context clues, you use details or restatements that surround the word or idea to determine its meaning.

② Practice the Skill

By mastering the skill of context clues, you will improve your study and test-taking skills, especially as they relate to science high school equivalency tests. Read the paragraph and strategies below. Use the information to answer question 1.

Ⓐ When you use context clues to figure out the meaning of a word or phrase, examine familiar words to get an idea of the general tone of the passage. This passage contains many words and phrases, such as those underlined in red, that have negative meanings. Although *algal bloom* is not specifically defined in the passage, you can tell that it is a negative thing or event.

Ⓑ Although the passage does not directly answer the question, you can use logic to figure it out. The passage states that nutrients can cause algal blooms and that farm fertilizers are a source of nutrients. From these clues, you can identify a solution to the problem of algal blooms.

"In addition to <u>toxic</u> pollutants, increased nutrients, especially nitrogen and phosphorus, from city sewage and fertilizers from agricultural areas (e.g., animal feed lots) have also proven to be very <u>damaging</u> to aquatic ecosystems. Certain levels of these nutrients are known to cause <u>harmful</u> algal blooms in both freshwater and marine habitats. In turn, algal blooms impact aquatic biodiversity by affecting water clarity, depleting oxygen levels, and <u>crowding out</u> organisms within an ecosystem. In some instances <u>algal blooms</u> have produced neurotoxins that have led to species die-offs and illnesses such as paralytic shellfish poisoning."

From *Aquatic Biodiversity*, EPA, 2007

💡 USING LOGIC

The word *bloom* often has a positive meaning, especially in the context of flowers blooming. You might assume that a bloom of any kind would be helpful in an ecosystem. A *bloom* in this context, however, is a sudden increase in population of algae, not a flowering.

1 Based on the information, which measure would help prevent algal blooms?
   A increasing the amount of oxygen in a body of water
   B decreasing the amount of fertilizer used on farms
   C developing a treatment for neurotoxins
   D adding nutrients to freshwater habitats

UNIT 1

Directions: Questions 2 through 4 are based on the information below.

"Wetlands and riparian areas can play a critical role in reducing . . . pollution by intercepting surface runoff, subsurface flow, and certain ground water flows . . . Their role in water quality improvement includes processing, removing, transforming, and storing such pollutants as sediment, nitrogen, phosphorus, and certain heavy metals."

From *National Management Measures to Protect and Restore Wetlands and Riparian Areas*, EPA, 2005

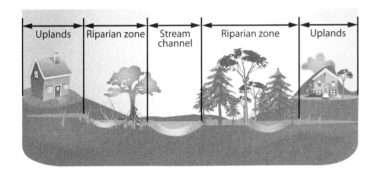

2   **Based on the information in the paragraph and in the diagram, what is the best definition of a riparian area?**
A   a heavily wooded area near farmland
B   a source of water pollution
C   a zone of vegetation along a body of water
D   a freshwater stream

3   **The cited source of the information in the paragraph is the EPA. This type of source is generally considered reliable. What category of source is the EPA?**
A   government agency
B   newspaper editorial
C   commercial Internet site
D   Web blog

4   **Based on the information, what argument is the EPA document most likely making?**
A   Riparian areas should be preserved to decrease pollution of water resources.
B   Riparian areas should be eliminated because they are a major source of heavy metals.
C   Riparian areas should be replaced by wetlands to decrease water pollution.
D   Preserving riparian areas will involve destroying farmland.

Directions: Question 5 is based on the paragraph below.

Common air pollutants can have harmful effects on the health and survival of plants and animals. The Clean Air Act (CAA) of 1970 established air quality monitoring for six criteria pollutants in the United States. Leaders in states where the criteria pollutants are above levels established in the CAA must submit plans to bring those levels down. The federal government can issue sanctions against a state that fails to comply with the law. In general, the CAA has helped reduce the level of these air pollutants over the last 40 years.

5   **Based on the information, what is a "criteria pollutant"?**
A   A pollutant that is no longer a threat to the health of plants and animals.
B   A pollutant that is common and must be tested regularly.
C   A pollutant that is generally rare.
D   A pollutant that does not cause health problems in humans.

WATERSHED QUALITY OF VARIOUS TEXAS WATERBODIES

WATERSHED	STATUS	ACRES
Lake Fork Reservoir	Good	5,518
Caddo Lake	Impaired	3,284
Lake Bob Sandlin	Good	2,379
Lake Meredith	Impaired	8,026
Benbrook Lake	Good	1,065
Upper Prairie Dog Town Fork Red River	Good	57

Source: Watershed Assessment Tracking and Environmental Results, EPA

6 **Based on context clues in the table, what does *impaired* mean?**
A   river
B   lake
C   bad
D   large

7 **Based on the table, what can you determine about watersheds in Texas?**
A   They include only lakes.
B   Almost all of them are environmentally impaired.
C   They all include at least 200 acres of land.
D   Some of them are environmentally healthy.

Directions: Questions 8 through 10 refer to the following paragraph from Section 303(d) of the Clean Water Act (2006).

Identification of areas with insufficient controls; maximum daily load; certain effluent limitations revision:

(1)(A) Each State shall identify those waters within its boundaries for which the effluent limitations required by section 1311(b)(1)(A) and section 1311(b)(1)(B) of this title are not stringent enough to implement any water quality standard applicable to such waters. The State shall establish a priority ranking for such waters, taking into account the severity of the pollution and the uses to be made of such waters.

8 **Use context clues to determine the meaning of the word *stringent* in this paragraph.**
A   healthy or useful
B   first in line
C   rigorous or strong
D   of uncertain quality

9 **What is the significance of the boldfaced paragraph above?**
A   It provides a summary of the text to follow.
B   It provides details that reinforce the main idea.
C   It provides an opinion about the information to come.
D   It provides certain key words for use as table headings.

10 **To which of the following does the paragraph from the Clean Water Act primarily apply?**
A   clean bodies of water
B   bodies of water outside each state's boundaries
C   a ratings system for water quality
D   elimination of water quality standards

UNIT 1

Directions: Question 11 is based on the information below.

Biofuel production seems to be the wave of the future. Many farmers have supplanted traditional crops with the more lucrative corn plant used in biofuel production. However, this dramatic switch has wreaked havoc on groundwater aquifers and other water bodies. Raising a monoculture, or only one crop, can be difficult to maintain. Many farmers use large amounts of pesticides and fertilizers to keep the corn strong. These substances contain nitrates and other pollutants that can contaminate groundwater. Also, farms in dry areas that could not naturally sustain corn crops have been irrigating without regulation, draining limited water resources.

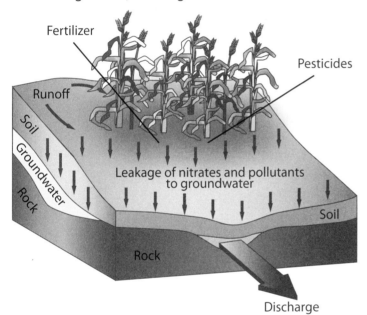

Directions: Questions 12 through 14 are based on the paragraph below.

Acid precipitation is a major air pollution problem in some parts of the country. It forms when pollutants containing acid (such as sulfur dioxide) mix with moisture in the air. The mixture then precipitates as acid rain or snow, or hangs in the air as acid mist. Acid precipitation damages trees. It builds up in freshwater sources, producing acid lakes and streams. The acidity in the water harms aquatic life. Acid precipitation is most serious downwind of large sources of acidic pollutants, such as power plants that burn coal.

12 Based on the paragraph, what does *precipitates* mean?
  A falls
  B hangs
  C burns
  D dries up

13 Which of the following combinations of words best describes the effects of acid precipitation?
  A *forms* and *hangs*
  B *damages* and *harms*
  C *builds* and *precipitates*
  D *acidity* and *air*

14 Based on the paragraph, what can you determine to be an effective response to the situation?
  A frequent water testing
  B the planting of new trees
  C a shift from coal to other forms of energy
  D the repopulation of certain animal species

11 What does the author mean by stating that the decision to plant corn has "wreaked havoc" on aquifers and other bodies of water?
  A The decision largely has been a success.
  B The decision prompted the growth of different varieties of corn.
  C The decision helped to purify aquifers and other bodies of water.
  D The decision resulted in contamination of groundwater.

Directions: Questions 15 through 17 are based on the information below.

Directions: Questions 18 through 20 are based on the information below.

CERP: RESTORING THE EVERGLADES

The largest freshwater restoration program in the United States began in 2000. The Comprehensive Everglades Restoration Plan, or CERP, is a 30-year undertaking to redirect freshwater that flows unused to the ocean back into the Everglades. The Army Corps of Engineers, spearheading the majority of the reconstruction efforts, is tasked with moving levees, building canals, and constructing new reservoirs and storage areas. During this process, the Corps must consider the ramifications of each move and look to protect the endangered wildlife in the area. The hope is that these efforts will make all of Florida more sustainable—the wildlife in the Everglades will be able to thrive, and the people of Florida will have access to all the freshwater they need.

THE EXXON VALDEZ

In March 1989, the Exxon Valdez supertanker, with an inebriated captain, ran aground on Bligh Reef, ruptured, and spilled 11 million gallons of crude oil into Alaska's Prince William Sound, contaminating about 900 miles of shoreline.

The damage to the fishing industry and to native subsistence hunting lasted for years. Exxon originally was ordered by a federal court to pay $5 billion in punitive damages in 1994. A federal appeal in 2006 reduced it to $2.5 billion.

---

15 What is the best definition for *sustainable,* based on the clues in this passage?
   A   able to take care of itself
   B   able to have access to water
   C   able to use new reservoirs
   D   able to preserve wildlife

16 Which words in the paragraph best highlight the complexity of the CERP program?
   A   *spearheading* and *constructing*
   B   *restoration* and *plan*
   C   *redirect* and *thrive*
   D   *undertaking* and *process*

17 Which of the following research questions will this study answer?
   A   How much freshwater flows into the ocean in Florida?
   B   How can freshwater be redirected back to the Everglades?
   C   How many endangered species live in the Everglades?
   D   How much freshwater do the people of Florida use everyday?

18 Using context clues, what does *ruptured* mean?
   A   spilled
   B   broke open
   C   marooned
   D   contaminated

19 The passage states that Exxon had to pay *punitive damages.* Within the context of the passage, the best definition for this term is
   A   payment for causing damage.
   B   a federal appeal for leniency.
   C   a halt in subsistence hunting.
   D   government regulations.

20 What would be a likely by-product of the Exxon Valdez oil spill?
   A   a sharp decrease in fishing revenue in Alaska
   B   a reduction of oil shipments to Alaska
   C   the retirement by Exxon of its fleet of supertankers
   D   an immediate increase in game hunting in Alaska

Analyze Information

① Learn the Skill

Graphical information, such as graphs, tables, and illustrations, often is used to support and clarify text. Graphics also may be used to present additional information. When you see text and graphical information together, you must **analyze information** in the text and the graphic to fully understand the material being presented.

② Practice the Skill

By mastering the skill of analyzing information, you will improve your study and test-taking skills, especially as they relate to science high school equivalency tests. Examine the text and graph. Use the information to answer question 1.

A Paragraphs and longer passages give important information in text form. If a graphic accompanies the text, the text may make a reference to that graphic. These references can help you determine the relationship between the text and the graphic.

B Text and graphics often give different, but related, information. In most cases, you will need to use information from both the text and the graphic to answer the questions.

A biome is a large region that has about the same temperature and precipitation (rainfall) everywhere. Most parts of the United States belong to one of three biomes: desert, grassland, or temperate deciduous forest. <u>The graph below shows the average yearly rainfall for several biomes.</u>

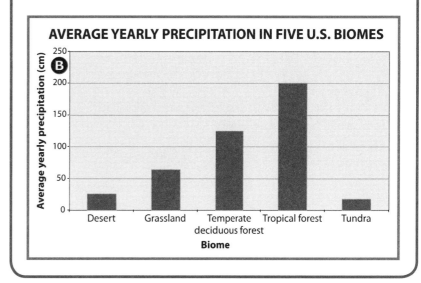

AVERAGE YEARLY PRECIPITATION IN FIVE U.S. BIOMES

Average yearly precipitation (cm) / *Biome*
(Desert, Grassland, Temperate deciduous forest, Tropical forest, Tundra)

USING LOGIC

In many cases, the correct answer is not specifically stated in the text or shown in the graphic. Instead, you must combine information from both to answer the question.

1 **The text and the graph support which generalization?**

   A Most of the United States is part of the grassland biome.

   B Most parts of the United States receive between 25 cm and 125 cm of rainfall each year.

   C The desert is the driest biome on Earth.

   D Tropical forests and grasslands receive about the same amount of rainfall each year.

Directions: Questions 2 through 4 are based on the information below.

The plants and animals that live in a particular biome have adaptations that help them survive that biome's climate. These adaptations take many forms. Some adaptations are physical characteristics. For example, plants that live in dense forests may grow very tall, allowing them to get sunlight by growing above other plants in the forest. Other adaptations involve behaviors. For example, animals that live in a biome with cold winters may hibernate or migrate to a warmer area during the winter.

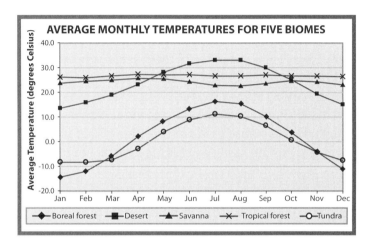

AVERAGE MONTHLY TEMPERATURES FOR FIVE BIOMES

2 Based on the information and graph, animals in which biomes are most likely to have thick fur to help them stay warm?
A   savanna and desert
B   boreal forest and tropical forest
C   desert and tundra
D   tundra and boreal forest

3 The information and graph support which of the following statements?
A   Plants in the desert grow very tall.
B   The average temperature in a savanna is warmer than in a tropical forest.
C   Plants and animals have different adaptations depending on the biome in which they live.
D   Temperatures in the tundra are always colder than in a boreal forest.

4 Based on the information and graph, animals living in the boreal forest and tundra biomes are most likely to have which of the following characteristics?
A   large ears to rid excess body heat
B   fur that changes color to provide protection from predators
C   the ability to hibernate during very cold weather
D   a great deal of exposed skin to increase the body's ability to stay cool

Directions: Question 5 is based on the information below.

The main factors that define a biome are temperature and precipitation. Regions that have similar temperatures and amounts of precipitation are generally placed into the same biome, even if they are very far apart geographically. The map shows the distribution of biomes in the world.

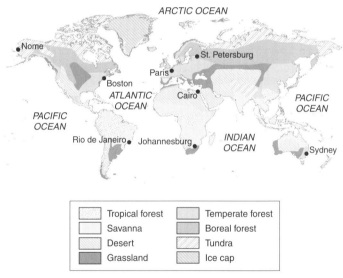

5 Based on the information in the paragraph and map, which two cities are most likely to have similar temperatures and amounts of precipitation?
A   Boston and Paris
B   Nome and Cairo
C   Sydney and St. Petersburg
D   St. Petersburg and Johannesburg

Directions: Questions 6 and 7 are based on the information below.

The desert biome is extremely dry. In general, a desert receives 25 cm or less of precipitation each year. In many deserts, most of the precipitation occurs within a relatively short amount of time (the rainy season). During the rest of the year, the desert receives little or no precipitation. In fact, in some deserts, the air is so dry that rain evaporates before it even hits the ground.

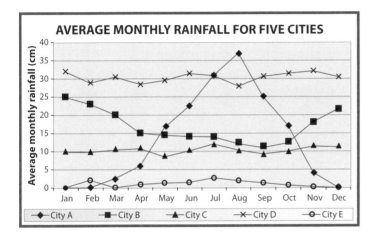

AVERAGE MONTHLY RAINFALL FOR FIVE CITIES

6   **The graph shows the average monthly rainfall for five different cities. Which city is most likely located in a desert biome?**
   A   city A
   B   city B
   C   city D
   D   city E

7   **The biome of a temperate deciduous forest receives between 75 and 150 cm of rainfall each year. Which of the above cities is most likely located in a temperate deciduous forest biome?**
   A   city A
   B   city B
   C   city C
   D   Not enough information is given.

Directions: Question 8 is based on the information below.

Temperate deciduous forests are found in the eastern and northeastern United States and across much of western Europe and eastern Asia. These forests are called temperate forests because their climates are relatively mild. They are neither extremely cold in the winter, nor extremely hot in the summer. Because most of the trees in these forests lose their leaves in the fall, the forests are deciduous forests (*deciduous* refers to trees that lose their leaves each year).

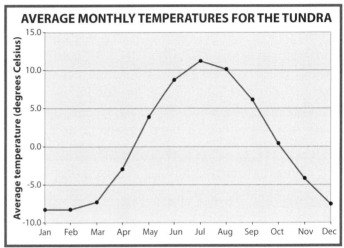

AVERAGE MONTHLY TEMPERATURES FOR THE TUNDRA

8   **Based on the information in the paragraph and graph, what is the main difference between the tundra biome and the temperate deciduous forest biome?**
   A   The tundra has a wider yearly temperature range than the temperate deciduous forest.
   B   More trees live in the tundra than in the temperate deciduous forest.
   C   The tundra receives more sunlight than the temperate deciduous forest.
   D   The temperate deciduous forest covers a larger area than the tundra.

Directions: Questions 9 through 12 are based on the information below.

The grassland biome is found mainly in the central United States and central Asia. The main plants that grow in grasslands are grasses and small shrubs. The deep roots of the grasses help prevent soil erosion. Decaying plant-matter in the soil makes the soil nutrient-rich. Although grasslands receive a moderately large amount of rainfall (50–90 cm per year), most of that rainfall occurs between March and September.

The savanna biome is similar to the grassland biome in that its main plants are grasses and shrubs. However, the soil in the savanna is generally not as thick or nutrient-rich as the soil in grasslands. The savanna is found mainly in central Africa, India, northern Australia, and eastern South America. Average temperatures in savannas tend to be higher than those in grasslands. The graph shows the average monthly rainfall in the savanna biome.

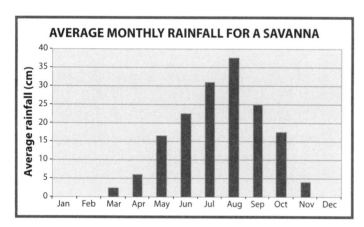

9   **Which statement is supported by the information in the paragraph and graph?**
   A   Grasslands and savannas have about the same average yearly temperature.
   B   The rainy season occurs at about the same time in the grassland and the savanna.
   C   Grasslands and savannas are found in similar parts of the world.
   D   Larger shrubs grow in grasslands than in savannas.

10   **Natural fires are common in both the savanna and the grassland. During which part of the year are fires most likely to occur in each biome?**
   A   in April in both biomes
   B   in June and July in the grassland, and in December and January in the savanna
   C   between November and February in both biomes
   D   in May in the savanna and in June in the grassland

11   **Grassland biomes make good farmland, but savanna biomes generally do not. What is the most likely reason for this?**
   A   The savanna does not receive enough rain for crops to grow.
   B   The savanna is too cold for crops to grow.
   C   More people live near the grassland than live near the savanna.
   D   The soil in the grassland is more fertile than the soil in the savanna.

12   **Based on the information in the passage and graph, what can you conclude about life in the grassland and savanna biomes?**
   A   The savanna's additional rainfall leads to lower average temperatures than in the grassland biome.
   B   Yearly rainfall in a grassland biome more closely approximates the yearly rainfall in a tundra biome.
   C   Soil in both biomes is of equal density.
   D   The rainfall and temperatures are similar enough in both biomes to produce the same types of plant life.

Directions: Question 13 is based on the information below.

Different plants and animals live in different biomes. In general, the plants and animals in a specific biome have adaptations that allow them to survive in that biome's climate. Temperature and amount of rainfall are two of the most important climate factors to which living things must adapt.

	BOREAL FOREST	TUNDRA
Average yearly temperature range	–40°C to 20°C	–40°C to 18°C
Average yearly precipitation	30 cm to 90 cm	15 cm to 25 cm
General climate description	Long, cold winters and short, cool summers	Very long, cold winters and short, cool summers
Common animals	Moose, coyote, bobcat, elk, porcupine, snowshoe hare	Caribou, lemming, arctic hare, arctic squirrel, arctic fox, wolf, polar bear
Common plants	Evergreen trees, mosses	Mosses, various flowers and shrubs

13 **Based on the information in the paragraph and table, how are the animals in boreal forests and tundras similar?**

 A They have adaptations that allow them to survive cold weather.

 B They all require large amounts of water to survive.

 C They all use tall trees for food and shelter.

 D None of them can survive without long periods of warm weather.

Directions: Questions 14 and 15 are based on the information below.

Some adaptations that allow an organism to survive in one biome are harmful to the same organism in a different biome. For example, desert animals and plants have adaptations that help them get rid of excess heat and prevent water loss. If these plants or animals were placed in a tundra biome, they would quickly freeze. However, animals and plants that are adapted to a specific biome may survive in a different biome if the climate of the new biome is similar to that of their native biome.

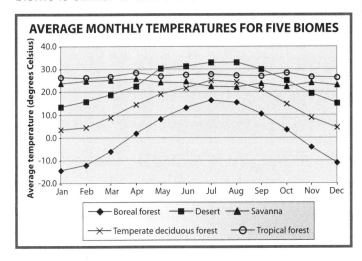

14 **Based on the information in the paragraph and graph, what would most likely happen to an animal from a boreal forest that was brought into a tropical forest?**

 A It would die from lack of water.

 B It would overheat in the new biome.

 C It would be too cold during the summer.

 D It would survive easily in the new biome.

15 **An animal is brought from a tropical forest to a savanna, but it does not survive. What is the most likely reason for this?**

 A The savanna is too dry.

 B The savanna is too hot.

 C The climate in the savanna is very similar to that of the tropical forest.

 D There is too much variation in temperature in the savanna.

Categorize and Classify

① Learn the Skill

When you **categorize**, you choose the criteria for placing organisms, objects, or processes into groups. Such groups are based on common features or relationships between things in the group. When you **classify**, you put things into groups that already exist.

② Practice the Skill

By mastering the skills of categorizing and classifying, you will improve your study and test-taking skills, especially as they relate to science high school equivalency tests. Read the table and strategies below. Use the information to answer question 1.

A Tables are good tools to use when categorizing and classifying information. Here, the heading atop each column represents one category of organism. The categories were designed to group organisms with common characteristics. For example, animals can move and take in food from their environment. Plants do not move. They make their own food using gases from the air and energy from sunlight.

B After categories have been determined, one can classify other organisms into these categories. For example, a palm tree could be classified with the plants.

Scientists organize all living things into categories for classification. Kingdoms are the broadest categories. There are six kingdoms. The table lists two of the kingdoms and several types of organisms in each one.

ORGANISMS IN TWO KINGDOMS	
ANIMAL	**PLANT**
Bison	Heather
Camel	Oak
Penguin	Orchid
Rattlesnake	Poison ivy
Shark	Redwood
Zebra	Rose

☑ TEST-TAKING TIPS

There is usually more than one way to categorize and classify organisms. If a question asks you to categorize, make sure to choose criteria that fit all the members of that group. If it asks you to classify, make sure the organism meets all criteria for that category.

1 Which phrase best describes the information in the table?

A different types of bison and heather

B an explanation of how plants and animals differ

C animals and plants that are similar

D two groups of organisms with different characteristics

Directions: Question 2 is based on the information below.

In 1735, botanist Carolus Linnaeus devised a system for categorizing and classifying organisms. Linnaeus categorized organisms by their physical traits. The broadest category is the kingdom. Kingdoms are divided into smaller groups called phyla (singular, *phylum*). Phyla are divided into even smaller categories called classes, and so on down to the smallest category, species. A species is one particular type of animal—a category of one. One kingdom can have millions of different species.

Kingdom

    ↘ **Phylum** (plural, *Phyla*)

       ↘ **Class**

         ↘ **Order**

           ↘ **Family**

             ↘ **Genus** (plural, *Genera*)

               ↘ **Species**

2 **Based on the information, which statement best describes the structure of the Linnaean classification system?**

   A more families than classes

   B fewer species than genera

   C the same number of phyla and classes

   D more kingdoms than species

Directions: Question 3 is based on the information below.

The six kingdoms into which scientists classify all living things are in the far left column of the table. Categories of information about each kingdom are in the other columns.

SIX SCIENTIFIC KINGDOMS		
Kingdom	**Characteristics of Organisms**	**Examples**
EUBACTERIA	Single-celled; some species form chains or mats	*E. coli*, which is found in the human digestive system
ARCHAEBACTERIA	Single-celled; many can survive in extreme environments	Organisms that live in hot springs
PROTISTA	Some single-celled, some multicellular; some make their own food, some eat other organisms	Paramecia, amoebas, algae
FUNGI	Most are multicellular; made of threadlike fibers	Yeasts, molds, mushrooms
PLANTAE	Contain many specialized cells; cells have rigid outer wall; feature structures to make own food	Mosses, ferns, flowering plants
ANIMALIA	Made up of many specialized cells; cells lack rigid outer wall; must collect and eat food	Sponges, worms, insects, fish, amphibians, reptiles, birds, mammals

3 **A scientist discovers a new organism and classifies it in kingdom Plantae. Based on the information in the table, what must be true about the organism?**

   A The organism has threadlike fibers.

   B The organism can survive in extreme environments.

   C The organism can produce its own food.

   D The organism is made up of a single cell.

Directions: Questions 4 through 6 are based on the paragraph below.

In the system scientists use to classify animals, the group called Vertebrata includes all animals with backbones. Two important groups within Vertebrata are amphibians and reptiles. The animals in each group share certain characteristics. Amphibians have soft, moist skin. They have no fur. Amphibians lay eggs without shells in water or in moist soil. They also have a two-stage life cycle. They start life in water, but usually live on land as adults. Reptiles have dry, scaly skin. They lay eggs with leathery shells. Many reptiles live on land. However, some live in water or spend some of their time there.

4 Based on the information, which characteristic allows scientists to classify amphibians and reptiles together?

A backbone

B dry skin

C scaly skin

D eggs with shells

5 Which statement best explains why reptiles and amphibians are categorized separately?

A The two groups share no common features.

B Reptiles and amphibians are more alike than they are different.

C They have little in common with other animal groups.

D All reptiles are more like one another than they are like amphibians.

6 A scientist discovers an animal in a shallow pond. It has a backbone, but it does not have fur. The animal lays eggs. How should the scientist classify the animal?

A Reptile: reptiles sometimes are found in water, and exhibit all of the other characteristics.

B Amphibian: Amphibians start life in water, and exhibit all of the other characteristics.

C The animal can be classified as both a reptile and an amphibian.

D There is not enough information to classify this animal.

Directions: Questions 7 and 8 are based on the diagram below.

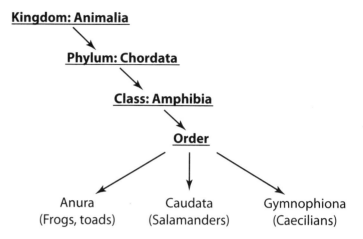

7 Based on the information, what must be true about animals in order Anura?

A Animals in order Anura must have identical characteristics to animals in other orders.

B Animals in order Anura must possess entirely different characteristics than other amphibians.

C Animals in order Anura must share characteristics with amphibians but not with chordates.

D Animals in order Anura must have characteristics that animals in other orders do not.

8 Which statement best describes the animals in class Amphibia?

A Amphibians include all animals that are not in phylum Chordata.

B Amphibians share more characteristics with one another than they do with other chordates.

C Amphibians are also classified in order Caudata.

D Amphibians have all the same characteristics.

CLASSIFICATION OF THE DOUGLAS SQUIRREL

Kingdom *ANIMALIA* *(Animals)*	Housefly	Snake	Platypus	Giraffe	Woodchuck	Prairie Dog	Red Squirrel	Douglas Squirrel
Phylum *CHORDATA* *(Animals with backbones)*		Snake	Platypus	Giraffe	Woodchuck	Prairie Dog	Red Squirrel	Douglas Squirrel
Class *MAMMALIA* *(Animals with backbones; feed milk to their young)*			Platypus	Giraffe	Woodchuck	Prairie Dog	Red Squirrel	Douglas Squirrel
Order *RODENTIA* *(Animals with backbones; feed milk to their young; possess long, sharp front teeth)*					Woodchuck	Prairie Dog	Red Squirrel	Douglas Squirrel
Family *SCIURIDAE* *(Animals with backbones; feed milk to their young; possess long, sharp front teeth and full tails)*						Prairie Dog	Red Squirrel	Douglas Squirrel
Genus *TAMIASCIURUS* *(Animals with backbones; feed milk to their young; possess long, sharp front teeth and full tails; live in trees)*							Red Squirrel	Douglas Squirrel
Species *DOUGLASII* *(Animals with backbones; feed milk to their young; possess long, sharp front teeth and full tails; live in trees; have brown and gray fur on their backs and light-to-dark orange fur on their bellies)*								Douglas Squirrel

9   What characteristic do members of genus *Tamiasciurus* have that makes them different from other members of the family Sciuridae?

A   fluffy tails
B   backbones
C   feed milk to their young
D   live in trees

10   Which of these animals can be classified into class Mammalia but not into order Rodentia?

A   giraffe
B   Douglas Squirrel
C   chipmunk
D   Eastern Red Squirrel

11   Based on the information, which of these statements is true of the Douglas Squirrel?

A   The Douglas Squirrel can be classified into only one category.
B   The Douglas Squirrel does not fit into an existing category.
C   The Douglas Squirrel shares more characteristics with a woodchuck than with a platypus.
D   The Douglas Squirrel is the only animal in the table classified as a rodent.

Directions: Question 12 is based on the paragraph below.

Biologists have classified reptiles in one class (Reptilia) and birds in another (Aves). However, some biologists think that this classification should change. Fossils show that birds evolved from a group of small, two-legged dinosaurs millions of years ago. Dinosaurs are classified as reptiles. Some biologists argue that birds are reptiles, too.

12 Which statement would further support the argument that birds should be classified with reptiles?
A Birds and reptiles show all the characteristics of animals.
B Birds and reptiles share many similar features.
C There are more birds than reptiles.
D Reptiles are extinct, whereas birds are not.

Directions: Question 13 is based on the table below.

CLASSIFICATION OF FOUR MAMMALS				
	BROWN BEAR	**CAT**	**DOG**	**KILLER WHALE**
Kingdom	Animalia	Animalia	Animalia	Animalia
Phylum	Chordata	Chordata	Chordata	Chordata
Class	Mammalia	Mammalia	Mammalia	Mammalia
Order	Carnivora	Carnivora	Carnivora	Carnivora
Family	Ursidae	Felidae	Canidae	Delphinidae
Genus	*Ursus*	*Felis*	*Canis*	*Orcinus*
Species	*Ursus arctos*	*Felis catus*	*Canis familiaris*	*Orcinus orca*

13 Into which genus would you classify a wolf?
A *Ursus*
B *Felis*
C *Canis*
D *Orcinus*

Directions: Questions 14 and 15 are based on the table below.

CLASSIFICATION FOR TWO REPTILES		
	AMERICAN ALLIGATOR	**AMERICAN CROCODILE**
Kingdom	**Animalia** (Animal)	**Animalia** (Animal)
Phylum	**Chordata** (Have backbone)	**Chordata** (Have backbone)
Class	**Reptilia** (Scaly skin, claws)	**Reptilia** (Scaly skin, claws)
Order	**Crocodilia** (Walk semi-erect; breathe partly submerged)	**Crocodilia** (Walk semi-erect; breathe partly submerged)
Family	**Alligatoridae** (U-shaped snout, prefer fresh water)	**Crocodylidae** (Pointier snout, live comfortably in saltwater)
Genus	*Alligator*	*Crocodylus*
Species	*mississippiensis*	*acutus*

14 Suppose that scientists find a new animal and think that they should classify it in one of the families within order Crocodilia. Which characteristic would scientists use to correctly classify the animal?
A skin texture
B presence of a backbone
C presence of claws
D shape of the snout

15 There is no description in the table for genus and species. Which of the following statements must be true about the missing information?
A It would be the same for the alligator and the crocodile.
B It would be the same for species but not for genus.
C It would be different for the genus and species of both.
D It would be the same for genus but not species.

Compare and Contrast

1 Learn the Skill

When you **compare**, you identify the ways in which organisms, objects, places, or events are similar and the ways in which they are different. When you **contrast**, you identify only how those organisms, objects, places, or events are different.

2 Practice the Skill

By mastering the skills of compare and contrast, you will improve your study and test-taking skills, especially as they relate to science high school equivalency tests. Examine the illustrations and strategies below. Use the information to answer question 1.

A When comparing objects or organisms, look for ways in which they are alike and different. Scan the illustrations and skim the passage to determine what these mammals have in common.

B When contrasting organisms, look only for ways in which they are different. Once again, examine the illustrations and text, this time for differences. Note that the front limbs of the animals in one group are wings and the front limbs of animals in the other group are legs. Type of limb is a way in which these groups differ.

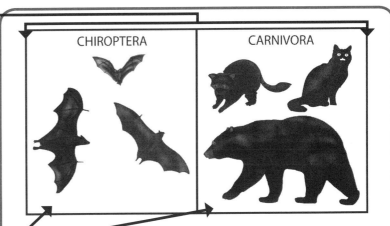

CHIROPTERA   CARNIVORA

The animals in both groups above are mammals. That means they all have hair and nurse their young with mother's milk. When you compare them, you can see that members of one group can fly and members of the other group cannot.

✓ TEST-TAKING TIPS

Words such as *both, as, similar, like,* and *alike* often show comparisons. Words such as *unlike, different,* and *but* often show contrasts. Consider possible similarities and differences before reading the answer choices. Then look for the correct answer.

1 In which way are animals in both mammal groups alike?
  A They both have the same type of limb.
  B They both have scales for skin.
  C They both are the same size.
  D They both have hair.

Directions: Questions 2 and 3 are based on the table below.

THREE CLASSES OF MAMMALS		
MONOTREMES	**MARSUPIALS**	**PLACENTAL MAMMALS**
Young hatch from eggs	Young born live	Young born live
Mothers make milk	Mothers make milk	Mothers make milk
After hatching, young nurse by licking milk the mother squirts on her fur	Young suck mother's milk while developing inside her pouch	Young suck mother's milk after developing inside her uterus
Warm-blooded	Warm-blooded	Warm-blooded
Hair or fur	Hair or fur	Hair or fur
Four-chambered hearts	Four-chambered hearts	Four-chambered hearts
Relatively large brains	Relatively large brains	Relatively large brains
Live only in Australia and New Guinea	Live mainly in Australia and New Zealand	Live in almost all parts of the world

2 **Compare these three classes of mammals. Which characteristic do they all share?**

   A They live only in Australia and New Zealand.

   B Their young hatch from eggs.

   C Mothers produce milk for their young.

   D Young mammals are born live.

3 **Unlike marsupials and placental mammals, the monotremes**

   A have hair or fur.

   B have young that develop in a uterus.

   C are warm-blooded.

   D lay eggs.

Directions: Questions 4 and 5 are based on the table below.

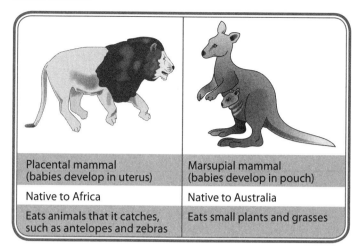

Placental mammal (babies develop in uterus)	Marsupial mammal (babies develop in pouch)
Native to Africa	Native to Australia
Eats animals that it catches, such as antelopes and zebras	Eats small plants and grasses

4 **Which statement accurately contrasts these two animals?**

   A Both the kangaroo and the lion are mammals.

   B The lion is a hunter, whereas the kangaroo is not.

   C Neither the kangaroo nor the lion is native to North America.

   D The lion and the kangaroo both have hair on their bodies.

5 **Which statement accurately compares kangaroos with lions?**

   A Both are monotremes.

   B Both graze on large prairies.

   C Both give birth to live young.

   D Both walk exclusively on four legs.

UNIT 1

Directions: Questions 6 and 7 are based on the Venn diagram below.

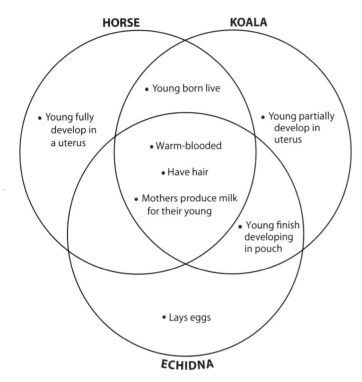

6 Which statement accurately compares the koala, the horse, and the echidna?
  A All of them are warm-blooded.
  B All of them have hair and are cold-blooded.
  C All of them have young that are born live.
  D All of them lay eggs and carry their young in pouches.

7 Which statement accurately contrasts the horse and the echidna?
  A Only one is warm-blooded.
  B Both animals have young that are born live.
  C Only one has young that develop fully in the uterus.
  D Both produce milk for their young.

Directions: Questions 8 through 10 are based on the paragraph below.

Mammals have been on Earth for more than 200 million years. However, ancient mammals were much different from mammals of today. There were no large mammals, such as the moose or the blue whale, 200 million years ago. Fossil evidence shows that the first mammals were probably all small animals. Mammals became bigger and more diverse only after large dinosaurs became extinct.

8 Based on the information, contrast early mammals and current mammals.
  A Early mammals dominated for 200 million years.
  B Early mammals were all relatively small.
  C Early mammals lived longer than modern mammals.
  D Early mammals towered over dinosaurs.

9 All mammals share certain basic characteristics. For example, they are warm-blooded, nurse their young, and have hair.

  Based on the information, which statement most accurately compares mammals of long ago with mammals of today?
  A They shared only some of the basic characteristics listed above.
  B Mammals of long ago were probably not warm-blooded.
  C Mammals of long ago had characteristics completely different from mammals today.
  D Both groups share the same basic characteristics.

10 For what purpose might you compare and contrast early mammals and current mammals?
  A a multimedia presentation about modern mammals
  B a documentary about the fossil record
  C a scientific study about the diversity of early mammals
  D a term paper on the history of mammals

Directions: Question 11 is based on the information below.

There are two major camel species: the dromedary camel and the Bactrian camel. They are easy to identify because the two animals differ in appearance. The Bactrian has two humps, dark and shaggy hair, and is smaller. The dromedary has one hump, short tan hair, and is taller. The camels also live in different environments. The graphs below show temperature data for one area of the world in which the Bactrian camel is common and for one area in which the dromedary camel is common.

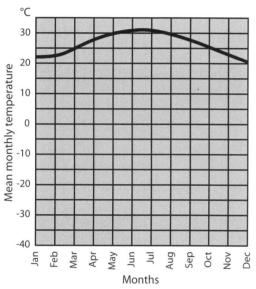

Average Monthly Temperature for a Region in the Middle East (Range of Dromedary Camel)

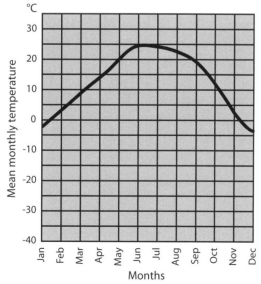

Average Monthly Temperature for a Region in Central Asia (Range of Bactrian Camel)

11 **Based on the information, which statement accurately contrasts the two camel species?**
- **A** Both camels can survive in basically the same climate conditions.
- **B** Dromedaries must endure much colder winters than Bactrian camels.
- **C** Dromedaries cannot endure long periods of high temperatures.
- **D** Bactrian camels are adapted for a colder climate than are dromedaries.

Directions: Questions 12 and 13 are based on the paragraph below.

Placental mammals are the most common mammals. The young of placental mammals develop fully inside the mother's body, attached to a placenta that brings them nourishment. Marsupials are a second and smaller group of mammals. In marsupials, young are undeveloped when they are born. Most finish their early development inside their mother's pouch, or marsupium. In North America, marsupial mammals are rare. The only common marsupial that is native to North America is the opossum. However, marsupials are the dominant mammals in Australia. There, marsupials include kangaroos, koalas, wallabies, and Tasmanian devils.

12 **Based on the information, which statement correctly contrasts the mammals of North America and Australia?**
- **A** In Australia, marsupial mammals are less likely to have pouches.
- **B** In Australia, marsupial mammals are undeveloped as adults.
- **C** In Australia, marsupial mammals are more common than placental mammals.
- **D** In Australia, marsupial mammals are larger than North American mammals.

13 **Contrast the opossum to most other mammals of North America.**
- **A** The opposum gives birth to undeveloped young.
- **B** The opposum lays eggs.
- **C** The opposum lacks a pouch for development of its young.
- **D** The opposum has a placenta instead of a marsupium.

Directions: Questions 14 and 15 are based on the information below.

The illustrations below show the limbs of four types of mammals. Although the limbs are somewhat similar in structure, each limb is adapted for movement in the environment in which that animal lives.

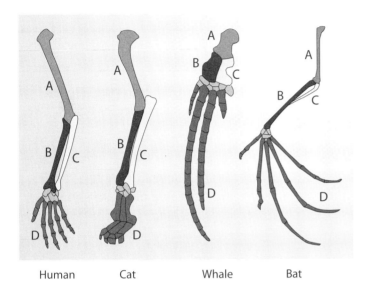

Human   Cat   Whale   Bat

14 **Based on the information in the diagram, compare the limbs of the different mammals.**
   A   The limbs all have the same basic parts.
   B   The limbs have parts that are generally the same size.
   C   The limbs move in the same way.
   D   The limbs are adapted to attract prey.

15 **Based on the diagram, how does the human limb contrast with the limbs of other mammals?**
   A   Structure A is relatively longer in humans.
   B   It is the only limb with long bones.
   C   The human limb is much smaller than the limbs of the other mammals.
   D   Its bones are much wider and thicker.

Directions: Questions 16 and 17 are based on the information below.

Primates are the order of mammals that includes humans. The diagram below shows the main groups of primates.

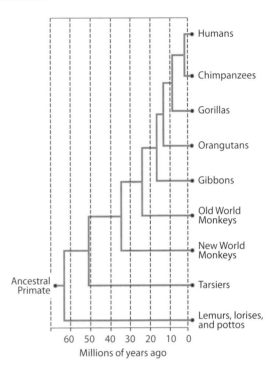

Millions of years ago

16 **What is being contrasted in this diagram?**
   A   the comparative body structure of different groups of primates
   B   the way that different groups of primates move from place to place
   C   the size of different types of primates
   D   when primate groups developed and how they are related

17 **What would be another means by which to show the information above?**
   A   a bar graph
   B   a Venn diagram
   C   a line graph
   D   a circle graph

Sequence

① Learn the Skill

When you place events or processes in **sequence**, you put them in a particular order. The sequence of events shows their relationship to, and with, one another.

② Practice the Skill

By mastering the skill of sequencing, you will improve your study and test-taking skills, especially as they relate to science high school equivalency tests. Examine the diagram and strategies below. Use that information to answer question 1.

Ⓐ Events in a sequence often are numbered. Those numbers indicate the order in which the events occur. In this illustration, the mouth is the organ in the first step in digestion, and the anus is the organ in the last step.

Ⓑ A sequence may be shown in a diagram, such as this one. The locations of the parts of the diagram can help show the sequence of events. In this diagram, the esophagus connects to the mouth. That connection shows that the esophagus comes after the mouth in the sequence.

During digestion, the body breaks down food into substances it can absorb and use. This diagram shows the major organs involved in digestion.

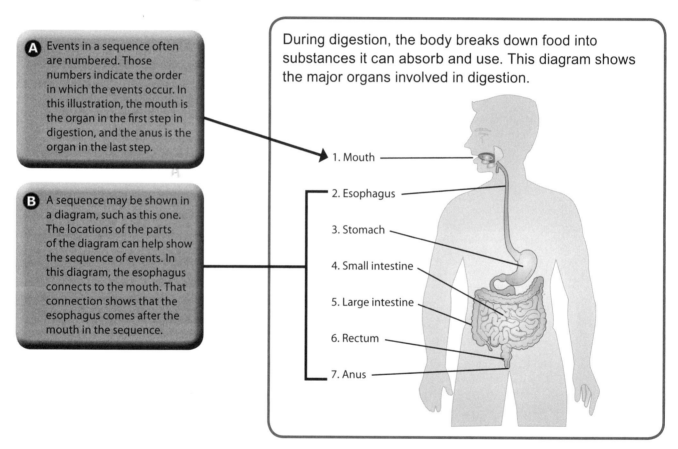

1. Mouth
2. Esophagus
3. Stomach
4. Small intestine
5. Large intestine
6. Rectum
7. Anus

☑ **TEST-TAKING TIPS**

When a sequence is shown horizontally (left to right), the first step is generally at the far left. When a sequence is shown vertically (up and down), the first step is generally at the top.

1 **Through which organ does food pass after the stomach?**

  A the rectum
  B the esophagus
  C the large intestine
  D the small intestine

Directions: Questions 2 and 3 are based on the paragraph below.

Digestion actually begins before you take the first bite of food. The sight of a piece of warm pie and its tempting smell cause your salivary glands to send saliva into your mouth. Substances in saliva start digestion when food enters your mouth. After you take a bite, your teeth cut, grind, and mash the food into smaller pieces that are easier to swallow. The substances in your saliva that aid digestion then can break down the food more easily. Your tongue also plays a part. You taste food with your tongue. But your tongue also moves the food around, forms it into a ball, and then pushes that ball to the back of your mouth.

2   **When does the body produce saliva?**
    A   The body first produces saliva when you put food into your mouth.
    B   The body first produces saliva when you take a bite of food.
    C   The body first produces saliva when you see and smell the food.
    D   The body first produces saliva when you taste the food.

3   **Which list shows the correct sequence of steps in part of the digestive process?**
    A   teeth grind up food; saliva breaks down food; teeth move food to back of mouth
    B   food moves to back of mouth; food moves to stomach; saliva released into mouth
    C   teeth grind food; food enters mouth; saliva enters mouth
    D   food enters mouth; tongue moves food around in the mouth; teeth grind food

Directions: Questions 4 and 5 are based on the information below.

After food leaves the mouth, it passes into the esophagus. From there, it passes through the following sequence of processes.

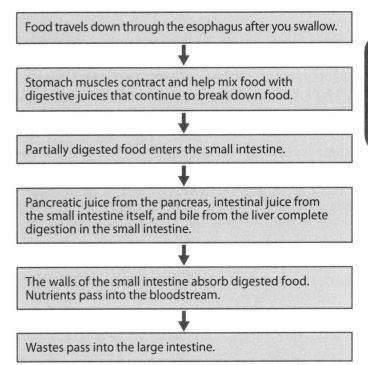

4   **Through which organ do substances from the pancreas and liver enter the digestive tract?**
    A   small intestine
    B   stomach
    C   large intestine
    D   esophagus

5   **Based on the information, at what point is digestion mostly complete?**
    A   Digestion is mostly complete when the food reaches the liver.
    B   Digestion is mostly complete when the food leaves the small intestine.
    C   Digestion is mostly complete when the food leaves the stomach.
    D   Digestion is mostly complete when the food enters the stomach.

UNIT 1

Directions: Questions 6 and 7 are based on the paragraph below.

When you swallow, food moves from your mouth to your esophagus. The esophagus is a long tube made up mainly of muscle tissue. The muscles relax and contract to push food along. If you imagine squeezing toothpaste out of a tube, you can get an idea of how the muscles work. First, muscles at the top of the esophagus contract. That pushes the food a short way down the esophagus. Then muscles a short distance down the esophagus contract, pushing the food farther. As the muscles contract, the food is pushed along toward the stomach. At the same time, muscles higher up relax, allowing you to swallow more food. The muscles in the esophagus are strong enough to push food toward the stomach even when you are upside down. The contractions in the esophagus stop when all the food enters the stomach.

6 **Based on the information, when do all the muscles in the esophagus stop contracting?**
  A immediately after food is swallowed
  B when all the food enters the stomach
  C when all the muscles in the stomach have contracted
  D as soon as food enters the esophagus

7 **In which stage of the digestion process does the movement of food through the esophagus occur?**
  A before the digestion process begins
  B in the early stages of the digestion process
  C in the middle stages of the digestion process
  D in the last stages of the digestion process

Directions: Questions 8 and 9 are based on the paragraph below.

After food moves out of the stomach, it moves to the small intestine. As the food moves through the small intestine, it continues to be digested. Most nutrients in the food are absorbed through the walls of the small intestine. The parts of the food that the body cannot digest are left behind as waste. Then the waste moves to the large intestine. In the large intestine, most of the water in the waste is absorbed. As the waste moves through the large intestine, more and more water is absorbed from it, and it becomes more compact. When most of the water has been absorbed from the waste, it is very compact. The compact waste, or feces, moves into the rectum. The feces are stored in the rectum until they are eliminated from the body through the anus.

8 **Based on the information in the paragraph, at what point in the digestion process is waste material the most compact?**
  A at the end of the small intestine
  B at the beginning of the large intestine
  C in the rectum
  D in the middle of the large intestine

9 **Which of the following is true of digestion in the large intestine?**
  A Digestion in the large intestine happens before the body has absorbed much of the nutrition from food.
  B Digestion in the large intestine happens mostly within the rectum.
  C Digestion in the large intestine adds water to waste materials to make them pass through the body more easily.
  D Digestion in the large intestine mainly involves indigestible material from earlier in the digestion process.

Directions: Questions 10 through 12 are based on the information below.

When you swallow, food moves from your mouth into your esophagus. From there, the food should move down the esophagus to the stomach. However, the process can sometimes go wrong. A person may eat too fast, swallow something too large, or sneeze or cough while chewing. As a result, food can lodge in a person's throat and block the trachea, which brings air from the nose or mouth to the lungs. When this occurs, a person chokes because he or she cannot get air. The Heimlich maneuver is a first-aid maneuver that removes blocked food and restores normal breathing. It also restores the normal swallowing process in digestion. The following diagram shows the steps in the Heimlich maneuver.

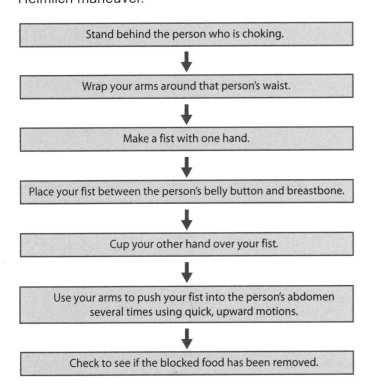

10 **Based on the information, if you are performing the Heimlich maneuver, what should you do immediately after placing your fist on the person's abdomen?**
  A   place your other hand over your fist
  B   push upward into the person's abdomen
  C   stand behind the person
  D   wrap your arms around the person's waist

11 **What is the last step in the Heimlich maneuver?**
  A   getting behind the person
  B   wrapping your arms around the person's waist
  C   checking to see if the blocked food has been removed
  D   pressing upward into the person's abdomen

12 **Between which two steps in the digestion process can choking happen?**
  A   food being chewed and food being swallowed
  B   food being swallowed and food moving into the esophagus
  C   food moving into the stomach and the stomach contracting
  D   food moving out of the esophagus and into the stomach

Directions: Question 13 is based on the paragraph below.

Although food does not pass through the liver and pancreas during digestion, these organs play an important part in the process. They send enzymes into the top part of the small intestine known as the duodenum. Enzymes are proteins that speed up reactions in cells. These enzymes are needed to break down partly digested foods that enter the small intestine from the stomach. The pancreas makes pancreatic juice, which helps break down starches and proteins. The liver makes bile, which helps break down fats. The gallbladder stores bile from the liver until it is needed in the small intestine.

13 **What must happen immediately before actions in the small intestine break down fats?**
  A   The duodenum must make bile.
  B   Food must pass through the liver.
  C   Starches must be broken down in the small intestine.
  D   Bile must move from the liver to the gallbladder.

Directions: Questions 14 and 15 are based on the information below.

It can take up to 36 hours from the time you bite into food to when waste from that food leaves your body. The diagram shows the time needed for food to pass through each of the major stages of digestion.

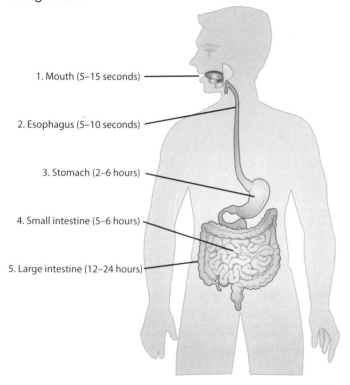

1. Mouth (5–15 seconds)

2. Esophagus (5–10 seconds)

3. Stomach (2–6 hours)

4. Small intestine (5–6 hours)

5. Large intestine (12–24 hours)

14 **The paragraph and diagram support the generalization that**
   A food spends more time in the stomach than in any other part of the digestive system.
   B each step in the process takes longer than the one before it.
   C the first two steps in the process take less than one hour to complete.
   D the last steps in the process take less time than do the first steps in the process.

15 **You eat a full dinner Thursday at 6 p.m. At what point will your body fully digest the dinner?**
   A by midnight Thursday
   B by 6 a.m. Friday
   C by 6 p.m. Friday
   D by 6 a.m. Saturday

Directions: Questions 16 and 17 are based on the paragraph below.

Blood carries nutrients from food to all the cells in a person's body. Blood also carries oxygen to the body's cells. The oxygen gets into the blood and to the rest of the body through a series of steps that involve the heart, lungs, and blood vessels. First, blood from the body's cells flows through blood vessels into the heart. This blood contains very little oxygen because the body's cells have used it up. The heart pumps the oxygen-poor blood to the lungs, where it flows through tiny blood vessels. Next, the oxygen in the air in the lungs moves through the walls of the blood vessels and into the blood. Special cells in the blood absorb the oxygen. Then the blood moves through larger blood vessels back to the heart. The heart pumps the oxygen-rich blood through blood vessels to the rest of the body. As the blood moves through the body, the cells absorb oxygen from it. Finally, the oxygen-poor blood moves back to the heart, and the cycle starts again.

16 **What happens to the blood after it arrives in the lungs and before it flows through the blood vessels in the rest of the body?**
   A The blood moves through tiny blood vessels into the heart.
   B The blood releases oxygen to the air.
   C The blood carries nutrients to the cells in the body.
   D The blood flows through tiny blood vessels in the lungs.

17 **What occurs after the heart pumps oxygen-rich blood throughout the body?**
   A The blood carries nutrients to cells in the body.
   B Cells absorb the oxygen, the oxygen-poor blood returns to the heart, and the process starts again.
   C The heart pumps the oxygen-poor blood to the lungs.
   D Blood from the body's cells flows through blood vessels into the heart.

Interpret, Analyze, and Evaluate Timelines

① Learn the Skill

Timelines display a sequence of events in a visual way. Remember that when you use a sequence, you place events or processes in a particular order. When you **interpret timelines**, you use a visual tool to determine when events happened and the amount of time that occurred between them. Timelines may be organized either horizontally or vertically.

② Practice the Skill

By mastering the skill of interpreting timelines, you will improve your study and test-taking skills, especially as they relate to science high school equivalency tests. Read the text, timeline, and strategies below. Use the information to answer question 1.

A Hash marks divide a timeline into equal intervals, or parts. Determine the size of an interval on a timeline by reading the years below or to the side of the hash marks. On this timeline, the interval is 10 years.

B When events occur at hash marks, the year is easy to identify. Here, you can see the Lacey Act was passed in 1900. When events occur between hash marks, you must estimate the year. The ESA was passed *between* 1970 and 1980. Based on where the event is marked, you can estimate that the year was about 1973.

Beginning in the early 1900s, the United States passed several laws to give greater protection to plants and animals in danger of extinction.

Lacey Act | Migrating Bird Act (limits hunting of migratory birds) | Endangered Species Preservation Act | Endangered Species Act (ESA)

1900 1910 1920 1930 1940 1950 1960 1970 1980 1990 2000

First national wildlife refuge | Bald Eagle Protection Act (outlaws killing of eagles) | Endangered Species Conservation Act

MAKING ASSUMPTIONS

A timeline can help you see trends in a sequence of events. For example, a timeline may show that the government passed few laws to protect plants and animals in the 1980s. This trend may support several ideas. Perhaps existing laws were working and no new laws were needed.

1 Which conclusion does the timeline support?

A Protection of wildlife was more important to people in 1900 than in 1973.

B National Wildlife Refuges were created as part of the Endangered Species Act.

C Protection of endangered species was still a concern in the second half of the 1900s.

D The Migrating Bird Act replaced the Bald Eagle Protection Act.

Directions: Question 2 is based on the information below.

Sometimes legal protection alone cannot save a species from extinction. The timeline shows several species that became extinct during the 1900s.

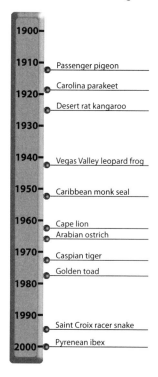

Directions: Questions 3 and 4 are based on the information below.

When the bald eagle became a national symbol in 1782, there were about 500,000 bald eagles in the United States. Hunting and habitat destruction, however, caused gradual declines in eagle populations. In the first part of the 1900s, the United States government gave eagles limited protection. Between the 1940s and 1960s, increased use of the pesticide DDT caused reproductive problems for eagles. As a result, their population numbers dropped. By 1963, the population of eagles was at an all-time low. The government passed laws in the 1960s and 1970s to give eagles greater protection.

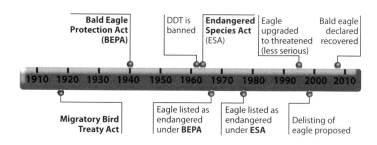

2 **Based on the timeline, which statement is accurate?**
  A Most of the animals listed became extinct in the first half of the 1900s.
  B Ten years passed between the extinctions of the Caspian tiger and the golden toad.
  C The timeline shows several extinctions between 2000 and present day.
  D The Cape lion, Arabian ostrich, and Caspian tiger became extinct within ten years.

3 **Based on the information and timeline, which statement was true of bald eagles in the 1960s?**
  A They were abundant in the wild.
  B Their populations had remained virtually unchanged for nearly 200 years.
  C They were removed from the endangered list.
  D They produced fewer chicks because of DDT.

4 **Which statement best describes the effect that federal actions had on bald eagle populations after 1950?**
  A No effect; bald eagles never required government protection.
  B Minor effect; the population of bald eagles seldom changed over a 90-year period.
  C Moderate effect; limited government protection kept the populations stable.
  D Major effect; protections allowed for the removal of eagles from the endangered list.

Directions: Questions 5 through 9 are based on the information below.

Pelican Island National Wildlife Refuge celebrated its 100th birthday in 2003. It was the first national wildlife refuge in the United States. Today, there are more than 540 national wildlife refuges. The mission of national wildlife refuges is to preserve wildlife and its habitat. Today's national wildlife refuges provide protected habitats for more than 250 endangered and threatened species. The timeline shows some key events in the formation of Pelican Island National Wildlife Refuge.

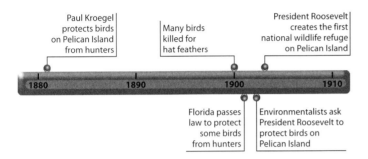

5   Based on the information in the timeline, when did President Roosevelt create the Pelican Island National Wildlife Refuge?
    A   at the start of the 1880s
    B   about 10 years after Paul Kroegel started protecting birds
    C   about one year after environmentalists asked him for help
    D   about five years after Florida passed a law to protect some birds

6   About how many years passed between when Paul Kroegel protected birds on Pelican Island and when President Roosevelt created the Pelican Island National Wildlife Refuge?
    A   about 3 years
    B   about 5 years
    C   about 10 years
    D   about 20 years

7   Based on the information in the paragraph and the timeline, which event happened most recently?
    A   Many pelicans were killed for their feathers.
    B   Pelican Island National Wildlife Refuge celebrated its 100th birthday.
    C   Paul Kroegel protected birds on Pelican Island.
    D   President Roosevelt was asked to protect birds on Pelican Island.

8   What does the information in the timeline suggest about President Roosevelt's contributions to wildlife preservation?
    A   He paid little attention to environmentalists.
    B   He acted promptly in response to environmental concerns.
    C   He listened only to the concerns of Paul Kroegel.
    D   Nothing happened until he left the presidency.

9   Where on the timeline would you place the following entry:

    President Roosevelt establishes a network of 55 wildlife refuges.
    A   between 1890 and 1900
    B   after the creation of Pelican Island National Wildlife Refuge
    C   immediately after environmentalists asked for protection for birds on Pelican Island
    D   at the same time Roosevelt created the first national wildlife refuge

Directions: Questions 10 and 11 are based on the information below.

Both alligators and crocodiles once were common in Florida, but over time hunting by humans reduced their populations. As a result, both animals have been listed as endangered species. The protection of federal and state endangered species laws has allowed alligator and crocodile populations to increase in Florida. Today, both alligators and crocodiles are listed as threatened. The timeline shows some events in the history of alligator and crocodile populations in Florida.

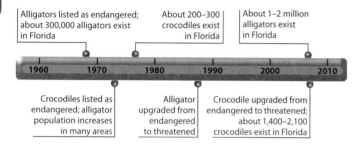

10 **Based on the information and the timeline, which of these statements is true?**
   A Crocodiles were listed as endangered before alligators were.
   B Alligator populations have increased, but crocodile populations have not.
   C Crocodile populations have increased, but alligator populations have not.
   D Federal and state protections have helped increase the populations of alligators and crocodiles.

11 **Based on the information in the timeline, about how long did it take for the crocodile population to increase from 200–300 to 1,400–2,100?**
   A about 3 years
   B about 5 years
   C about 10 years
   D about 30 years

Directions: Questions 12 through 14 are based on the information below.

Gray wolves once were common across North America. However, to prevent wolves from attacking their cattle, settlers killed many wolves. By the 1920s, gray wolves were gone from most of the Rocky Mountains. By 1950, few wolves were left in the United States. The 1973 Endangered Species Act helped protect remaining wolf populations. In the following years, scientists made plans to re-introduce wolves to areas west of where hunters once had eliminated them. In 1995, a new plan began to put wolves back into Yellowstone National Park and surrounding areas. In 2013, there were nearly 1,700 wolves in the area around the Rocky Mountains.

12 **Suppose you wanted to use the information in the paragraph to construct a timeline showing the history of gray wolf populations in the United States. Which of the following would make the best range for your timeline?**
   A 1950–2000
   B 1920–1995
   C 1973–2007
   D 1910–2020

13 **Where on your timeline should you put the entry "Endangered Species Act passes"?**
   A about halfway between the 1960 tick mark and the 1970 tick mark
   B about one-third of the way between the 1970 tick mark and the 1980 tick mark
   C very close to the 1980 tick mark
   D lined up with the 1970 tick mark

14 **To more fully tell the story of the gray wolf on the timeline, what additional piece of information would you need?**
   A the predicted population of the gray wolf in the Rocky Mountains in 50 years
   B the exact population of wolves in each state in 1950
   C the population of the gray wolf in the Rocky Mountains in the late 1800s, before many were killed
   D the text of the 1973 Endangered Species Act

Lesson 12 | Interpret, Analyze, and Evaluate Timelines

Directions: Question 15 is based on the information below.

Hundreds of years ago, there may have been as many as 30 million bison roaming on the Great Plains. But as settlers moved west and bison hides became valuable, millions of bison were killed. Soldiers also killed many bison to weaken Plains Indians who depended on bison meat and hides. As a result, bison nearly disappeared from the Great Plains in the late 1800s. The timeline below shows some of the major events in the history of the bison on the Great Plains.

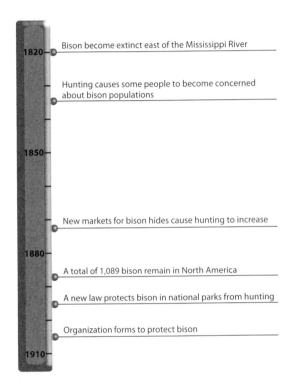

15 Based on the information in the timeline, about how many years passed between when some people began to be concerned about the bison populations and when an organization formed to protect bison?

A about 10 years
B about 25 years
C about 70 years
D about 80 years

Directions: Questions 16 and 17 are based on the information below.

Human actions once nearly caused the California condor to become extinct. Human actions also may have helped to save the condor from extinction. For example, the federal Endangered Species Act helped California make saving the condor a priority. Today, the condor population is increasing slowly. The timeline below shows some of the major events in the history of the California condor.

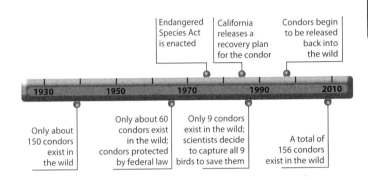

16 Based on the information in the timeline, how many years passed between the time when the California condor was protected by federal law and when the state of California released a recovery plan for the condor?

A about 1 year
B about 5 years
C about 10 years
D about 20 years

17 Based on the information in the timeline, when did scientists decide to capture all of the wild condors in order to save them?

A when there were only about 150 condors left in the wild
B in the early 1990s
C before passage of the Endangered Species Act
D around 1986

Cause and Effect

① Learn the Skill

A **cause** is an object or action that makes an event happen. The **effect** is the event that results from the cause. Often, a cause is stated directly. In other cases, it is implied. A cause may have more than one effect, and a single effect may have more than one cause.

② Practice the Skill

By mastering the skill of cause and effect, you will improve your study and test-taking skills, especially as they relate to science high school equivalency tests. Look at the diagram and strategies below. Use the information to answer question 1.

A Here, one cause can trigger several effects. The cause is an object that cuts the skin and inserts bacteria. The initial effect is that the bacteria cause the release of chemicals such as histamines.

B The histamines then become the cause of a secondary effect—the swelling and redness around the wound.

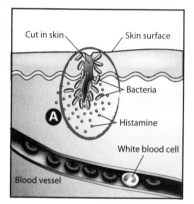
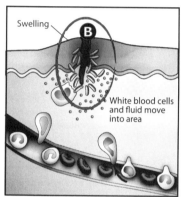

When a sharp object breaks the skin, bacteria can enter the body. Bacteria trigger a part of the body's immune system. As a first step to fighting infection, the body releases a chemical called histamine.

💡 USING LOGIC

Just because events occur at or around the same time does not ensure a cause-and-effect relationship. When answering questions on cause and effect, consider whether it is logical that a given object or event influenced the other.

1 What is the body's response to this chemical signal?
  A The body drains blood and fluids from the injured area.
  B The body sends in its own bacteria to attack the foreign bacteria.
  C The body increases the flow of blood and other fluids to the area, which produces swelling.
  D The body decreases the amount of oxygen in the area.

Directions: Questions 2 and 3 are based on the information below.

In the late 1700s, the deadly disease smallpox was widespread. Edward Jenner, a doctor, found that most people who caught a related but milder disease called cowpox recovered. He further discovered that later exposure to smallpox did not affect these people. Jenner decided to expose a healthy young boy to the cowpox virus. The boy became mildly ill and then recovered. Jenner then exposed the boy to smallpox. The boy did not become ill. Without knowing it, Jenner had given the first vaccination. Vaccination involves injecting people with dead or weakened bacteria or viruses. As a result, a person's immune system produces antibodies to a particular bacterium or virus. Antibodies are proteins that identify disease-causing invaders. If a person is later exposed to the same microbe, the antibodies from his or her immune system can quickly recognize the invader. Today, vaccination is a major weapon in preventing disease.

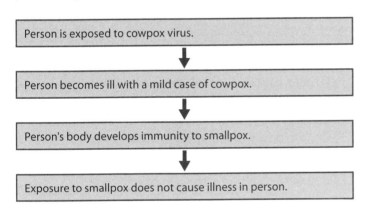

Person is exposed to cowpox virus.

↓

Person becomes ill with a mild case of cowpox.

↓

Person's body develops immunity to smallpox.

↓

Exposure to smallpox does not cause illness in person.

2 What does the body produce as a result of exposure to cowpox?
 A antibodies that protect against cowpox and, to some degree, smallpox
 B red blood cells that protect against antibodies
 C bacteria that cause cowpox
 D antibodies that protect against any disease

3 What limitations were inherent in the procedure that Edward Jenner carried out?
 A It resulted in immunity to both cowpox and smallpox.
 B It produced poisons that killed the test subjects exposed to smallpox.
 C The results could not explain why the test subjects became immune to cowpox and smallpox.
 D The procedure could not be repeated.

Directions: Question 4 is based on the paragraph below.

It wasn't until the 1850s and the efforts of scientist Louis Pasteur that people began to understand the cause of disease. Pasteur correctly believed that disease was caused by microscopic germs that attacked the body from outside. However, many scientists of that time thought it ridiculous that unseen organisms could destroy vastly larger ones. Pasteur's discovery, known as the germ theory of disease, convinced them otherwise. Pasteur later used his germ theory as a basis to explain the causes of and treatments for diseases such as anthrax and rabies. Later scientists built upon Pasteur's theory with the development and treatment of various types of vaccines.

4 What effect did Pasteur's research have on the understanding and prevention of disease?
 A No effect; levels of disease remained unchanged.
 B Minor effect; levels of disease decreased, but only slightly.
 C Moderate effect; Pasteur's findings worked on certain diseases, but not others.
 D Major effect; Pasteur's efforts changed how people understand and treat diseases.

Directions: Questions 5 and 6 are based on the paragraph below.

Some snakes have poisonous venom that can kill a person with a single bite. To counteract the effects of a snakebite, doctors give snakebite victims a type of drug called antivenin. Antivenin neutralizes the poison in snake venom. To make antivenin, scientists take poisonous venom from snakes. They give a horse or a sheep several shots of the venom over several weeks. Because the amount of injected venom is small, the animals do not die. However, the amount is enough to cause the animals' blood to make antibodies to the venom. Scientists then can make antivenin for humans with antibodies from the horse and sheep blood.

5   Based on the information, what causes the production of antibodies that are used to make antivenin?
   A   the injection of snake venom into a horse or a sheep
   B   the production of bacteria in the body of a venomous snake
   C   the injection of snake venom directly into the blood of snakebite victims
   D   the injection of human antibodies into a venomous snake

6   What effect does antivenin have on human snakebite victims?
   A   The antivenin makes it so that snakes no longer produce harmful venom.
   B   The antivenin stops the spread of the snakebite venom from one person to another.
   C   The antivenin acts as a lasting vaccine against various viruses.
   D   The antivenin neutralizes the poison in snakebite venom.

Directions: Questions 7 and 8 are based on the information below.

Antigens are any foreign substances that enter the body. Antibodies are proteins in the blood that attach to antigens. Antibodies help the cells of the immune system recognize and destroy harmful antigens. When antigen particles enter the body, antibodies bind to them. This forms a large cluster of antigens and antibodies. The clusters then become easier for other cells of the immune system to find and destroy.

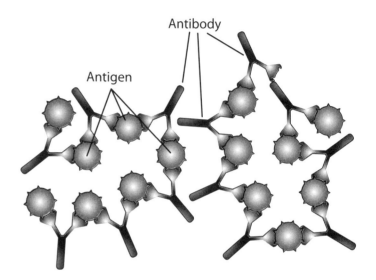

7   Based on the information, what effect do the antibodies have on antigen particles in the body?
   A   They assist in the development of additional antigens.
   B   They eliminate all foreign substances, including antigens.
   C   They help produce additional proteins in the blood.
   D   They bind with the antigens, forming a large and noticeable cluster.

8   Based on the information, what must happen before the antigens and antibodies can form clusters?
   A   The antibodies must recognize the antigens.
   B   The antigens must recognize foreign substances.
   C   The antigens must destroy the immune cells.
   D   The blood must get rid of antibodies.

Directions: Questions 9 and 10 are based on the information below.

Until the 1950s, polio was a common disease that left many people paralyzed. Jonas Salk and others worked for several years to develop a vaccine for the polio virus. In 1955, the government approved Salk's vaccine. From that point on, the number of polio vaccinations increased. Today, most children in the United States are vaccinated for polio at very young ages.

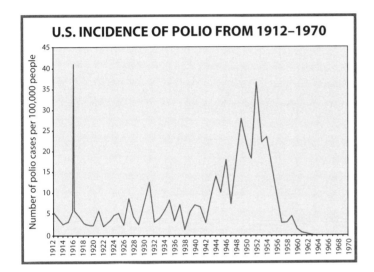

U.S. INCIDENCE OF POLIO FROM 1912–1970

9 **Based on the information and line graph, what was the effect of the Salk polio vaccine?**
   A The number of new polio cases increased sharply.
   B The number of new polio cases decreased sharply.
   C The number of new polio cases increased and then decreased.
   D The number of new polio cases decreased and then increased.

10 **Based on the information, what most likely caused the rate of polio vaccination in the United States to increase in the late 1950s?**
   A a decrease in the amount of polio cases in the early 1950s
   B an increase in the number of young children in the United States
   C reduced funding for polio research
   D government approval of the Salk polio vaccine in 1955

Directions: Questions 11 and 12 are based on the paragraph below.

Albert Sabin thought he could improve upon the Salk polio vaccine. The Salk vaccine used a dead virus to cause the body to make polio antibodies. Sabin experimented with a weakened, live virus. He thought a live virus would give longer and better protection against the disease. In 1960, the U.S. government approved the use of the Sabin vaccine. Today, doctors use the Sabin vaccine more often than Salk's version. The Sabin vaccine, which a person swallows, is easier to give than the Salk vaccine. Its protection also lasts longer.

11 **What effect did the use of a live polio virus have on Sabin's polio vaccine?**
   A Using a live virus made the protection from the vaccine last longer.
   B Using a live virus caused more people to become ill from the vaccine.
   C Using a live virus led to the discontinuation of the Salk vaccine.
   D Using a live virus caused the body to make fewer antibodies to the polio virus.

12 **Based on the information in the paragraph, why did the Sabin vaccine become more commonly used than the Salk vaccine?**
   A Polio rates continued to rise, even after the Salk vaccine began to be used.
   B The Salk vaccine is more likely to cause illness than is the Sabin vaccine.
   C People who receive the Sabin vaccine cannot also receive the Salk vaccine.
   D The Sabin vaccine lasts longer than the Salk vaccine.

Directions: Questions 13 through 15 are based on the information below.

Usually, the human immune system responds only to harmful substances. Sometimes, though, the immune system reacts in an extreme way to relatively harmless substances, such as pollen, molds, dust, or pet fur. These reactions are called allergies. Some allergic reactions are mild. They cause sneezing or a runny nose. Other allergic reactions are more severe. In people with asthma (an illness of the lungs), allergic reactions can cause severe breathing problems.

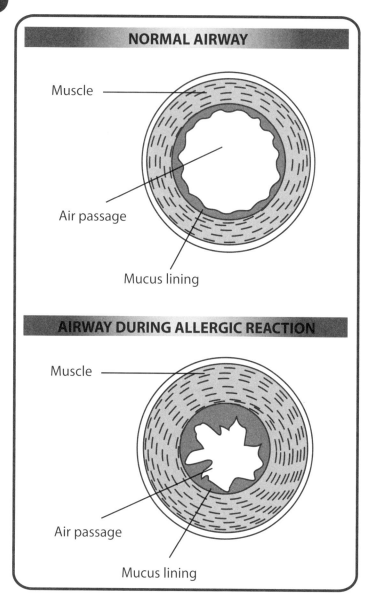

NORMAL AIRWAY

Muscle

Air passage

Mucus lining

AIRWAY DURING ALLERGIC REACTION

Muscle

Air passage

Mucus lining

13 Based on the diagram, what happens to small air passages when a person with asthma is exposed to certain substances?
  A The air passages swell as more air moves inside.
  B The air passages dry out as the body absorbs more water from the lungs.
  C The air passages narrow as muscles tighten, and the lining makes extra mucus.
  D Small air passages in the lungs fill completely with water.

14 Based on the information, what is a typical cause of an asthma attack?
  A dust or pollen
  B muscle contractions
  C sneezing and a runny nose
  D certain medications

15 Which symptom would be the most likely effect of an asthma attack?
  A upset stomach
  B headache
  C leg cramps
  D shortness of breath

Directions: Question 16 is based on the paragraph below.

HIV is a virus that can cause the body to develop acquired immunodeficiency syndrome (AIDS). AIDS is a disease in which the immune system stops working as it should. As a result, the body becomes susceptible to various diseases and infections. Many of these diseases would have little to no effect on individuals with healthy immune systems. However, AIDS patients typically die from infections that their immune systems cannot fight.

16 Based on the information, what causes the deaths of most people with AIDS?
  A infections the immune system cannot fight
  B overactive immune systems
  C undeveloped immune systems
  D antibodies triggered by the HIV virus

Make Inferences

① Learn the Skill

An **inference** is a logical guess based on facts, evidence, experience, or reasoning. If you know several related facts, you can **make inferences** about their meaning. That meaning could be implied, or hinted at, through several details. When meaning is implied, the reader must use prior knowledge to connect facts.

② Practice the Skill

By mastering the skill of making inferences, you will improve your study and test-taking skills, especially as they relate to science high school equivalency tests. Read the excerpt and the strategies below. Use the information to answer question 1.

Ⓐ Before the author made an inference, he collected and presented his observations. Making an inference requires the use of logic to determine the truth based on available information.

Ⓑ Scientists generally make inferences about objects or events that they cannot or did not observe directly. Darwin did not know from direct observation that small eyes help prevent infection. Instead, Darwin made an inference from the evidence he had.

Excerpt fom Charles Darwin's *On the Origin of Species by Means of Natural Selection* (1859)

"....The eyes of moles and of some burrowing rodents are rudimentary in size, and in some cases are quite covered up by skin and fur. This state of the eyes is probably due to gradual reduction from disuse . . . In South America, a burrowing rodent, the tuco-tuco . . . is even more subterranean in its habits than the mole; and . . . they were frequently blind; one which I kept alive was certainly in this condition, the cause, as appeared on dissection, having been inflammation of the nictitating membrane. As frequent inflammation of the eyes must be injurious to any animal, and <u>as eyes are certainly not indispensable to animals with subterranean habits, a reduction in their size . . . might in such case be an advantage</u>. . . ."

💡 USING LOGIC

As you analyze a passage, note that a writer generally will state his or her inference after presenting all the facts. Inferences often can be recognized by the following wording: *if . . . then; as . . . then; might be; could be; probably.*

1 **Which inference did Darwin make about the connection between eye size and living underground?**
   A Animals with large eyes are unable to survive underground.
   B The eyes of burrowing animals are smaller, but the animals' eyesight is stronger.
   C Burrowing in the ground can cause an animal to develop larger eyes.
   D The small eyes of burrowing animals are beneficial to survival.

Directions: Questions 2 through 4 are based on the information below.

Charles Darwin left England in 1831 for a voyage around the world. The trip gave him the chance to observe and collect plants and animals from many different places. In late 1835, Darwin spent several weeks on the Galápagos Islands off the coast of South America. He collected several finches from the islands and brought the specimens back to London. Once home, Darwin studied the birds. He was amazed to find that, although they were all finches from the same group of islands, they had beaks of different sizes and shapes. Darwin wrote that, "One might really fancy that . . . one species had been taken and modified for different ends."

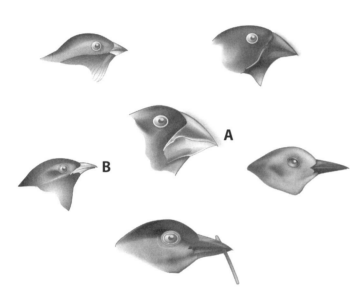

2 In the passage, Darwin states that one might think one species had been modified for different purposes. What inference did Darwin make?
  A The different beaks prove that all birds have different purposes.
  B Finches from different islands had different beak shapes.
  C Birds on the Galápagos are different from birds in London.
  D The different finches had come from the same ancestor.

3 On what did Darwin base his inference?
  A personal experience
  B the work of another scientist
  C his own observations
  D a prediction about life on the Galápagos

4 Based on the information in the illustration, what inference can you make about Bird A and Bird B?
  A Bird A is more likely than Bird B to survive in its environment.
  B Bird B is an ancestor of Bird A.
  C Bird B's beak is thicker than Bird A's beak.
  D The birds probably do not have to compete for food.

Directions: Question 5 is based on the paragraph below.

As a young scientist, Charles Darwin spent five years observing nature while on board the *Beagle*. While exploring parts of South America, Darwin experienced first-hand the devastation caused by an earthquake. The earthquake caused a tsunami that destroyed the Chilean city of Concepción. Darwin walked through the rubble of the city and was intrigued by the damage as well as by a strange sight: Local mussel beds, all dead, were now above the high tide level.

5 What is a logical inference Darwin could have made about the surrounding land from his observation of mussel beds above high tide level?
  A The land had risen.
  B The land had fallen.
  C The earthquake had replenished the mussel population.
  D The mussel beds had been buried beneath the city of Concepción.

Directions: Questions 6 and 7 are based on the information below.

Charles Darwin traveled around the world, observing plants and animals in many different places. He used his observations to make inferences as he developed his theory of evolution.

OBSERVATION 1

Resources such as food and shelter are limited in a given ecosystem.

OBSERVATION 2

If all individuals in a population reproduce, the population quickly grows out of control.

OBSERVATION 3

In most cases, the size of a population stays basically stable over time.

INFERENCE

---

6 **Based on the information, what inference can be made?**
   A Over time, a population will have more and more individuals with beneficial traits.
   B An increase in population size must lead to an increase in available resources.
   C Availability of resources has no effect on population size.
   D Competition for resources keeps many members of a population from surviving to reproduce.

7 **If a trait helps an individual to survive and reproduce, that trait can be passed on to offspring. Based on this information, which inference can you make?**
   A Over time, more individuals in the population will have this trait.
   B Offspring are identical to their parents.
   C Competition for resources will decrease over time.
   D Parents will choose which traits to pass on to their offspring.

Directions: Question 8 is based on the paragraph below.

Darwin inferred that types of organisms alive today evolved slowly in form from organisms of the past. But he had no direct evidence because the fossil record was incomplete. He concluded that if scientists could find fossils that covered every period of time, they would see the gradual evolution in the forms of organisms. Since Darwin's time, scientists have discovered many more fossils. Though the fossil record is still far from complete, newly discovered fossils help scientists piece together the story of how the structures of living things changed over time.

8 **Based on the information, which evidence best supports Darwin's inference?**
   A living animals of the same species with different characteristics
   B living animals of the same species with the same characteristics
   C fossils from different time periods with characteristics that become more similar to those of living animals
   D fossils of animals of the same species from the same time period but with different characteristics

Directions: Questions 9 and 10 are based on the information below.

Two types of moths, one light gray and the other dark gray, lived in the same area. The light gray moths could easily blend in and hide from predators when resting on light-colored tree trunks. Predators could easily see the darker moths, however. When factories were built in the area, soot from smokestacks blackened the tree trunks. A scientist counted the number of individuals in each moth population and compared her numbers to population data from before the factories were built.

	LIGHT MOTHS	DARK MOTHS
Population Numbers Before Factories	243	104
Population Numbers After Factories	150	227

9 **Which of the following best summarizes the data in the table?**
   A The population of light moths increased over time; the population of dark moths decreased.
   B The populations of both light and dark moths increased.
   C The populations of both moth types remained stable.
   D The population of light moths decreased over time; the population of dark moths increased.

10 **Based on the information, what can you infer?**
   A Light color was an advantage when tree trunks were light; dark color became an advantage when trunks got darker.
   B Dark-colored moths always have a better chance of survival than light-colored moths.
   C Color is unlikely to determine the survival of a population.
   D Dark-colored animals live for a long time in polluted environments.

Directions: Questions 11 through 13 are based on the following excerpt from the writings of Charles Darwin.

"Although each [rock] formation may mark a very long lapse of years, each perhaps is short compared with the period . . . [needed] to change one species into another. . . . When we see [the fossil of] a species first appearing in the middle of any formation, it would be rash . . . to infer that it had not elsewhere previously existed . . . [or that] it had become wholly extinct. We forget how small the area of Europe is compared with the rest of the world . . ."

11 **In this excerpt, Darwin argues that the fossil record is incomplete. What inference does Darwin make?**
   A All the fossils that show the past form of a species have been discovered.
   B If a species existed, scientists would have discovered a fossil proving it.
   C Fossils are not useful in confirming the existence of past species.
   D Species could have lived in many places where fossils have not yet been found.

12 **Which of the following supports Darwin's inference?**
   A the relatively large size of Europe
   B the growing extinction of species
   C the presence of similar species on different continents
   D the accuracy of the existing fossil record

13 **Based on Darwin's writings, what can you infer would provide a more complete fossil record?**
   A the comparison of like fossils from other places
   B new fossil discoveries within Europe
   C a comparison of fossils over a shorter span of time
   D the comparison of fossils from areas similar to Europe

Directions: Questions 14 through 16 are based on the information below.

A scientist is observing interactions of different species along a white, sandy beach. She observes that seagulls often feed on clams partially buried in sand at the waterline. The seagulls snatch the clams and then drop them from several feet off the ground onto rocks. Once the shells are broken, the seagulls can eat the clams inside. Some of the clams in this area have white shells, while others have dark pink shells. The table below summarizes some of the scientist's observations.

CLAM POPULATION NUMBERS BY SHELL COLOR		
	NUMBER OF INDIVIDUALS	PERCENT OF TOTAL CLAM POPULATION
White	425	68%
Pink	201	32%

EMPTY CLAM SHELLS FOUND BY SHELL COLOR		
	NUMBER OF SHELLS	PERCENT OF TOTAL SHELLS
White	296	43%
Pink	390	57%

14 Based on the tables, what inference can you make about the seagulls?
A The seagulls have no clam color preference.
B The seagulls prefer to feed on the pink clams.
C The seagulls must compete with other animals for the clams.
D The seagulls prefer to feed on the white clams.

15 Based on the information and tables, what inference can you make about the clam populations on this particular beach?
A White clams are protected from seagulls because their shells are too hard to break.
B White clams are more difficult to locate in the white sand than pink clams.
C The clam populations are in danger of extinction from heavy predation.
D The two clam populations compete for the same resources.

16 Scientists have found that traits helpful to a species become more common in a population of that species over time. With that in mind, which inference can you make?
A The ratio of white to pink clams will stay the same in the future.
B White clams will disappear from the population.
C White clams will remain a larger percentage of the total clam population.
D Pink clams will make up a larger percentage of the total population in the future.

Directions: Question 17 is based on the paragraph below.

In the spring and summer, the dark coat of the arctic fox blends into the abundant brown dirt of its environment. This provides it with an advantage in hunting prey such as lemmings, ground squirrels, and birds. In the winter, the arctic fox's coat changes color to white.

17 What can you infer about the change in the fox's coat during the winter?
A The white coat keeps the fox warmer.
B The white coat enables the arctic fox to blend into the snowy conditions.
C The white coat reflects the sunshine, keeping the arctic fox cooler.
D The thicker white coat allows the arctic fox to hibernate during the winter months.

Draw Conclusions

① Learn the Skill

Remember that an inference is an educated guess based upon facts, evidence, experience, or reasoning. A **conclusion** is an explanation or judgment that generally relies on inferences. When you **draw conclusions**, you make a statement that explains your observations and the facts that you have.

② Practice the Skill

By mastering the skill of drawing conclusions, you will improve your study and test-taking skills, especially as they relate to science high school equivalency tests. Look at the diagram and strategies below. Use the information to answer question 1.

Ⓐ A conclusion is the answer to a researcher's main question. In this case, Mendel carried out his experiments to determine how traits are passed from one generation to the next.

Ⓑ A conclusion differs from a summary. For example, the statement, "Some offspring produced purple flowers and some produced white flowers" is a summary of the observations, not a conclusion. A conclusion is an explanation or judgment that is based on an educated guess.

Gregor Mendel's experiments with pea plants in the mid-1800s laid the foundation for the science of genetics. Mendel wanted to learn how traits were passed down and combined through generations. The diagram shows the results of an experiment in which Mendel bred plants with purple flowers to plants with white flowers.

Parent generation — Purple flowers X White flowers

First generation of offspring — All plants have purple flowers

Second generation of offspring — $\frac{3}{4}$ of plants have purple flowers, $\frac{1}{4}$ of plants have white flowers

✓ TEST-TAKING TIPS

For a conclusion to be valid, it should explain all observations. When drawing a conclusion, consider any and all results or other relevant information.

1 **Based on the information, which statement is a valid conclusion for Mendel's experiment?**
  A The purple flower trait destroys the white flower trait.
  B A trait may reappear unchanged even if it is "hidden" in one generation by another trait.
  C Plants with purple flowers are less likely to survive than plants with white flowers.
  D A single offspring shows a blending of all the traits of both parents.

Directions: Questions 2 through 4 are based on the information below.

Mendel drew certain conclusions from the results of his experiments with pea plants. He realized that each plant carried pairs of "heritable factors" (what we now call *genes*) for all its visible traits. Mendel's results demonstrated that certain inherited traits show dominance or recessiveness. The Punnett square below represents the cross between two purple flowers, both of which had one copy of the white-flower trait (*p*) and one copy of the purple-flower trait (*P*). The boxes inside the square show the possible combinations of flower-color traits in the offspring.

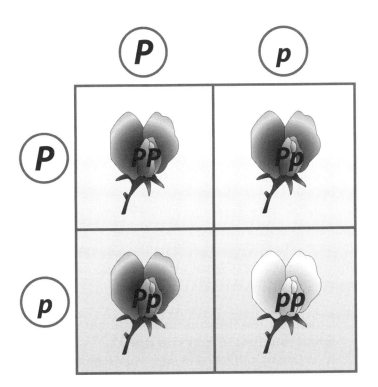

2 **Based on the information, what conclusion can you make about the relationship between the white-flower trait and the purple-flower trait?**
   A The white-flower trait shows even when the individual also has a copy of the purple-flower trait.
   B The white-flower trait never appears in the offspring of two purple-flowered plants.
   C The white-flower trait is dominant to the purple-flower trait.
   D The white-flower trait is recessive to the purple-flower trait.

3 **Based on the information in the diagram, what can you conclude about why the color of the pea flowers in each generation alone does not predict the flower color of the next generation?**
   A Color changes randomly with each generation.
   B An individual showing the dominant trait may be able to pass on a copy of the recessive trait to its offspring.
   C Plants generally lack sufficient offspring for a recessive trait to appear.
   D An individual showing the recessive trait may carry a hidden version of the dominant trait.

4 **Based on the information, what conclusion can you make about the parents of all pea plants with white flowers?**
   A The parents have white flowers.
   B The parents each have at least one copy of the white-flower trait.
   C The parents produce only offspring with white flowers.
   D The parents each have two copies of the white-flower trait.

Directions: Questions 5 and 6 are based on the information below.

Chromosomes are tiny thread-like structures that carry genetic material in each cell. Each species, such as humans, has a certain number of chromosomes in its cells. In most organisms, the chromosomes form pairs. Chromosomes make copies of themselves when cells divide. This allows each new cell to have a complete copy of the organism's genetic material.

Deoxyribonucleic acid, or DNA, is the molecule that stores genetic material. Chromosomes are made up of tightly coiled molecules of DNA. The thin, ladder-shaped DNA molecules are made of millions of tiny units called nucleotides. Each nucleotide contains one of four different bases: adenine (A), guanine (G), thymine (T), or cytosine (C). Sugars and phosphates form the ladder's sides. The bases form the rungs of the ladder, as shown in the figure below.

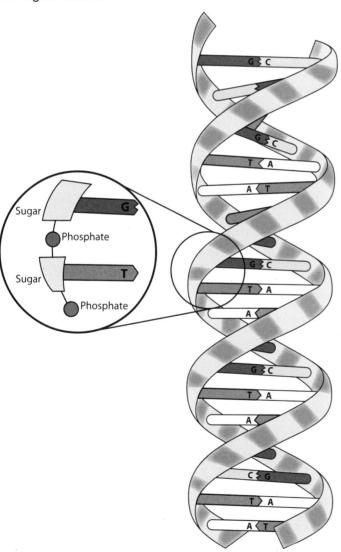

5 Based on the information in the paragraph and illustration, what can you conclude about the number of guanine (G) and cytosine (C) nucleotides in a DNA molecule?

A   A DNA molecule has the same number of C nucleotides as G nucleotides.

B   There are more G nucleotides than C nucleotides in a DNA molecule.

C   Some DNA molecules contain no C nucleotides.

D   Most DNA molecules contain very few G nucleotides.

6 Based on the paragraph and illustration, what can you conclude about the structure of DNA?

A   Sugars are located along the sides and middle of a DNA molecule.

B   One side of a DNA molecule is longer than the other.

C   Sugars and phosphates form the rungs of the ladder.

D   There are four different possible nucleotides in a DNA molecule.

Directions: Question 7 is based on the paragraph below.

By the early 1950s, scientists knew about the chemical composition of a DNA molecule. They knew that each DNA molecule contains sugars, phosphates, and bases. In 1953, Francis Crick and James Watson proposed a "double helix" structure for DNA. That's the ladder structure we know today. They won the Nobel Prize for Medicine in 1962 for their discovery.

7 Based on the information in the paragraph, what conclusion can you draw?

A   Watson and Crick did not understand the chemical composition of DNA.

B   Scientists in the 1950s did not know that DNA has a role in heredity.

C   Scientists in the 1950s did not know that chromosomes exist.

D   Until 1953, scientists did not know what the structure of a DNA molecule looked like.

Directions: Question 8 is based on the information below.

When scientists discovered chromosomes and DNA, they were able to explain many of Gregor Mendel's observations about inherited traits. Scientists learned that inherited traits are controlled by DNA. A segment of DNA that controls a specific trait is called a gene. All the members of a species have the same genes. However, members of the same species may have different forms of their genes. For example, the flower-color gene in the pea plants Mendel studied has two forms: a purple-flower form and a white-flower form. The diagram shows how gene forms affect flower color in pea plants.

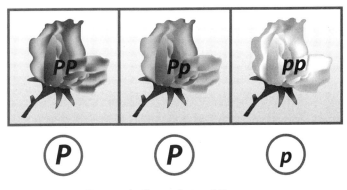

P = purple-flower form of the gene
p = white-flower form of the gene

8 **Based on the paragraph and diagram, which of the following is a valid conclusion?**
   A All of the members of a species have exactly the same traits.
   B Each pea plant has two copies of the flower-color gene.
   C Every trait is controlled by a single gene.
   D All genes have exactly two different forms.

Directions: Questions 9 and 10 are based on the information below.

Each plant has two copies of a gene for a trait. The two copies both may be of the same form or may be of different forms of the gene. The Punnett square shows how different forms of one pea-plant trait (seed color) is determined by the form of a plant's gene.

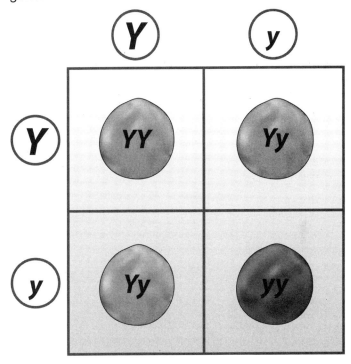

Y = yellow-seed form of the gene
y = green-seed form of the gene

9 **Based on the information and the diagram, what can you conclude about the seed-color trait?**
   A It does not appear in some plants.
   B It is related to several other pea-plant traits.
   C It is not passed on to all pea-plant offspring.
   D It is controlled by one gene with two forms.

10 **Based on the information, which of these is a valid conclusion?**
   A Only plants with two copies of the green-seed form of the gene have green seeds.
   B Yellow seeds appear in all pea plants.
   C Plants with yellow seeds produce only offspring with yellow seeds.
   D All pea plants with yellow seeds have two copies of the yellow-seed form of the gene.

Directions: Questions 11 through 15 are based on the information below.

Mendel's results demonstrated that certain inherited traits show dominance or recessiveness. If a plant has two copies of the recessive form of the gene, the plant shows the recessive trait. If the plant has one or two copies of the dominant form of the gene, the plant shows the dominant trait. One trait that Mendel studied was the shape of pea seeds. Some pea plants have smooth seeds, and others have wrinkled seeds. Mendel did several experiments to study the shapes of pea seeds. The illustration shows three of his experiments and their results.

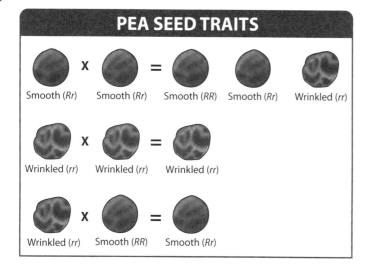

PEA SEED TRAITS

Smooth (*Rr*) X Smooth (*Rr*) = Smooth (*RR*) Smooth (*Rr*) Wrinkled (*rr*)

Wrinkled (*rr*) X Wrinkled (*rr*) = Wrinkled (*rr*)

Wrinkled (*rr*) X Smooth (*RR*) = Smooth (*Rr*)

11 What would be the most likely conclusion to the crossing of two smooth (*Rr*) seeds?
  A   25 percent chance of a smooth seed
  B   50 percent chance of a wrinkled seed
  C   50 percent chance of a smooth seed
  D   75 percent chance of a smooth seed

12 The breeding of one dominant (*RR*) smooth seed to another type of seed produces offspring that are all smooth (*Rr*). What conclusion can you draw about the gene form of the second parent seed?
  A   The second parent had *RR* forms of the trait.
  B   The second parent had *Rr* forms of the trait.
  C   The second parent had *rr* forms of the trait.
  D   The second parent had no recessive forms of the trait.

13 Based on the information in the paragraph, which of the following is a valid conclusion?
  A   The dominant form of a gene is present in all members of a species.
  B   The dominant form of a gene can be passed on only to male offspring.
  C   The dominant form of a gene, if present, is expressed as a visible trait.
  D   The dominant form of a gene is hidden if a recessive form is present.

14 Based on the paragraph and the diagram, which of the following is a valid conclusion about the seed-shape gene in pea plants?
  A   The wrinkled-seed form of the gene is dominant.
  B   The smooth-seed form of the gene is dominant.
  C   All peas with smooth seeds have a copy of the wrinkled-seed form of the gene.
  D   Peas with wrinkled seeds can be produced only by two plants with wrinkled seeds.

15 Suppose you bred a plant with wrinkled seeds to a plant with smooth seeds, and some of the offspring had wrinkled seeds. What could you conclude?
  A   The wrinkled-seed parent plant must have had two copies of the smooth-seed form of the gene.
  B   The smooth-seed parent plant must have had one copy of the wrinkled-seed form of the gene.
  C   Both parent plants had dominant forms of the gene.
  D   The offspring all had only one copy of the seed-shape gene.

UNIT 1

Generalize

① Learn the Skill

When you **generalize**, you make a broad statement that applies to an entire group of people, places, or events. A generalization can be valid or invalid. **Valid generalizations** are conclusions supported by facts and examples. **Invalid generalizations** are conclusions that are unsupported by facts or examples.

② Practice the Skill

By mastering the skill of generalizing, you will improve your study and test-taking skills, especially as they relate to science high school equivalency tests. Read the paragraph and strategies below. Use the information to answer question 1.

A To make a generalization, first gather and compare information about a topic. Then bring this information together to make a general statement. In some cases, you'll add your own knowledge to the information. This becomes your generalization.

B Even if a fact or definition describes all the members of a particular group, it is not a generalization. In this case, the fact that producers make their own food is their defining characteristic. So this statement is not a *generalization* about producers. It is a *fact* about producers.

An ecosystem is made up of a community of living organisms and the nonliving parts of the environment. Energy flows through the living components of an ecosystem. An organism gets energy from its food and passes on energy to any organism that feeds on it. Living things in an ecosystem can be classified into two broad groups based on how they obtain energy. **B** <u>Producers can make their own food.</u> Consumers must feed on other organisms to obtain energy. In most ecosystems, the producers are plants and other organisms that can use energy from sunlight to make food.

✓ TEST-TAKING TIPS

When you make a generalization, consider several examples of people, places, or things. Then consider what they have in common. Generalizations may contain key words such as *all, always, every,* and *never,* as well as *most, mostly, typically, in general, generally, often, overall, almost,* and *usually.*

1 **Which of the following statements is a generalization that can be made from the information in the passage?**
   A Every ecosystem has living and nonliving parts.
   B Most producers use energy from sunlight to make food.
   C Energy flows between the organisms in an ecosystem.
   D Organisms in an ecosystem can be divided into two main groups—producers and consumers.

Directions: Questions 2 and 3 are based on the paragraph below.

An ecosystem contains different kinds of living things. Scientists often think of the living things in an ecosystem as being organized into different levels. The lowest level of organization is the individual organism. Individual organisms are organized into populations. A population is a group of organisms that are all the same species and that all live in the same area. For example, all of the blue jays in a forest make up a population. Populations are organized into communities. A community is all of the populations in an area. Most communities contain many different populations.

2 **Based on the information in the paragraph, which statement is a valid generalization about the living things in an ecosystem?**
   A The communities in most ecosystems are made up of many different species.
   B Populations in an ecosystem are made up of individual communities.
   C All of the organisms in a population are of different species.
   D The individual organisms in a population are of many different species.

3 **Which statement is an <u>invalid</u> generalization about the living things in an ecosystem?**
   A A population includes only organisms from the same species that live in the same area.
   B Each community includes the same populations.
   C Communities contain individual organisms from different areas.
   D Organisms are organized into populations, which in turn make up communities.

Directions: Questions 4 and 5 are based on the paragraph below.

Nonliving things are very important in an ecosystem. For example, all living things need water to survive, but different living things need different amounts of water. So the amount of rainfall that an ecosystem receives helps to determine which organisms can live within it. In addition, an ecosystem's amount of sunlight and temperature similarly affect the organisms that can live there. Most organisms survive best within a narrow range of conditions. Only a few kinds of organisms can survive in very hot, very cold, very dry, or very dark environments.

4 **Which statement is a valid generalization based on information in the paragraph?**
   A Most organisms live in ecosystems with extreme temperatures.
   B The nonliving factors in an ecosystem affect which organisms live in the ecosystem.
   C All living things need water to survive.
   D All living things can live in all ecosystems.

5 **Which statement is a valid generalization based on information in the paragraph?**
   A Living things depend only on nonliving things to survive.
   B Some organisms need more water than others.
   C Most organisms need specific environmental conditions to survive.
   D The amount of sunlight in an ecosystem affects the organisms that live there.

Directions: Questions 6 and 7 are based on the information below.

Although there are many benefits to exercise, more than half of all adults in the United States fail to participate in regular physical activity. Understanding why certain individuals fail to exercise also requires understanding a person's culture, family life, and community.

PERCENTAGE OF AMERICANS WHO MET NONE OF THE GUIDELINES SET FORTH IN THE 2008 PHYSICAL ACTIVITY GUIDELINES FOR AMERICANS

ETHNICITY	YEARS		
	2000	2010	2012
African-American	65	59	55
American Indian or Alaska Native	67	54	51
Asian	67	54	51
Hispanic or Latino	67	60	55
White	53	48	46

Source: Center for Disease Control and Prevention, 2013

6 Based on the paragraph, what is an <u>invalid</u> generalization about regular physical activity?

A Regular physical activity is important to a healthy lifestyle.

B Most adults in the U.S. exercise regularly.

C An individual's environment can influence how often he or she exercises.

D Not enough American adults participate in regular physical activity.

7 Based on the table, what can you generalize about racial or ethnic groups and physical activity?

A Hispanics or Latinos tend to exercise more often than Whites.

B American Indians or Alaska Natives receive more physical activity than Asians.

C Physical activity varies from group to group.

D White individuals exercise the least of any group.

Directions: Questions 8 and 9 are based on the paragraph below.

Excessive alcohol use has many effects on the human body. Heavy drinking (at least two drinks a day for men and at least one drink a day for women) and binge drinking (five or more drinks in a sitting for a man, four or more for a woman) can increase the risk of health problems. Underage alcohol use is also a major health issue. Alcohol is the most abused drug among youth in the United States. Many health and social problems in youth, including tobacco use, physical violence, and poor academic performance, can be tied to excessive drinking.

8 Which of the following is a valid generalization about drinking alcohol?

A Heavy drinking is safe, but binge drinking is unsafe.

B Women can drink more alcohol than men without being impaired.

C Drinking alcohol in excess can cause health problems.

D Drinking large amounts of alcohol is important to maintain good health.

9 Based on the paragraph, which of the following is an <u>invalid</u> generalization about excessive underage drinking?

A There is no issue with underage alcohol use in the United States.

B Alcohol is the most abused drug by youth in the United States.

C Drinking alcohol can lead to poor academic performance.

D Excessive drinking is associated with tobacco use and physical violence.

Directions: Questions 10 and 11 are based on the information below.

There are many safe and effective methods of birth control available to prevent unintended pregnancy and the spread of sexually transmitted diseases (STDs).

CONTRACEPTIVE	PERCENT OF EFFECTIVENESS (IN PREVENTING PREGNANCY)	ADVANTAGES	DISADVANTAGES
IUD	99	Lasts up to 10 years	Does not protect against STDs
The Pill	91	Convenient	Does not protect against STDs
Male Condom	82	Inexpensive; can protect against sexually transmitted diseases	Can leak or break
Female Condom	79	Can protect against sexually transmitted diseases	Can cause irritation
Fertility Awareness	76	No cost or side effects	Does not protect against STDs

Sources: National Center for Chronic Disease Prevention and Health Promotion, 2011

10 **Based on the chart, which of the following is an <u>invalid</u> generalization about birth control?**
  A Fertility awareness is the most inexpensive form of birth control.
  B Using birth control is a safe and effective way to prevent unintended pregnancy.
  C No method of birth control can protect against STDs.
  D Male and female condoms are the best forms of birth control to protect against STDs.

11 **What can you generalize about the effectiveness of birth control methods in preventing pregnancy?**
  A No birth control method is 100 percent effective in preventing pregnancy.
  B The pill is the most effective method of birth control.
  C Female condoms have a better rate of effectiveness than IUDs.
  D Fertility awareness is the most effective method of birth control.

Directions: Question 12 is based on the paragraph below.

Experts on child development believe family relationships, specifically the relationship between a parent and a child, have a great deal of influence on the health of that child. Research suggests that unfavorable childhood experiences, such as violence, can lead to negative health effects and social behaviors. A good childhood can decrease the risk for serious health issues such as heart disease, diabetes, and mental illness.

12 **What can you generalize about the effect that parents have on a child's development?**
  A A parent's relationship with a child has no influence on a child's mental and physical development.
  B A positive parent/child relationship can have a positive effect on a child's health.
  C Positive childhood experiences have no connection to risk factors for disease.
  D A negative parent/child relationship can have a positive effect on a child's health.

Directions: Questions 13 and 14 are based on the information below.

Studies show that families with higher incomes tend to have higher-quality diets than families with lower incomes. According to the United States Department of Agriculture, only 8 percent of people with low household incomes have healthy diets. Lower-income Americans tend to consume more sodium and fat and fewer fruits and vegetables than Americans with higher incomes. Researchers believe that increased income provides families with better access to higher education, well-stocked grocery stores, and greater diet and health knowledge. These lead to better food choices and improved diet quality.

LIFE EXPECTANCY (IN AVERAGE NUMBER OF YEARS) VS. INCOME			
	YEAR		
	1980	**1990**	**2000**
High-income life expectancy	75.8	77.4	79.2
Low-income life expectancy	73	73.9	74.7

Source: International Journal of Epidemiology

13 **Based on the paragraph, what is a valid generalization about the relationship between diet and income?**
- A Less than 10 percent of high-income families have healthy diets.
- B Lower-income families tend to have less healthy diets than higher-income families.
- C Income has no effect on a family's nutrition or eating habits.
- D Higher-income families tend to have unhealthy diets.

14 **Based on the information, what can you generalize about the relationship between nutritional habits and life expectancy?**
- A Lower-income families are less healthy but live longer than higher-income families.
- B Income has no effect on health or life expectancy.
- C A longer, healthier life is associated with a better quality diet.
- D Higher-income families live healthy lives but tend to die at younger ages.

Directions: Questions 15 and 16 are based on the information below.

The graph below shows exponential population growth. In the presence of unlimited resources, a population experiencing exponential growth would increase continuously.

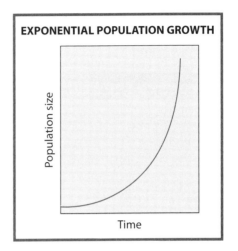

EXPONENTIAL POPULATION GROWTH

15 **Based on the information, what valid generalization can be made about exponential growth of populations?**
- A Typically, exponential growth will continue beyond carrying capacity.
- B Rapid exponential growth of populations is always due to a decrease in predation.
- C During periods of exponential growth, populations are always inhibited by factors such as limited resources and competition.
- D In populations that are growing exponentially, the rate of reproduction increases as time passes.

16 **Which of the following is an <u>invalid</u> generalization about a graph of exponential population growth?**
- A The more time that passes, the faster the population grows.
- B The more time that passes, the larger the population grows.
- C With more time, the line showing population size would continue almost straight upward.
- D With more time, the line showing population size would begin to curve downward.

Questioning

① Learn the Skill

Questioning is the process in which you ask a question about something that you observe. Questioning helps you review and understand what you read. It also helps you to identify any gaps in knowledge about a subject and then find ways to fill in those gaps with missing information.

② Practice the Skill

By mastering the skill of questioning, you will improve your study and test-taking skills, especially as they relate to science high school equivalency tests. Look at the text, illustration, and strategies below. Use the information to answer question 1.

A Questioning can help you interpret drawings and other graphics. Ask questions such as "What does this drawing show?" In this case, the drawing shows two kinds of living things interacting with one another.

Organisms can have different relationships with one another. One type of relationship is mutualism. In a mutualistic relationship, both organisms benefit. The illustration shows an example of a mutualistic relationship between a rhinoceros and oxpecker birds. In this relationship, the oxpecker birds eat insects off the rhinoceros. The birds get food, and the rhinoceros gets rid of biting insects.

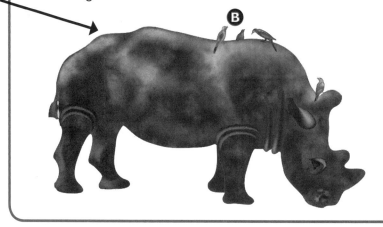

B Some questions can draw upon what you already know. For example, you may know that oxpecker birds pick insects off oxen. That may lead you to consider this: "Remora fish clean sharks' teeth, and the sharks don't hurt the remoras. Is that also an example of mutualism?"

USING LOGIC

Asking questions about the material, such as "What do I already know about this subject?" can help you make connections to your prior knowledge.

1 **Which question could you ask to help you understand why the illustration is an example of a mutualistic relationship?**
A   How large are the oxpecker birds?
B   How many insects does an oxpecker bird eat in a day?
C   Where do the oxpecker birds and rhinoceros live?
D   How do the oxpecker birds and rhinoceros help each other?

Directions: Questions 2 and 3 are based on the paragraph below.

Symbiosis is a situation in which two organisms from different species live closely together. There are several types of symbiotic relationships. One type is commensalism. In a commensal relationship, one organism benefits. The other organism does not benefit, but it is not harmed, either. For example, some types of orchids have a commensal relationship with the trees on which they grow. These orchids grow on the branches of large trees in tropical forests. The trees receive no benefit, but the orchids do not harm them.

2 **Which question should you ask to help you understand why the orchid-tree relationship is a commensal relationship?**
   A How large are the orchids?
   B How tall do the trees grow?
   C How do the orchids benefit from the relationship?
   D How are the orchids attached to the tree?

3 **What question could you ask to determine whether the orchid-tree relationship is also an example of mutualism?**
   A Is either organism harmed by the relationship?
   B Do the trees benefit in any way from the relationship?
   C How would a more moderate climate affect the relationship between trees and orchids?
   D Are the trees harmed by the orchids?

Directions: Questions 4 and 5 are based on the information below.

Some animals have a predator-prey relationship. A predator is an animal that catches and eats organisms of another species. The organisms that it catches and eats are its prey. The graph below shows the relationship between the populations of lynxes and hares in an ecosystem over time. In this ecosystem, the lynx is a predator, and the hare is its prey.

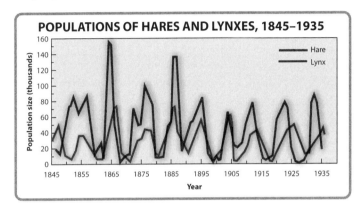

POPULATIONS OF HARES AND LYNXES, 1845–1935

4 **Which question could the graph help you answer?**
   A What are characteristics that make lynxes good predators?
   B What happens to the number of lynxes when the number of hares increases?
   C How do hares hide from lynxes?
   D How do lynxes and hares survive cold weather?

5 **If you wanted to understand more about predator-prey relationships, which question would it be most useful for you to ask?**
   A Is the lynx-hare population graph similar to graphs of other predator-prey populations?
   B Where do lynxes and hares live?
   C How many hares can a lynx kill in its lifetime?
   D Why were there so many hares in 1865?

Directions: Questions 6 and 7 are based on the information below.

A community contains many types of organisms. They live together, forming different relationships. For some members of the community, these relationships are beneficial. For others, they are not. The table below summarizes some of the major relationships among organisms in a community and their effects.

RELATIONSHIP	EFFECT ON SPECIES A	EFFECT ON SPECIES B
Competition	Negative	Negative
Commensalism	Positive	No effect
Mutualism	Positive	Positive
Predation	Positive	Negative
Parasitism	Positive	Negative

6   Which question should you ask to help explain why predation and parasitism have similar effects?
   A   When is predation or parasitism similar to competition?
   B   How is mutualism similar to predation or parasitism?
   C   What is the difference between predation and parasitism?
   D   Are humans involved in these relationships?

7   Which of the following questions would frame a discussion of mutualism?
   A   Why do mosquitoes bite humans?
   B   How does a lion stalk a zebra?
   C   How do clownfish and sea anemones protect one another from attack?
   D   Why do barnacles attach to the skin of a whale?

Directions: Questions 8 through 10 are based on the diagram below.

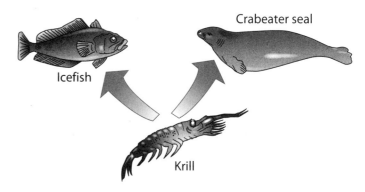

Icefish   Crabeater seal   Krill

The diagram shows the feeding patterns of two different species in an ecosystem.

8   Which question can you ask to better understand the diagram?
   A   Where is the ecosystem located?
   B   Why does a crabeater seal eat krill?
   C   What do the arrows in the diagram represent?
   D   What is the population of each type of animal in the ecosystem?

9   If you wanted to know more about the relationship between these animals, which question would you ask?
   A   Do the icefish and crabeater seal compete for krill?
   B   How is the life cycle of these animals similar?
   C   What does the krill consume?
   D   What consumes the icefish?

10 What question would you ask if an arrow in the diagram pointed away from the icefish?
   A   Which animal is eating krill?
   B   How has the feeding pattern of the crabeater seal changed?
   C   Which animal is preying on the icefish?
   D   Why is the crabeater seal no longer consuming krill?

Directions: Questions 11 and 12 are based on the information below.

A farmer has a dairy farm on which he keeps a small herd of cows. A stream runs along one edge of the field where the cows graze. A road with a fence alongside runs along another edge of the field. The area is slowly developing. There are new homes, and a food processing plant opened a couple of months ago upstream from the farm. The herd always has been healthy. But during the last couple of weeks, some of the cows have become ill. The farmer took the following notes:

JULY 15:
• Several cows listless, not eating for last week
JULY 22:
• Several more cows not eating
JULY 29:
• One cow with mouth sores; called in veterinarian to check herd
AUGUST 5:
• Cows with sores treated; two more showing signs of illness

---

11 Which is the best question to ask to identify the problem with the farmer's cows?

A Why did the farmer go a full week, from July 22 and July 29, without entering notes?

B Has the water quality changed in the stream since the opening of the food processing plant?

C Have any of the cows given birth recently?

D Is there any way to encourage the cows to eat?

12 Which is the best question to help the farmer scientifically investigate the problem?

A What would happen if I only fed the cows water from the well?

B Should I take my own family to see the doctor, too?

C Should I write a letter to all my neighbors alerting them of the problem?

D Are there plans to develop more of the land nearby?

Directions: Questions 13 through 15 are based on the paragraph below.

Jane Goodall is a biologist. She spent many years living with and studying chimpanzees and other primates in their natural environment in east Africa. Dr. Goodall discovered that chimpanzees live in groups. She noted that cooperation and good relations among members of the group were important for the survival of individuals. She states that scientists recognize the similarity in the structure of the brain of chimpanzees and humans. Through her observations, she also has found similarities in the emotions and behavior of the species.

13 Which question might best help you identify the main idea of the paragraph?

A Why did Dr. Goodall go to east Africa?

B What was challenging about living with chimpanzees?

C How did Dr. Goodall conduct her research?

D What did Dr. Goodall learn about chimpanzee and human societies?

14 You find Dr. Goodall's research interesting and want to read more about the way in which animals live together. Which scientist's work might answer your questions?

A a climatologist studying global warming in east Africa

B an ecologist studying the interactions of several species in the forests of east Africa

C a doctor doing research on the effectiveness of immunization

D a geologist studying the rocks and soils of east Africa

15 Which question would help you understand Dr. Goodall's motivation for scientific research?

A Why did she move to east Africa?

B How did her observations improve understanding of chimpanzee emotions?

C When did she become a biologist?

D How did she become interested in primate behaviors and emotions?

Directions: Questions 16 through 18 are based on the information below.

Honeybees are disappearing. All over the United States, beekeepers are finding their hives mysteriously empty. Bees leave the hive as usual to find nectar, but many just don't return. It is called colony collapse disorder. Between 2008 and 2014, the USDA estimates 30 percent of honey bee colonies have been lost. The problem could be a fungus or virus. It could be pesticides, but scientists are not yet sure. The major problem with the loss of the bees is that farmers need the bees to pollinate the plants that grow many of the most common food crops. The bar graph below shows the importance of bees to several crops.

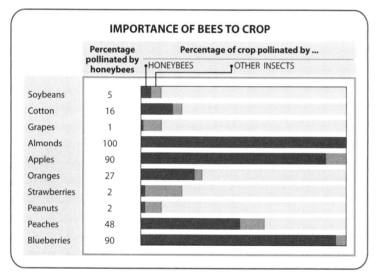

16 Which question might best help you identify the main idea of the paragraph?
A How do pesticides affect honeybees?
B What kinds of diseases harm honeybees?
C How many honeybee hives have been lost?
D What causes colony collapse disorder?

17 Which question is best answered by the graph?
A When do honeybees pollinate crops?
B How many different kinds of honey do honeybees make?
C What countries are affected by honeybee pollination?
D Which crops do honeybees pollinate?

18 Which is the best question to help scientists investigate the problem?
A Why do some food crops require pollination by bees?
B Can people still get honey from the remaining bees?
C Are other species of animals mysteriously disappearing, too?
D What is causing the change in bee behavior?

Directions: Questions 19 and 20 are based on the paragraph below.

Meerkats are small, slender mammals that live in southwestern Africa. Scientists have been studying meerkats for years to learn more about their way of life and, in particular, certain behaviors. Although evolutionary thinking states that an individual's success is measured by the number of offspring it raises, meerkats instead spend part or all of their lives helping raise the young rather than breeding themselves. That type and degree of cooperation sets meerkats apart from many other mammals, including apes. Scientists believe that human cooperation has its roots in evolutionary history. By studying meerkats, scientists gain insights into the evolution of another cooperative species.

19 Which question would you ask to learn more about the cooperative efforts of meerkats?
A Why are scientists studying meerkats?
B How are meerkats similar to apes?
C Why do meerkats live in southwestern Africa?
D Why do meerkats concentrate on raising their young rather than on breeding?

20 Which question would you ask to better understand why scientists are studying meerkats?
A Why is an individual's success measured by the number of offspring it raises?
B What insights into human cooperation could scientists glean from studying meerkats?
C How are meerkats similar to other animals?
D Why do scientists believe that human cooperation has its roots in history?

Unit 1 Review

UNIT 1

The Unit Review is structured to resemble science high school equivalency tests. Be sure to read each question and all possible answers carefully before choosing your answer.

To record your answers, fill in the numbered circle that corresponds to the answer you select for each question in the Unit Review.

Do not rest your pencil on the answer area while considering your answer. Make no stray or unnecessary marks. If you change an answer, erase your first mark completely.

Mark only one answer space for each question; multiple answers will be scored as incorrect.

Sample Question

How does a diagram differ from other forms of graphics?

A A diagram organizes information in rows and columns.
B A diagram shows relationships visually among objects or events.
C A diagram summarizes information in a passage.
D A diagram shows parts of a whole.

Ⓐ●ⒸⒹ

Directions: Questions 1 and 2 are based on the graph below.

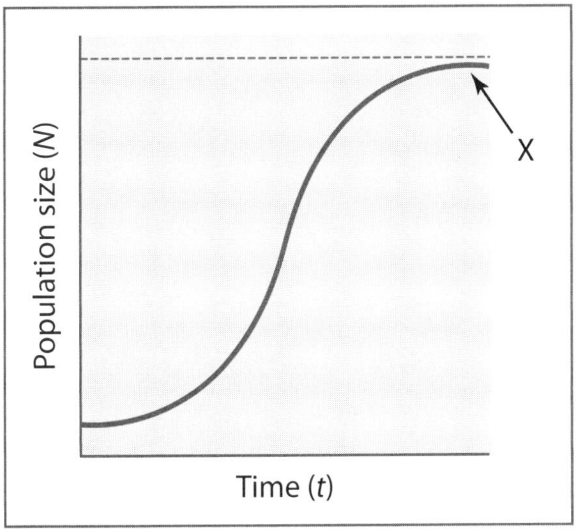

1 **The graph shows the growth of one population in a grassland ecosystem. What happened to the population at point *X*?**

A The population began to grow more quickly.
B The population suddenly decreased.
C The population stopped growing.
D The population began to grow more slowly.

ⒶⒷⒸⒹ

2 **Based on the graph, which of the following is a logical cause for what happened to the population at point *X*?**

A a limited food supply
B an introduced predator
C a sudden disease
D availability of unlimited resources

ⒶⒷⒸⒹ

Directions: Questions 3 and 4 are based on the paragraph below.

Plants adapt to the environment in which they live. Many desert plants have adaptations that decrease water loss, such as thick stems and waxy leaves. Thin, wax-coated needles on pine trees limit heat and moisture loss in the cold of winter.

3 **Which statement best summarizes the paragraph above?**
   A Plants have adaptations that allow them to live in different environments.
   B Desert plants have adaptations for surviving in hot climates.
   C Desert plants often have stems that help them retain scarce water.
   D Pine tree adaptations allow them to survive in cold climates.

   Ⓐ Ⓑ Ⓒ Ⓓ

4 **The illustration below represents the nitrogen cycle.**

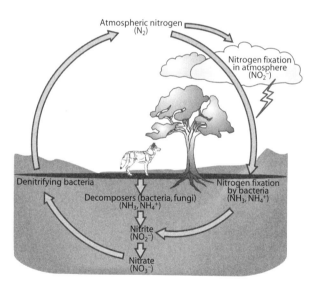

Which statement correctly describes an event of the nitrogen cycle?
   A Plants take N_2 directly from the air.
   B Plants release N_2 to the atmosphere, where it is converted to nitrites.
   C Some bacteria in the soil recycle nitrogen back into the atmosphere.
   D Trees release N_2 to the atmosphere.

   Ⓐ Ⓑ Ⓒ Ⓓ

Directions: Questions 5 and 6 are based on the information below.

In pea plants, purple flower color is a dominant trait, and white flower color is a recessive trait. This means that white flower color will appear only if an individual offspring receives the recessive trait from both parents. *P* represents the dominant trait, and *p* represents the recessive trait. A cross between two particular pea plants resulted in an individual offspring that produced white flowers. The Punnett square below shows all the possible flower colors for other offspring from this cross.

	P	*p*
P	*PP*	*Pp*
p	*Pp*	*pp*

5 **What conclusion can you draw about the parent plants?**
   A Both parents carried a trait for pink flowers.
   B One parent carried the dominant trait for purple flowers, and the other parent carried the recessive trait for white flowers.
   C Each parent had at least one recessive trait for white flowers.
   D Both parents could produce both purple and white flowers.

   Ⓐ Ⓑ Ⓒ Ⓓ

6 **Based on the diagram, what percent of total offspring of this cross will most likely have purple flowers?**
   A 20%
   B 25%
   C 50%
   D 75%

   Ⓐ Ⓑ Ⓒ Ⓓ

Directions: Questions 7 through 9 are based on the information below.

Sea otters live in kelp forests along the Pacific coast of North America. Biologists found that when the population of sea otters decreases, the population of sea urchins increases. The urchins then deplete the kelp populations.

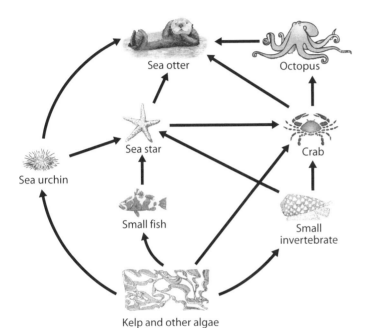

Sea otter
Octopus
Sea star
Crab
Sea urchin
Small fish
Small invertebrate
Kelp and other algae

7 **Which of these organisms in a kelp forest ecosystem is a producer?**
   A   sea otter
   B   kelp
   C   sea urchin
   D   sea star

Ⓐ Ⓑ Ⓒ Ⓓ

8 **Which organism does NOT feed on kelp and other algae?**
   A   sea urchin
   B   small invertebrate
   C   small fish
   D   sea star

Ⓐ Ⓑ Ⓒ Ⓓ

9 **Based on the information and diagram, which statement about organisms in a kelp forest is most accurate?**
   A   The otter provides food for all other species of animals in this ecosystem.
   B   Sea otters are the most important producers in this ecosystem.
   C   Without the otter, the populations of many other species in this ecosystem would increase.
   D   All of the other plants and animals in this ecosystem would disappear without the sea otter.

Ⓐ Ⓑ Ⓒ Ⓓ

Directions: Question 10 is based on the following excerpt about the Galápagos Islands from Charles Darwin.

"Considering that these islands are placed directly under the equator, the climate is far from being excessively hot, but this seems chiefly to be caused by the singularly low temperature of the surrounding water, brought here by the great southern Polar current . . ."

10 **Based on the excerpt, what did Darwin infer about the climate of the Galápagos Islands?**
   A   The climate was hot because the islands are near the equator.
   B   The relatively cool climate was due to cool waters around the islands.
   C   The islands have a polar climate because they are near the polar current.
   D   The islands have fairly low temperatures because they are below the equator.

Ⓐ Ⓑ Ⓒ Ⓓ

Directions: Questions 11 and 12 are based on the timeline below, which shows major events in the history of red wolf conservation in the United States.

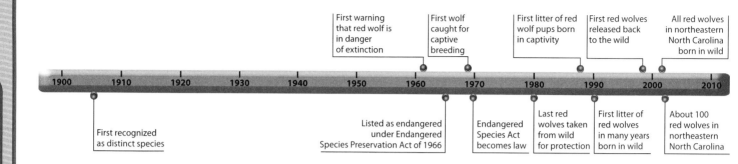

11 Based on the timeline, which of the following statements is true?

A   There have been no red wolves in the wild since 1980.

B   About eight years passed before captive red wolves were bred successfully.

C   Red wolves became extinct in the wild in 1962.

D   Captive breeding of wolves made the Endangered Species Act unnecessary.

Ⓐ Ⓑ Ⓒ Ⓓ

12 Based on the timeline, which statement summarizes the history of red wolf conservation in the United States?

A   The Endangered Species Act was the starting point for efforts to protect red wolves.

B   A combination of laws and captive breeding has had a positive effect on red wolf populations.

C   Red wolves remain entirely in captivity today.

D   Red wolves were recognized as a separate wolf species in the early 1900s.

Ⓐ Ⓑ Ⓒ Ⓓ

Directions: Question 13 is based on the information below.

Carnivores are organisms that feed only on animals. Herbivores are organisms that feed only on plants. Omnivores feed on plants and animals.

EXAMPLES OF ANIMAL SPECIES AND THEIR FEEDING ROLES IN ECOSYSTEMS	
SPECIES (COMMON NAME)	**FEEDING ROLE**
American alligator	Carnivore
Lion	Carnivore
Black bear	Omnivore
Rat snake	Carnivore

13 Based on the information and table, what inference can you make about the alligator?

A   The alligator is found in the same ecosystem as the rat snake.

B   The alligator is not prey for any other organism.

C   The alligator is higher on the food chain than the lion.

D   The alligator may feed on herbivores, carnivores, and omnivores.

Ⓐ Ⓑ Ⓒ Ⓓ

Directions: Questions 14 and 15 are based on the paragraph below.

A virus is basically a bundle of genetic material surrounded by a protein shell. Viruses are tiny—even smaller than bacteria. Scientists classify viruses as microbes, but viruses are not living things like other microbes. Unlike living things, viruses cannot reproduce themselves. Instead, they need living cells to reproduce. When a virus enters a living cell, it takes over the cell's processes. The virus directs the cell to copy the genetic material of the virus, making new virus particles. The new viruses kill the host cell. Then they spread to neighboring cells. If nothing stops them, the viruses keep reproducing and spreading through living cells.

14 Which statement best expresses the main idea of the passage?

A Viruses reproduce inside living cells.
B Viruses kill their host cells after reproducing inside them.
C Viruses are made of both protein and genetic material.
D Viruses are not alive.

Ⓐ Ⓑ Ⓒ Ⓓ

15 Which of these details supports the main idea of the passage?

A Viruses are smaller than bacteria.
B Viruses are surrounded by a protein shell.
C Viruses contain genetic material.
D Viruses take over a cell's processes to reproduce themselves.

Ⓐ Ⓑ Ⓒ Ⓓ

Directions: Question 16 is based on the paragraph below.

Biologists interested in protecting polar bear populations have fitted individual bears with radio collars and tracked the individuals throughout several years. The radio collars give scientists information about a bear's location and movements, and can allow scientists to determine whether a particular bear is still alive.

16 Which of the following questions could be answered with the wildlife study method described above?

A How many polar bears exist in the wild?
B What is the average survival rate of adult polar bears over a five-year period?
C What is the preferred food of polar bears?
D How many cubs does a female polar bear have each year?

Ⓐ Ⓑ Ⓒ Ⓓ

Directions: Question 17 is based on the paragraph below.

Acid precipitation can affect the growth of plants. Over time, acid precipitation raises the acid level of soil. The acid can cause water in the soil to leach important nutrients, such as magnesium and calcium. Plants do not grow as well when the soil does not contain a sufficient supply of these nutrients.

17 Based on the information in the passage, what is the meaning of *leach?*

A to poison
B to accumulate
C to make stronger
D to remove

Ⓐ Ⓑ Ⓒ Ⓓ

Unit 2

Unit Overview

From cooking and baking to developing new technologies and on through unlocking the secrets of the universe, physical science literally guides our every move. Physical science often is divided into chemistry (the study of matter) and physics (the study of the relationship between matter and energy).

Physical science is prominent in science high school equivalency tests, where it makes up about 25 percent of questions. As with the rest of the science test, physical science questions will assess your ability to successfully interpret passages and visuals. In Unit 2, the introduction of certain skills and the continuation of others, in combination with essential science concepts, will help you prepare for science high school equivalency tests.

Table of Contents

Key Physical Science Terms

acid: any compound that increases the number of hydrogen ions when dissolved in water; acids turn blue litmus paper red

amplitude: the maximum distance a wave vibrates from its rest position

base: any compound that increases the number of hydroxide ions when dissolved in water; bases turn red litmus paper blue

chemical change: a change that occurs when one or more substances are changed into entirely new substances with different properties

circuit: a complete, closed path through which electric charges flow

condensation: the change of state from a gas to a liquid

crest: the highest point of a transverse wave

electrons: the negatively charged particles found in all atoms

element: a pure substance that cannot be separated or broken down into simpler substances by physical or chemical means

enzymes: molecules that help chemical reactions occur more quickly

evaporation: the change of state from a liquid to a gas

frequency: the number of waves produced in a given amount of time

friction: a force that opposes motion between two surfaces that are touching

gas: the state in which matter has no definite shape or volume

liquid: the state in which matter takes the shape of its container and has a definite volume

longitudinal wave: a wave in which the particles of the medium vibrate back and forth along the path that the wave travels

magnetic field: the region around a magnet in which magnetic forces can act

mechanical advantage: a number that tells how may times a machine multiplies force

molecule: a neutral group of atoms held together by covalent bonds

Newton's second law: $F = ma$, where F stands for the net force (expressed in newtons), m stands for the object's mass, and a stands for the object's acceleration

Newton's third law: for every action force, there is an equal and opposite reaction force

nucleus: the tiny, extremely dense, positively charged region in the center of an atom made up of protons and neutrons

physical change: a change that affects one or more physical properties of a substance; no new substances are formed

solid: the state in which matter has a definite shape and volume

speed: a measure of how fast an object moves; $s = d/t$

sublimation: the change of state from a solid directly into a gas

synthesis: a chemical reaction in which an enzyme helps join two substrates together

transverse wave: a wave in which the particles of the wave's medium vibrate perpendicular to the direction the wave is traveling

trough: the lowest point of a transverse wave

velocity: the speed of an object in a particular direction

wavelength: the distance between one point on a wave and the corresponding point on an adjacent wave

UNIT 2

Interpret Complex Diagrams

① Learn the Skill

As you know, **diagrams** are visual aids that show relationships between ideas, objects, or events. Complex diagrams show more sophisticated information than do simple diagrams. When **interpreting complex diagrams,** keep in mind that they may show more than one concept or piece of information.

② Practice the Skill

By mastering the skill of interpreting complex diagrams, you will improve your study and test-taking skills, especially as they relate to science high school equivalency tests. Examine the diagram below. Use the information to answer question 1.

Ⓐ When studying a complex diagram, first read the title and headings to determine the main idea. In this example, the title and headings indicate that particle spacing is important in defining states of matter.

Ⓑ The illustrations at the bottom of the diagram represent magnified views of water particles in each state: solid, liquid, and gas. Compare these illustrations to learn the relationship between the state of matter and the arrangement of the particles in the matter.

STATES OF MATTER AND PARTICLE SPACING

Solid	Liquid	Gas
Ice	Liquid water	Water vapor

Particles packed tightly together in orderly arrangement

Particles close together in random arrangement

Particles very far apart in random arrangement

USING LOGIC

Information in a diagram is often arranged in a logical sequence. Therefore, you can use logic to infer the relationships between parts of the diagram. In this diagram, the states of matter are displayed in order of least to greatest spacing between particles.

1 Based on the diagram, the spacing between particles is generally

   A smallest in gases.

   B largest in liquids.

   C smallest in solids.

   D constant across all states.

UNIT 2

Directions: Questions 2 and 3 are based on the information below.

Substances can undergo changes in state. These changes occur when the energy of a system changes. For example, energy must be added to melt a solid into liquid form or to vaporize a liquid into a gas. Energy is released when a gas condenses into a liquid or when a liquid freezes as a solid.

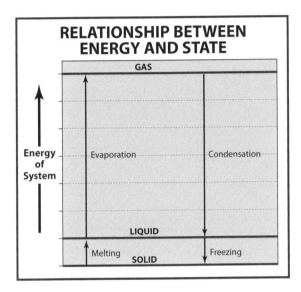

RELATIONSHIP BETWEEN ENERGY AND STATE

2 Which statement accurately reflects information presented in the diagram?
A Removing energy from liquid water changes it to water vapor.
B Adding energy to liquid water changes it to ice.
C The temperature of liquid water does not change as it evaporates.
D Different state changes involve different amounts of energy.

3 The kilojoule (kJ) is a unit of energy. If a sample of ice requires 6 kJ of energy to melt, how many kilojoules are most likely needed to evaporate the water that is produced?
A about 3 kJ
B about 6 kJ
C about 12 kJ
D about 36 kJ

Directions: Questions 4 and 5 are based on the information below.

A heating curve shows how the temperature of a substance changes as heat is added to it. The melting and boiling points of the substance can be identified from the curve. The diagram shows a heating curve for water.

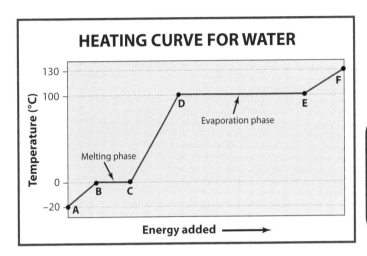

HEATING CURVE FOR WATER

4 Which statement accurately reflects information presented in the diagram?
A Water continually increases in temperature as it is heated.
B The temperature of a substance changes only during changes of state.
C The addition of energy to a system is always accompanied by an increase in temperature.
D During changes of state, temperature stays constant.

5 Which part of the diagram could tell you the freezing point of water?
A point A
B point B
C the segment between points C and D
D the segment between points D and E

Directions: Questions 6 through 8 are based on the information below.

PROPERTIES OF SOLIDS, LIQUIDS, AND GASES

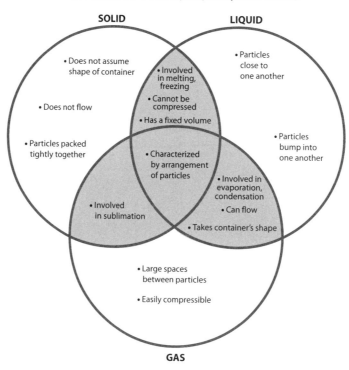

In our everyday lives, we encounter three basic states of matter—solids, liquids, and gases. The amount of space between particles in a substance changes as the substance's state changes. In the solid state, the particles are packed tightly in an orderly fashion and do not move relative to one another. In the liquid state, particles are spaced close together, but not as closely as in solid particles. Particles in liquids move around and constantly bump into one another. Particles in gases are spaced very far apart and move around freely.

6   **Matter in which of the following states retains its shape regardless of the shape of its container?**
   A   solids and liquids
   B   liquids and gases
   C   solids only
   D   liquids only

7   **Based on the diagram, what unique characteristic distinguishes gases from liquids and solids?**
   A   Gases are compressible.
   B   Gases are involved in evaporation and condensation.
   C   Gases are involved in sublimation.
   D   Gases do not assume the shapes of their containers.

8   **Based on the information, which of the following statements is true?**
   A   During melting, the spacing between particles decreases.
   B   The spacing between particles has no effect on the properties of a substance.
   C   The spacing between particles changes more during sublimation than during freezing.
   D   During condensation, the spacing between particles increases.

Directions: Questions 9 and 10 are based on the diagram below.

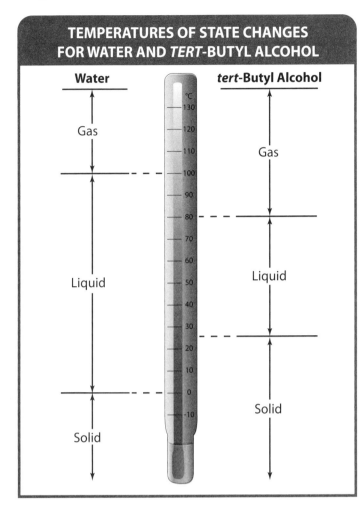

TEMPERATURES OF STATE CHANGES FOR WATER AND *TERT*-BUTYL ALCOHOL

9 **Based on the diagram, how does the freezing point of *tert*-butyl alcohol compare to the boiling and freezing points of water?**

A The freezing point of *tert*-butyl alcohol is about 18° lower than the freezing point of water.

B The freezing point of *tert*-butyl alcohol is about 18° lower than the boiling point of water.

C The freezing point of *tert*-butyl alcohol is about 75° lower than the freezing point of water.

D The freezing point of *tert*-butyl alcohol is about 75° lower than the boiling point of water.

10 **Within the range of temperatures at which water is a liquid, in which state or states can *tert*-butyl alcohol exist?**

A gas or liquid only

B liquid or solid only

C gas, liquid, or solid

D liquid only

Directions: Question 11 is based on the information below.

Under certain conditions, substances can change from solid to gas without first going through a liquid state. This process is called sublimation. Frozen carbon dioxide, or "dry ice," is a good example of a solid that undergoes sublimation at ordinary room temperature and air pressure. Carbon dioxide can exist as a liquid only under high pressure.

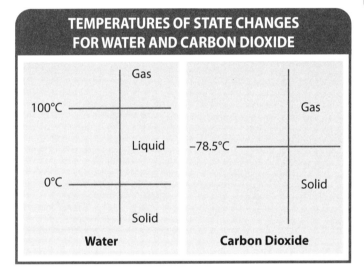

TEMPERATURES OF STATE CHANGES FOR WATER AND CARBON DIOXIDE

11 **If you heated samples of water and carbon dioxide from –100°C to –50°C, what would happen?**

A The water would boil, and the carbon dioxide would melt.

B The water and carbon dioxide would both sublimate.

C The water would freeze, and the carbon dioxide would boil.

D The water would remain frozen, and the carbon dioxide would sublimate.

Directions: Questions 12 through 16 are based on the information below.

Distillation is a process that takes advantage of differences in boiling points to separate mixtures of liquids. During distillation, a mixture is heated until it boils. The liquid with the lower boiling point evaporates more readily at this temperature than does the liquid with the higher boiling point. The vapor that is produced therefore contains more of the lower boiling-point liquid. As the vapor travels through the condenser, it condenses and drips into a clean collection vessel. While not pure, this liquid is enriched in the lowest boiling-point liquid found in the original mixture. This low boiling-point liquid can be further enriched by repeated distillations.

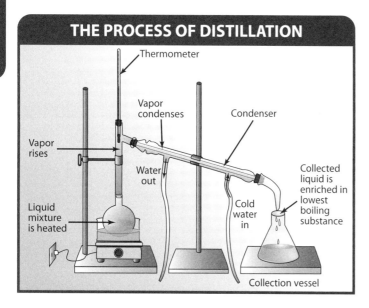

THE PROCESS OF DISTILLATION

Thermometer
Vapor condenses
Condenser
Vapor rises
Water out
Collected liquid is enriched in lowest boiling substance
Liquid mixture is heated
Cold water in
Collection vessel

12 Based on the information, distillation could best be used to separate the components of which of the following mixtures?
  A sand and water
  B alcohol and sugar
  C gasoline and alcohol
  D water and salt

13 Based on the information, what state changes does the mixture in a distillation apparatus undergo?
  A liquid to solid only
  B vapor to liquid only
  C vapor to liquid, then liquid to vapor
  D liquid to vapor, then vapor to liquid

14 The boiling point of ethanol is 78.5°C; the boiling point of toluene is 110.6°C. Based on the information, what would be the composition of the liquid collected from distillation of a 50:50 mixture of ethanol and toluene?
  A an ethanol/toluene mixture having more ethanol than toluene
  B an ethanol/toluene mixture having more toluene than ethanol
  C a 50:50 mixture of ethanol and toluene
  D pure ethanol

15 What is the purpose of the cold water that flows into the apparatus?
  A to support the apparatus
  B to condense the vapor
  C to flush out the distilled liquid
  D to trap impurities

16 The boiling point of Liquid A is only a few degrees higher than the boiling point of Liquid B. Which of the following statements about a mixture of the liquids is most likely true?
  A Many distillations will be required to separate Liquid A from Liquid B.
  B The liquid collected during a distillation of the mixture will be enriched in Liquid A.
  C A wide range of temperatures can be used to separate the two liquids.
  D The vapor produced during the distillation will not condense easily.

Interpret Complex Tables

① Learn the Skill

As you learned, a **table** is a graphic tool used to display complex information in an organized and concentrated way. To **interpret complex tables**, you must carefully read the column headings to make sure you know exactly the type of information contained in the table. You also might need to examine information surrounding the table, such as a key or footnotes that provide additional details.

② Practice the Skill

By mastering the skill of interpreting complex tables, you will improve your study and test-taking skills, especially as they relate to science high school equivalency tests. Examine the table below. Use the information to answer question 1.

A Typically, all entries in one column provide a particular type of information. Individual row entries are typically related to the entry in the far left column.

B In many cases, important details do not fit into a particular part of the table. Additional symbols may refer you to another place to find the information. Look at the area below the table to find out the meaning of the asterisks.

THE ALKALI METALS

A ELEMENT	ATOMIC NUMBER* **B**	**B** ATOMIC WEIGHT** (AMU)
Lithium	3	6.94
Sodium	11	22.99
Potassium	19	39.10
Rubidium	37	85.47
Cesium	55	132.91
Francium	87	223

B *atomic number: the number of protons in a single atom of a particular element
**atomic weight: the average mass of atoms of a particular element

🧩 MAKING ASSUMPTIONS

In tables that provide numerical data, units are typically stated in the column heading only. All values in the column are expressed in those same units.

1 **Based on the table, what trend can you identify?**

   A The larger the atomic number of an element, the smaller its atomic weight.

   B The larger the atomic number of an element, the greater its atomic weight.

   C The larger the atomic number of an element, the fewer protons it contains.

   D The larger the atomic number of an element, the fewer atoms it contains.

UNIT 2

Directions: Questions 2 through 4 are based on the information below.

An ionic compound is made up of particles of two or more elements; one of those particles donates an electron to another particle. A covalent compound is made up of two or more atoms in which atoms share electrons.

BOILING POINTS OF SELECT COMPOUNDS

COMPOUND	FORMULA	TYPE OF COMPOUND	BOILING POINT (°C)
Sodium chloride	NaCl	Ionic	1,413
Hydrogen fluoride	HF	Covalent	20
Hydrogen sulfide	H_2S	Covalent	−61
Calcium iodide	CaI_2	Ionic	1,100
Magnesium fluoride	MgF_2	Ionic	2,239

2 Which compound boils at the highest temperature?
A NaCl
B H_2S
C CaI_2
D MgF_2

3 A scientist studies an unknown compound and concludes that the compound is ionic. Which of the following is a likely boiling point for the compound?
A 15°C
B 80°C
C 110°C
D 1,050°C

4 Room temperature is about 25°C. Which of the following compounds would you expect to be gases at room temperature?
A NaCl only
B HF and H_2S
C H_2S only
D NaCl, CaI_2, and MgF_2

Directions: Questions 5 and 6 are based on the information below.

Six elements listed on the periodic table are known as "noble gases." These elements are very stable and do not naturally form compounds with other elements. Their properties make them important for many commercial uses.

NOBLE GASES AND COMMON USES

ELEMENT	SYMBOL	ATOMIC NUMBER	COMMON USES
Helium	He	2	Balloons, refrigeration*
Neon	Ne	10	Lighting, refrigeration*
Argon	Ar	18	Lighting
Krypton	Kr	36	Lighting
Xenon	Xe	54	Lighting, research
Radon	Rn	86	Medicine

* in liquid form

5 Based on the information, what is the most common commercial use of noble gases?
A refrigeration
B medicine
C balloons
D lighting

6 Based on the information, what can you conclude about the noble gas elements?
A Noble gases do not occur naturally.
B Noble gases can exist as liquids as well as gases.
C Noble gases are the most common elements.
D Noble gases have large atomic numbers.

Directions: Questions 7 through 11 are based on the information below.

Of all the atoms that make up the human body, 99% come from just four elements: oxygen, carbon, hydrogen, and nitrogen. The remaining 1% is made up of atoms of macronutrients and micronutrients. Both macronutrients and micronutrients are necessary for good health, but macronutrients are needed in greater amounts. Even some elements such as sodium that might be harmful at high levels are necessary for proper health in small amounts.

SELECT MACRO- AND MICRONUTRIENTS NEEDED BY THE HUMAN BODY		
ELEMENT	**AMOUNT NEEDED**	**MAJOR ROLE IN BODY**
Macronutrients		
Calcium	More than 0.1 g[1]	Strengthening teeth and bones; muscle contraction
Potassium		Nerve function
Sodium		Nerve and muscle function
Micronutrients		
Zinc	15×10^{-9} g[1]	Immune system function
Copper		Nervous system development
Iodine		Proper thyroid function; metabolism

[1] per day

7 **Which of the following elements is needed in the body in the smallest amount?**
   A   sodium
   B   carbon
   C   potassium
   D   iodine

8 **Scientists have reported that the body needs less than 0.0004 g of a particular element over a lifetime for proper health. Which of the following elements would this most likely be?**
   A   calcium
   B   nitrogen
   C   hydrogen
   D   copper

9 **Based on the information, a lack of which element in the diet will affect the function of muscles directly?**
   A   zinc
   B   iodine
   C   potassium
   D   calcium

10 **Based on the information, what can you conclude about sodium?**
   A   Less than 0.1 g should be consumed each week.
   B   In the proper amount, sodium supports good muscle functioning.
   C   An unlimited sodium intake is beneficial to the body.
   D   It is more important to the body than iodine.

11 **Based on the information, what can you conclude about micronutrients and macronutrients?**
   A   All micronutrients support immune system function.
   B   Deficiencies in micronutrients or macronutrients can affect many different body systems.
   C   The nervous system depends solely on macronutrients for proper development.
   D   Macronutrients must be consumed in much smaller quantities than micronutrients.

Directions: Questions 12 through 16 are based on the information below.

Periodic Table of Elements

Main-Group Elements

Main-Group Elements

Transition Metals

Inner-Transition Metals

6
C
Carbon
12.01

Atomic number
Symbol
Element name
Atomic weight

1 1A																	18 8A
1 H Hydrogen 1.01	2 2A											13 3A	14 4A	15 5A	16 6A	17 7A	2 He Helium 4.00
3 Li Lithium 6.94	4 Be Beryllium 9.01											5 B Boron 10.81	6 C Carbon 12.01	7 N Nitrogen 14.01	8 O Oxygen 16.00	9 F Fluorine 19.00	10 Ne Neon 20.18
11 Na Sodium 22.99	12 Mg Magnesium 24.31											13 Al Aluminum 26.98	14 Si Silicon 28.09	15 P Phosphorus 30.97	16 S Sulfur 32.07	17 Cl Chlorine 35.45	18 Ar Argon 39.95
19 K Potassium 39.10	20 Ca Calcium 40.08	21 Sc Scandium 44.96	22 Ti Titanium 47.87	23 V Vanadium 50.94	24 Cr Chromium 52.00	25 Mn Manganese 54.94	26 Fe Iron 55.85	27 Co Cobalt 58.93	28 Ni Nickel 58.69	29 Cu Copper 63.55	30 Zn Zinc 65.41	31 Ga Gallium 69.72	32 Ge Germanium 72.64	33 As Arsenic 74.92	34 Se Selenium 78.96	35 Br Bromine 79.90	36 Kr Krypton 83.80
37 Rb Rubidium 85.47	38 Sr Strontium 87.62	39 Y Yttrium 88.91	40 Zr Zirconium 91.22	41 Nb Niobium 92.91	42 Mo Molybdenum 95.94	43 Tc Technetium (98)	44 Ru Ruthenium 101.07	45 Rh Rhodium 102.91	46 Pd Palladium 106.42	47 Ag Silver 107.87	48 Cd Cadmium 112.41	49 In Indium 114.82	50 Sn Tin 118.71	51 Sb Antimony 121.76	52 Te Tellurium 127.60	53 I Iodine 126.90	54 Xe Xenon 131.29
55 Cs Cesium 132.91	56 Ba Barium 137.33	57 La Lanthanum 138.91	72 Hf Hafnium 178.49	73 Ta Tantalum 180.95	74 W Tungsten 183.84	75 Re Rhenium 186.21	76 Os Osmium 190.23	77 Ir Iridium 192.22	78 Pt Platinum 195.08	79 Au Gold 196.97	80 Hg Mercury 200.59	81 Tl Thallium 204.38	82 Pb Lead 207.2	83 Bi Bismuth 208.98	84 Po Polonium (209)	85 At Astatine (210)	86 Rn Radon (222)
87 Fr Francium (223)	88 Ra Radium (226)	89 Ac Actinium (227)	104 Rf Rutherfordium (261)	105 Db Dubnium (262)	106 Sg Seaborgium (266)	107 Bh Bohrium (264)	108 Hs Hassium (277)	109 Mt Meitnerium (268)	110 Ds Darmstadtium (269)	111 Rg Roentgenium (272)	112 Uub Ununbium (285)	114 Uuq Ununquadium (289)		116 Uuh Ununhexium (292)			

*Lanthanides

58 Ce Cerium 140.17	59 Pr Praseodymium 140.91	60 Nd Neodymium 144.24	61 Pm Promethium (145)	62 Sm Samarium 150.36	63 Eu Europium 151.96	64 Gd Gadolinium 157.25	65 Tb Terbium 158.93	66 Dy Dysprosium 162.50	67 Ho Holmium 164.93	68 Er Erbium 167.26	69 Tm Thulium 168.93	70 Yb Ytterbium 173.04	71 Lu Lutetium 174.97

**Actinides

90 Th Thorium 232.04	91 Pa Protactinium 231.04	92 U Uranium 238.03	93 Np Neptunium (237)	94 Pu Plutonium (244)	95 Am Americium (243)	96 Cm Curium (251)	97 Bk Berkelium (247)	98 Cf Californium (251)	99 Es Einsteinium (252)	100 Fm Fermium (257)	101 Md Mendelevium (258)	102 No Nobelium (259)	103 Lr Lawrencium (262)

Metal
Metalloid
Nonmetal

The columns in the periodic table are called groups. Elements in the same group have a number of common traits, including similar physical and chemical properties. In each column, atomic mass increases from top to bottom. The rows in the periodic table are called periods. Across a period from left to right, atomic number increases. Atomic radius decreases across a period and increases down a group.

12 Based on the information, where on the periodic table would you look to find the most massive element?
   A   top right corner
   B   bottom right corner
   C   center row
   D   top left corner

13 What is the atomic number of radon (Rn)?
   A   6
   B   18
   C   86
   D   88

14 Which pair of elements would you expect to have the most similar properties?
   A   nitrogen and oxygen
   B   sodium and magnesium
   C   chlorine and bromine
   D   hydrogen and helium

15 Based on the periodic table, which of the following elements is a nonmetal?
   A   magnesium
   B   sodium
   C   potassium
   D   phosphorus

16 Which of the following elements would have characteristics of both metals and nonmetals?
   A   lithium
   B   silicon
   C   bromine
   D   sodium

Directions: Questions 17 and 18 are based on the information below.

The six alkali metals are found in Group 1 of the periodic table. These metals are soft and pliable and can conduct heat and electricity. However, they melt at relatively low temperatures and also can explode if they become wet.

SELECT PROPERTIES OF ALKALI METALS

ELEMENT	ATOMIC NUMBER	ATOMIC WEIGHT	MELTING POINT (°C)
Lithium	3	6.94	180.54
Sodium	11	22.99	97.72
Potassium	19	39.1	63.65
Rubidium	37	85.47	38.89
Cesium	55	132.91	28.5
Francium	87	223.0	27.0

17 Which alkali metal will melt at the lowest temperature?
   A   francium
   B   sodium
   C   potassium
   D   cesium

18 Based on the table, which trend can you identify?
   A   The greater the atomic weight, the lower the element's melting point.
   B   The smaller the atomic weight, the lower the element's melting point.
   C   The greater the atomic number, the higher the element's melting point.
   D   The smaller the atomic weight, the lower the element's boiling point.

UNIT 2

Interpret Illustrated Models

① Learn the Skill

An **illustrated model** can be used to represent objects that are too large or too small to be shown in actual size. By **interpreting illustrated models**, you can understand processes that occur too quickly or too slowly to be directly observed. An illustrated model can be expressed in two-dimensional form, in three-dimensional form, or as a mathematical equation.

② Practice the Skill

By mastering the skill of interpreting illustrated models, you will improve your study and test-taking skills, especially as they relate to science high school equivalency tests. Examine the model below. Use the information to answer question 1.

A Even if you could magnify an atom to the point that it became visible, the atom would still not appear the way that it is represented in almost any model. Models aid understanding, but they cannot always show strict reality.

B Different models serve different purposes. The illustrated model is most helpful for visualizing the major parts of atoms and how they interact.

MODEL OF A HYDROGEN MOLECULE

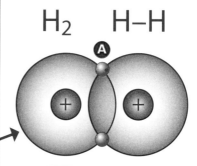

H_2 H–H

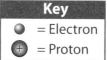

Key	
⚬	= Electron
⊕	= Proton

Most matter is a collection of atoms joined through the process of chemical bonding. One way atoms bond is by sharing electrons. A bond formed by sharing electrons is a covalent bond. When two or more atoms share their electrons in covalent bonds, they form a molecule. The model shows how two hydrogen atoms, each having one electron, bond to form a hydrogen molecule.

MAKING ASSUMPTIONS

In many cases, it is not possible to represent all aspects of a model, such as size of components and distance from one another, to scale. Unless an illustrated model states directly that it is drawn to scale, you should assume that the model is *not* to scale.

1 **What happens to the number of electrons when two atoms form a covalent bond?**
   A The number of electrons remains the same.
   B The total number of electrons doubles.
   C The number of electrons is halved.
   D The number of electrons is multiplied by two.

UNIT 2

Directions: Questions 2 through 4 are based on the information below.

Hydrogen is the simplest of the elements, with each atom consisting of a single proton and a single electron. Its name comes from the Greek words for "that which forms water." The electron moves so quickly around the proton that it cannot be seen. Although the location of the electron is represented in the model by a ring for simplicity, a "cloud" might represent the location of the electron more accurately.

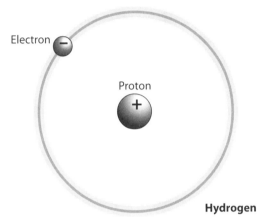

Hydrogen

2 **What does the large ring surrounding the "+" particle indicate?**
A   the location of the "−" particle
B   the location of the "+" particle
C   the structure of a hydrogen molecule
D   the location of the atom's positron

3 **The hydrogen atom is too small to be shown in actual size. What is another reason that the atom is shown as an illustrated model?**
A   The electron is much larger than the nucleus.
B   The electron moves too quickly to be seen directly.
C   Hydrogen atoms are too rare to be seen easily.
D   The positive charge of the proton makes it hard to see.

4 **How could you change this two-dimensional model into a three-dimensional model?**
A   add another electron to the model
B   use two balls and a long wire to recreate the model
C   draw an arrow on the model showing the direction of movement
D   display the model on posterboard

Directions: Questions 5 and 6 are based on the information below.

Each of the models below represents a hydrogen molecule.

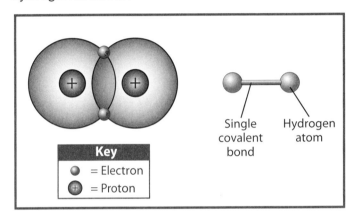

Single covalent bond   Hydrogen atom

Key
⚪ = Electron
⊕ = Proton

5 **Based on the models, which of the following is the best description of a covalent bond?**
A   a stick-like connection between two atoms
B   a proton shared by two atoms
C   a set of electrons shared between atoms
D   an overlap of the circular borders of two atoms

6 **For which of the following purposes would the ball-and-stick model be most useful?**
A   showing the relative positions of atoms in a molecule
B   showing the overlap between atoms in a true bond
C   showing the size of a molecule
D   showing the actual appearance of each atom

UNIT 2

Directions: Questions 7 and 8 are based on the information below.

Ancient people believed that water was a basic element. Then, in the late 1700s, a French chemist discovered that water was actually a compound of hydrogen and oxygen. Because of the way the hydrogen and oxygen atoms are bonded together, one side of the molecule has a slight positive charge, and the other side has a slight negative charge. In a sample of water, which contains large numbers of water molecules, the positive end of each molecule attracts the negative end of another molecule. This attraction is not as strong as the bonds between the hydrogen and oxygen atoms. However, it is strong enough to produce many important properties of water, including its high surface tension and ability to absorb heat.

A WATER MOLECULE

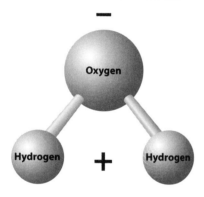

7 **Based on the information, which of the following best describes the attractions in a sample of water?**
  A The hydrogen atoms on one molecule are attracted to the oxygen atom on another molecule.
  B One hydrogen atom in a molecule is attracted to the other hydrogen atom in the molecule.
  C The oxygen atom on one molecule is attracted to the oxygen atom on another molecule.
  D The hydrogen atoms on one molecule are attracted to the hydrogen atoms on another molecule.

8 **Which piece of information that is not given in the passage can be inferred from looking at the model?**
  A A water molecule is magnetic.
  B Each water molecule is made of hydrogen and oxygen.
  C The three atoms in the water molecule do not form a straight line.
  D Water molecules are attracted to one another.

Directions: Question 9 is based on the information below.

Atoms form molecules through a process called covalent bonding. Bonding occurs when two atoms each have room for additional electrons. When two or more such atoms share their electrons with one another, they form a molecule.

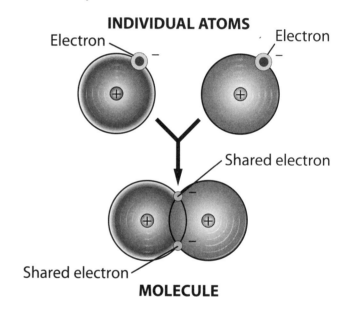

9 **What happens to electrons when two atoms covalently bond?**
  A The electrons are destroyed.
  B The electrons are shared between the atoms.
  C Four new electrons are formed.
  D Half of the electrons become protons.

Directions: Questions 10 through 12 are based on the information below.

Hydrogen is a colorless, odorless gas. However, when hydrogen is burned in the presence of oxygen, the molecules react to form water. The chemical equation below shows this process.

$$2H_2 + O_2 \rightarrow 2H_2O + energy$$

If you pass an electric current through a sample of water, the water molecules will break apart and form hydrogen gas and oxygen gas. This reaction is the opposite of the one shown in the equation above. The process of breaking water apart using electricity is known as electrolysis. *Lysis* means "to break apart," so *electrolysis* means "to break apart using electricity."

10 Which of the following is another way to state the equation shown above?
   A Two hydrogen molecules are removed from an oxygen molecule to form a water molecule.
   B Two hydrogen molecules react with energy to form a water molecule and an oxygen molecule.
   C Oxygen gas combines with energy to form hydrogen gas and water.
   D Two hydrogen molecules react with one oxygen molecule to form two water molecules and energy.

11 Based on the information, how many hydrogen and oxygen molecules are required to produce 100 molecules of water?
   A 50 hydrogen molecules and 100 oxygen molecules
   B 100 hydrogen molecules and 50 oxygen molecules
   C 50 hydrogen molecules and 50 oxygen molecules
   D 100 hydrogen molecules and 100 oxygen molecules

12 Which of the following equations most likely represents electrolysis?
   A $2H_2 + O_2 \rightarrow 2H_2O$
   B $H_2O \rightarrow 2H_2 + H_2$
   C $2H_2O + 2H_2 \rightarrow O_2$
   D $2H_2O \rightarrow 2H_2 + O_2$

Directions: Question 13 is based on the information below.

Osmosis is the movement of water molecules from an area of greater concentration to an area of lower concentration. The diagram below shows saltwater on one side of a membrane, and water on the other side. Because the concentration of water molecules on the right side is higher, the water molecules will move to the left side, where the concentration of water molecules is lower.

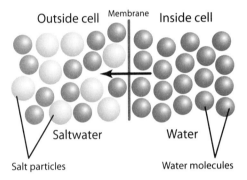

Because of osmosis, fish that live in the ocean (marine fish) use water differently from freshwater fish. Because the fluids inside of a marine fish have a higher water concentration than the ocean water, water molecules from inside the fish move through the gills into the ocean. The gills act as a membrane. Therefore, many marine fish drink a lot of water and rarely urinate. Freshwater fish, on the other hand, often take in water molecules through osmosis. Therefore, they rarely drink water and urinate often.

13 What does the arrow in the model indicate?
   A the direction of the movement of salt particles
   B the direction of the movement of water molecules
   C the location of the fish's gills
   D the location of the membrane

Directions: Questions 14 through 19 are based on the information below.

Chemical reactions occur constantly in your body. These reactions are what keep you alive. Most reactions in your body involve enzymes. Enzymes are molecules that help reactions occur more quickly. The enzymes are not used up during the reactions. Instead, they help the molecules involved in the reactions react more readily.

The molecules that react with the help of an enzyme are called substrates. In the figure below, two substrates are joining together to form a single product. The substrates fit perfectly onto the active site of the enzyme. The enzyme helps a chemical reaction occur, and the reaction joins the two substrates together into a product.

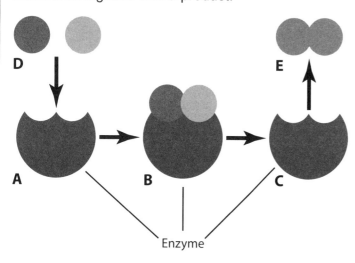

The term *synthesis* is used to describe a chemical reaction in which an enzyme helps join two substrates. The term *hydrolysis* is used to describe a chemical reaction in which the enzyme helps break one substrate into two pieces.

14 **What is the role of the enzyme in the reaction shown above?**
  A It produces the substrates.
  B Its presence assists in hydrolysis.
  C The substrates break it apart during synthesis.
  D It helps the substrates react.

15 **Which letter or letters in the model show the *product* of the chemical reaction?**
  A A, B, and C
  B D
  C E
  D D and E

16 **Which word would best describe the entire illustrated model?**
  A enzyme
  B substrate
  C synthesis
  D hydrolysis

17 **Which of the following statements about the enzyme and substrates shown in the model is most likely true?**
  A The enzyme can work with any two substrates.
  B The substrates break down the enzyme as they react.
  C The enzyme and the substrates are made of the same elements.
  D The reaction requires the presence of a specific enzyme.

18 **Based on the information, what must happen before a reaction can take place with the help of an enzyme?**
  A The enzyme must break apart.
  B The enzyme and substrates must be heated.
  C The reaction must occur slowly.
  D The substrates must bind to the enzyme.

19 **If the direction of the arrows in the model were reversed, what would the model represent?**
  A hydrolysis
  B destruction of an enzyme
  C energy created from matter
  D synthesis

UNIT 2

Interpret Observations

① Learn the Skill

Observations are pieces of information gathered with the senses. To **interpret observations** means to figure out what those observations mean. Understanding the meaning of observations is an important part of the scientific process.

② Practice the Skill

By mastering the skill of interpreting observations, you will improve your study and test-taking skills, especially as they relate to science high school equivalency tests. Examine the paragraph and diagram below. Use the information to answer question 1.

A A chemical reaction occurs when the particles from two or more substances are rearranged to form new substances.

B The substance or substances initially involved in a chemical reaction are called reactants. The particles in these substances are rearranged to form one or more products, or the new substances that are made. In this reaction, the reactants are iron and oxygen from air. The product is iron oxide (rust).

Moistened steel wool was placed into a test tube as shown here. The test tube with the moist steel wool and an empty test tube then were placed upside-down into a pan of water about $\frac{1}{2}$-inch deep and set aside undisturbed for 24 hours. During this time, the iron (Fe) in the steel wool reacted with oxygen (O) in the air inside of the test tube to form iron oxide (Fe_2O_3), which is the chemical name for rust. After 24 hours, the water in the test tube with the steel wool in it rose about $\frac{1}{5}$ of the way up the tube. In contrast, the empty tube showed no change in the water level.

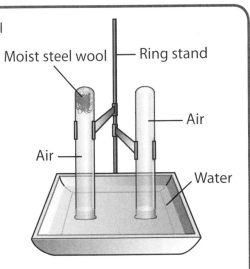

Moist steel wool — Ring stand
Air — Air
Water

MAKING ASSUMPTIONS

You might assume that any combination of chemicals represents a chemical reaction. However, if no new substances can be observed, then a chemical reaction has not occured.

1 **If removing the oxygen from the air in the test tube raised the water level about $\frac{1}{5}$ the volume, what conclusion could be made about oxygen in air?**
   A Air does not contain oxygen.
   B Air is 80% oxygen.
   C Oxygen comprises about $\frac{1}{5}$ the volume of air.
   D Oxygen is the main component of air.

Directions: Questions 2 and 3 are based on the information below.

When a metal reacts with an acid, a salt and hydrogen gas are formed. The general word equation for this reaction is:

Metal + acid ⟶ salt + hydrogen

The activity series is often used to predict whether certain reactions will occur. More reactive metals appear at the top of the list, while less reactive metals appear at the bottom. Metals listed below hydrogen on the activity series do not react with acids to produce hydrogen gas.

Three small pieces of three different metals were placed in separate test tubes as shown here. Acid was added to each test tube.

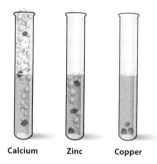

Calcium   Zinc   Copper

2 **Which of the following correctly lists the metals in order of decreasing reactivity?**
A   copper, zinc, calcium
B   calcium, copper, zinc
C   copper, calcium, zinc
D   calcium, zinc, copper

3 **Based on the information and illustration, which of the following statements is true?**
A   Copper is listed above hydrogen on the activity series.
B   Zinc is listed below hydrogen on the activity series
C   Both zinc and calcium are listed above hydrogen on the activity series.
D   Calcium is listed below hydrogen on the activity series.

Directions: Questions 4 and 5 are based on the information below.

Chemical change requires a chemical reaction. In a chemical reaction, the particles of subtances are rearranged to form new substances. Physical changes are those changes that do not result in a new substance being formed.

CHEMICAL AND PHYSICAL CHANGES		
MATERIAL	**CHANGE**	**OBSERVATION**
Candle	Melted	Solid candle became liquid wax.
Candle	Burned	Candle seemed to disappear.
Silver	Melted	Solid silver became liquid silver.
Silver	Tarnished	Silver developed a dark-colored coating on it.
Paper	Torn	A large piece of paper became smaller pieces.
Paper	Burned	Paper became ashes and smoke.

4 **Based on the information, which of the following statements is true?**
A   Melting silver is an example of a chemical change.
B   Burning paper is an example of a chemical change.
C   Tearing paper is an example of a chemical change.
D   Silver tarnishes as a result of a physical change.

5 **Based on the information, which of the following is the best indication that when silver tarnishes, a chemical reaction takes place?**
A   Solid silver becomes liquid silver.
B   No new substances are formed.
C   The color of the silver remains the same.
D   The dark coating is a new substance.

Directions: Questions 6 and 7 are based on the information below.

Chemical reactions take place when bonds between atoms are formed and broken. Sodium (Na) and chlorine (Cl) form sodium chloride (NaCl)—also known as table salt—in a process called ionic bonding. Ionic bonding occurs between ions, or charged particles. The sodium ions in salt are positively charged. The chloride ions are negatively charged. The electrical attraction between the ions holds them together; that attraction is called an ionic bond.

PROPERTIES OF THREE SUBSTANCES	
SUBSTANCE	**CHARACTERISTICS**
Sodium (Na)	Silver-colored soft metal
Chlorine (Cl_2)	Yellow-green gaseous nonmetal
Sodium chloride (NaCl)	White or colorless crystal or powder

6 **Based on the information, which of the following statements is true?**
   A Ionic bonding is caused by a physical change.
   B The properties of sodium chloride are similar to the properties of both sodium and chlorine.
   C The chemical reaction between sodium and chlorine results in the formation of a new substance with different properties.
   D Sodium chloride is a mixture of sodium and chlorine.

7 **Based on the information, sodium chloride is made of which of the following?**
   A two nonmetals
   B elements that have similar properties
   C a metal and a nonmetal
   D two metals

Directions: Questions 8 and 9 are based on the information below.

Most elements are metals. Certain properties distinguish metals from other elements. Most metals have the properties shown in the table below.

PROPERTIES OF METALS
Can be pulled into wires or flattened into sheets
Conduct electricity as solids or liquids
Conduct heat well as solids or liquids

A scientist makes observations about the properties of several substances. The table shows the scientist's observations.

PROPERTIES OF FOUR SUBSTANCES	
SUBSTANCE	**PROPERTIES**
A	Clear; does not conduct electricity or heat well
B	Gray; conducts electricity and heat well
C	Gray; conducts electricity and heat
D	Yellow; breaks easily; does not conduct electricity

8 **Based on the information, which of the substances are metals?**
   A Substance A only
   B Substances B and C
   C Substance D only
   D Substances C and D

9 **A scientist observes the properties of a fifth substance and concludes that it is not a metal. Which of the following statements about the substance is most likely true?**
   A It conducted electricity when melted.
   B It broke apart when hit with a hammer.
   C It conducted heat well.
   D It was easy to form into wires.

Directions: Questions 10 through 13 are based on the information below.

During chemical reactions, atoms bond, or join together, to form compounds. There are two main ways in which atoms can bond: by sharing electrons or by exchanging electrons. A bond formed by sharing electrons is called a covalent bond. Substances that contain covalent bonds are called covalent compounds. A bond that forms when atoms exchange electrons is called an ionic bond. Substances that contain ionic bonds are called ionic compounds or salts. The tables below give some common properties of covalent and ionic compounds.

COMMON PROPERTIES OF COVALENT COMPOUNDS
May be solids, liquids, or gases at room temperature
Brittle in the solid state
Low melting points
Do not conduct heat or electricity well
May dissolve in water

COMMON PROPERTIES OF IONIC COMPOUNDS (SALTS)
Generally solid at room temperature
Brittle in the solid state
High melting points
Conduct electricity when melted or dissolved in water
Generally dissolve in water

10 A scientist is studying a substance. Which of the following tests would best help the scientist determine whether the substance is an ionic compound or a covalent compound?

A   determining whether the solid is brittle

B   determining whether the substance is solid at room temperature

C   determining whether the substance has a high melting point

D   determining whether the substance dissolves in water

11 A scientist is studying two substances, Substance A and Substance B. She concludes that Substance A is a covalent compound, and that Substance B is an ionic compound. Which of the following observations did the scientist most likely make?

A   A solution of Substance B in water conducts electricity, but a solution of Substance A in water does not.

B   Substance A is a solid at room temperature, and Substance B is a liquid at room temperature.

C   Substance A dissolves in water, and Substance B does not.

D   The melting point of Substance B is lower than that of Substance A.

12 A solution of table salt in water conducts electricity, but a solution of table sugar in water does not. What is most likely true about table salt and table sugar?

A   The atoms in table salt share electrons, and the atoms in table sugar have exchanged electrons.

B   Both table salt and table sugar conduct electricity when melted.

C   Table sugar is brittle, but table salt is not.

D   Table salt has a higher melting point than table sugar.

13 Which of the following statements best explains why ionic compounds are generally not used in electrical wiring?

A   Most of them are brittle.

B   They generally have high melting points.

C   Some of them do not dissolve in water.

D   Most of them are solid at room temperature.

Directions: Questions 14 and 15 are based on the information below.

Whenever a chemical reaction occurs, there is nearly always an observable change in the original substances' appearance, temperature, or both. At least one of the following should be apparent as substances change form:
- fizzing, bubbling, or a release of gas
- changes in color
- formation of a precipitate (a solid forming within a liquid)
- a change in temperature

CHEMICAL REACTIONS IN COMPOUNDS		
COMPOUND	**APPEARANCE BEFORE REACTION**	**OBSERVATIONS DURING REACTION WITH AMMONIA**
Sodium chloride	White crystals	Looks the same as before the reaction
Iron chloride	Yellow-brown crystals	Brown precipitate forms
Copper chloride	Light blue crystals	Bubbles form; dark blue precipitate forms

14 **Based on your knowledge and the above information, which response is an accurate evaluation of the data?**
  A   A release of gas occurred in the reaction of ammonia with iron choride and sodium chloride.
  B   A release of gas occurred in the reaction of ammonia with iron chloride only.
  C   A release of gas occurred in the reaction of ammonia with copper chloride only.
  D   A release of gas occurred in the reaction of ammonia with sodium chloride only.

15 **The observation that the sodium chloride looked the same before and after the reaction is an indication of which of the following?**
  A   A new substance was formed.
  B   A chemical reaction occurred.
  C   Sodium atoms combined with chlorine atoms.
  D   No chemical reaction took place.

Directions: Questions 16 and 17 are based on the information below.

An exothermic chemical reaction is one that produces heat. In an exothermic reaction, the energy content of the products is lower than that of the reactants. The difference in energy content is the heat that is released. A match burning is an example of an exothermic reaction.

Other chemical reactions are endothermic, which means that they take in energy from their surroundings. An observable example of this is the reaction of citric acid with baking soda. When citric acid and baking soda react, the temperature of the system decreases. Energy is absorbed from the surroundings to drive the reaction.

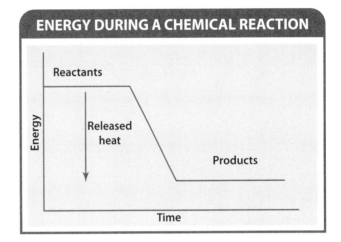

16 **The graph shows how the energy of a reaction system changed over time. Which of the following observations best explains why this is an exothermic reaction?**
  A   The reactants had more energy than the products.
  B   Time passed during the reaction.
  C   The reaction had both reactants and products.
  D   The products were formed after the reactants reacted.

17 **If you put your finger into a beaker containing citric acid and baking soda, the solution would feel cold. Why?**
  A   Energy is going into your finger.
  B   It is generating an electrical charge.
  C   Liquids are always cooler than their surroundings.
  D   Energy is being drawn from your finger.

Predict Outcomes

① Learn the Skill

Scientists follow the general sequence of 1) observation, 2) analysis, and 3) **predicting outcomes** as they carry out experiments to discover new knowledge about the universe. By looking for patterns in data and observations, they are able to develop hypotheses that can be tested through further experimentation.

② Practice the Skill

By mastering the skill of predicting outcomes, you will improve your study and test-taking skills, especially as they relate to science high school equivalency tests. Examine the paragraph and table below. Use the information to answer question 1.

A Use similarities that you see among the acid examples to learn defining characteristics of acids. Notice that all of the example acids ionize to produce H$^+$ ions.

B Use similarities that you see among the base examples to learn defining characteristics of bases. Notice that all of the example bases ionize to produce OH$^-$ ions.

We encounter acids, bases, and salts frequently in the world around us. Acids, bases, and salts are similar in that they have molecular compositions: two or more types of atoms bond together to form them. In addition, all three ionize when they are dissolved in water. This means that the parent molecules break into charged particles called ions. Several examples are shown below.

ACIDS, BASES, AND SALTS		
	EXAMPLE	**IONIZATION REACTION**
Acids	HCl HBr HI	HCl $\longrightarrow$ H$^+$ + Cl$^-$ HBr $\longrightarrow$ H$^+$ + Br$^-$ HI $\longrightarrow$ H$^+$ + I$^-$
Bases	NaOH KOH LiOH	NaOH $\longrightarrow$ Na$^+$ + OH$^-$ KOH $\longrightarrow$ K$^+$ + OH$^-$ LiOH $\longrightarrow$ Li$^+$ + OH$^-$
Salts	NaCl LiBr KI	NaCl $\longrightarrow$ Na$^+$ + Cl$^-$ LiBr $\longrightarrow$ Li$^+$ + Br$^-$ KI $\longrightarrow$ K$^+$ + I$^-$

USING LOGIC

Looking for patterns and trends in groups of data or observations can help you to make generalizations. The ability to generalize about a concept can make it easier to predict future outcomes.

1 **Based on the patterns you see in the table above, which set of compounds would have the most properties in common with the compound HF?**
   A NaCl, KI, LiOH
   B HBr, HI, HCl
   C NaOH, LiOH, KOH
   D LiBr, KI, NaCl

Directions: Questions 2 through 6 are based on the information below.

Acids are compounds that ionize to form H+ (hydrogen ions). The concentration of H+ in solution is used to measure the acidity of a solution. The greater the H+ concentration, the more acidic the solution is. HCl and H_2SO_4 are examples of acids. Their ionization reactions are shown below.

$$HCl \longrightarrow H^+ + Cl^-$$
$$H_2SO_4 \longrightarrow 2H^+ + SO_4^{2-}$$

Bases are compounds that can react with H+ ions to reduce their concentration in solution. Bases can therefore neutralize acidic solutions. An example of a base is NaOH. When NaOH is mixed with an acid, OH− (hydroxide ion) combines with H+ from the acid to form water. The overall equation showing the reaction of NaOH with HCl is shown below. A general reaction scheme is shown underneath.

$$HCl + NaOH \longrightarrow H_2O + NaCl$$
Acid + Base $\longrightarrow$ Water + Salt

Notice that water is one product of the reaction and salt is another product. These reactions are called neutralization reactions because both H+ and OH− ion concentrations are lowered as a result of the reaction.

2   **A student mixes the following pairs of compounds in solution. What is predicted to occur in each case?**

$$KOH + NaOH$$
$$HI + KBr$$
$$H_2SO_4 + KOH$$

   A   no reaction, reaction, reaction
   B   no reaction, reaction, no reaction
   C   reaction, no reaction, no reaction
   D   no reaction, no reaction, reaction

3   **Using the definition of acidity given in the text, what would you predict to be the relative acidity of two different solutions prepared using equal numbers of molecules of HCl and H_2SO_4?**
   A   The HCl solution would be exactly as acidic as the H_2SO_4 solution.
   B   The HCl solution would be twice as acidic as the H_2SO_4 solution.
   C   The HCl solution would be half as acidic as the H_2SO_4 solution.
   D   The HCl solution would be three times as acidic as the H_2SO_4 solution.

4   **Water and a salt are formed when HCl (an acid) is mixed with LiOH (a base). Which is the correct formula for the salt that forms?**
   A   HOH
   B   LiHCl
   C   OHCl
   D   LiCl

5   **Which reaction correctly represents the reaction of hydrocyanic acid (HCN) with potassium hydroxide (KOH)?**
   A $HCN + H_2O \longrightarrow KOH + NaCl$
   B $HCN + KOH \longrightarrow HK + CNOH$
   C $HCN + KOH \longrightarrow KCN + H_2O$
   D $KOH + H_2O \longrightarrow HCN + KCN$

6   **Potassium bromide (KBr) is a salt. It could be produced by which of the following reactions?**
   A   HBr + KOH
   B   HF + NaI
   C   HCl + NaOH
   D $H_2SO_4 + KOH$

UNIT 2

Directions: Questions 7 and 8 are based on the information below.

The acidity or basicity (alkalinity) of a solution is determined by the concentration of H^+ ions in the solution. Because H^+ concentration can vary over an extremely wide range, the pH scale was developed to deal with this range of values. The diagram below shows the pH scale, which runs from 0 to 14.

THE pH SCALE		
pH	[H^+]	[OH^-]
14	1×10^{-14}	1×10^{0}
13	1×10^{-13}	1×10^{-1}
12	1×10^{-12}	1×10^{-2}
11	1×10^{-11}	1×10^{-3}
10	1×10^{-10}	1×10^{-4}
9	1×10^{-9}	1×10^{-5}
8	1×10^{-8}	1×10^{-6}
7	1×10^{-7}	1×10^{-7}
6	1×10^{-6}	1×10^{-8}
5	1×10^{-5}	1×10^{-9}
4	1×10^{-4}	1×10^{-10}
3	1×10^{-3}	1×10^{-11}
2	1×10^{-2}	1×10^{-12}
1	1×10^{-1}	1×10^{-13}
0	1×10^{0}	1×10^{-14}

More basic ↑ (pH 7 Neutral) More acidic ↓

7 Based on the information, what is the most likely pH of battery acid, an example of a concentrated acid?

A pH 14
B pH 12
C pH 7
D pH 0

8 Based on the diagram, what pH change would be expected for a solution if its H^+ concentration were changed from 1×10^{-7} to 1×10^{-6}?

A It would increase from 6 to 7.
B It would decrease from 7 to 6.
C It would increase from 5 to 6.
D It would decrease from 6 to 5.

Directions: Questions 9 and 10 are based on the information below.

Combining an acid and a base results in a reaction in which H^+ from the acid reacts with OH^- from the base to produce water. The pH of pure water is 7. Therefore, if sodium hydroxide (a base) is mixed with hydrochloric acid, the resulting solution is neutral. Below are some solutions and their measured pH.

SOLUTIONS		
NUMBER	SOLUTION	pH
1	Lemon juice	3
2	Vinegar	3
3	Grape juice	4
4	Cola	5
5	Spot remover	9
6	Cleaning solution	10
7	Drain cleaner	11

9 Based on the information, which of the solutions could be mixed with lemon juice to produce a solution of pH 7?

A only solutions 2, 3, or 4
B only solutions 3, 4, or 5
C only solutions 5, 6, or 7
D only solutions 2 or 7

10 If water with a pH of 7 is added to grape juice, which of the following is the most likely pH that will result?

A pH 3
B pH 5
C pH 10
D pH 12

UNIT 2

Directions: Question 11 is based on the information below.

Litmus paper is sometimes used to determine the acidity or basicity of a solution. Litmus paper is covered with a colored dye. An acid turns blue litmus paper red. A base turns red litmus paper blue. Dipping the paper strip into a solution reveals whether the solution is acidic or basic.

A scientist wanted to neutralize an acidic solution. She added small amounts of sodium hydroxide (a basic solution) to it. After each addition, she tested the solution with blue litmus paper. Below are her results.

NEUTRALIZING AN ACID SOLUTION: RESULTS	
SODIUM HYDROXIDE ADDITION	**LITMUS PAPER COLOR**
1st addition	Blue paper turned red
2nd addition	Blue paper turned red
3rd addition	Blue paper turned red
4th addition	Blue paper turned red
5th addition	Blue paper remained blue

11 If the scientist makes two more additions of sodium hydroxide to the solution, what will most likely happen to a piece of blue litmus paper dipped into the final solution?
A The blue litmus paper will turn red.
B The blue litmus paper will remain blue.
C The blue litmus paper will lose its color.
D The blue litmus paper will become half red and half blue.

Directions: Questions 12 and 13 are based on the information below.

A pH meter is an electronic device that measures H^+ concentration in a solution and gives its pH as a numerical output. Although much more costly to use than litmus paper, a pH meter must be used when exact values for pH are needed. The following table compares pH meter readings with litmus paper readings for three of four different solutions.

pH METER AND LITMUS PAPER READINGS		
SAMPLE TESTED	**pH METER READING**	**LITMUS PAPER RESULT**
Strong acid	2.3	Blue paper turned red
Weak acid	5.2	Blue paper turned red
Weak base	8.5	Red paper turned blue
Strong base		

12 Based on the information in the paragraph and table above, what set of data would most likely fill in the missing spots in the table?
A 12.2, blue paper turned red
B 7.4, red paper turned blue
C 2.0, red paper turned blue
D 12.6, red paper turned blue

13 If the weak acid and weak base shown in the table above were mixed together, what pH would most likely result?
A 4.4
B 10.7
C 7.2
D 2.5

Directions: Questions 14 and 15 are based on the information below.

Titration is a technique used to determine the exact quantity of an acid in a sample. In a titration, a known concentration of a base is added slowly to a sample of an acid. Addition of the base continues until the acid is completely neutralized. The total amount of base added is calculated. The amount of base added is directly proportional to the amount of acid that was present in the original sample. For example, one molecule of sodium hydroxide, a strong base, is required to neutralize each molecule of hydrochloric acid, a strong acid.

The diagram below shows the experimental setup. The base is added from the buret into the flask containing the unknown quantity of acid. Because the buret has markings etched on its exterior, the total amount of base added can be tracked.

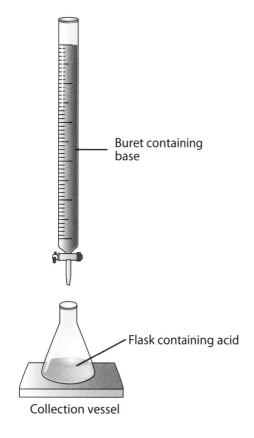

Buret containing base

Flask containing acid

Collection vessel

14 A mole is a unit used to specify a quantity of a chemical compound. If the flask contained 10 moles of hydrochloric acid, how many moles of sodium hydroxide would be required to neutralize it?
A   1
B   5
C   10
D   20

15 Of the possibilities below, what solution pH most likely would be found in the flask at the end of the titration?
A   2.2
B   6.8
C   7.1
D   10.7

Directions: Question 16 is based on the information below.

Some acids are strong and some are weak. Strong acids ionize completely so that all hydrogen is in the H^+ form. An example is HCl:

$$HCl \rightarrow H^+ + Cl^-$$

Weak acids do not ionize completely. In these cases, some of the hydrogen remains bonded to the parent molecule. An example is HNO_2:

$$HNO_2 \Leftrightarrow H^+ + NO_2^-$$

In this equation, the double arrow indicates that not all of the HNO_2 ionizes.

16 Acetic acid is a weak acid. According to the information presented in the paragraph, acetic acid would be expected to
A   not undergo ionization in solution.
B   completely ionize in solution.
C   have fewer H^+ ions in solution than HCl.
D   have more H^+ ions in solution than HCl.

Lesson 5 | Predict Outcomes

Use Calculations to Interpret Outcomes

① Learn the Skill

Scientific texts often include diagrams with numerical values listed on them. The diagrams may describe an event that occurred in an experiment or a test. To help make the numbers more meaningful, you could include them in a calculation of a rate or force that was tested in the experiment. When you use this process, you are **using calculations to interpret outcomes**.

② Practice the Skill

By mastering the skill of using calculations, you will improve your study and test-taking skills, especially as they relate to science high school equivalency tests. Examine the text and diagram below. Use the information to answer question 1.

A This text provides information related to a calculation. It states that to calculate speed, you divide time into distance, or $s = \frac{d}{t}$.

B This question asks you to use a calculation to interpret an outcome. To calculate speed, use the formula $s = \frac{d}{t}$. Use data from the diagram to find numbers for distance and time.

Speed is a measure of how fast an object moves, and it is calculated by dividing the distance that the object moved by the time required for the movement. Displacement describes how far an object travels, or its total change in position.

A commuter uses a scooter to travel 4 miles to work each day. The commuter's route is a direct route to the hospital where she works and then a direct route home. The chart below shows her average speed during a one-way trip to work or a one-way trip home.

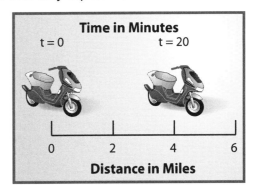

Time in Minutes

t = 0   t = 20

0   2   4   6

Distance in Miles

☑ **TEST-TAKING TIPS**

The diagram uses minutes as a unit of measurement, but the question uses hours. To convert units, multiply the speed per minute by the minutes in an hour.

1   Based on the text and the diagram, which best describes the speed and displacement of the scooter after the commuter's routine workday?

A   4 mph, 4 miles

B   4 mph, 8 miles

C   12 mph, 0 miles

D   12 mph, 8 miles

UNIT 2

Directions: Questions 2 and 3 are based on the information below.

Newton's second law states that the net force on an object equals its mass multiplied by its acceleration. This law is stated in the equation $F = ma$, where F stands for the net force (expressed in newtons), m stands for the object's mass, and a stands for the object's acceleration.

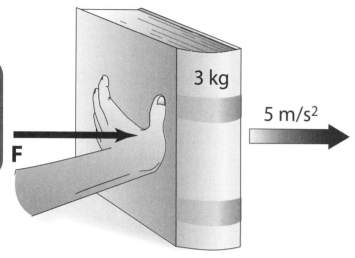

2   **How much force is being applied to the book in the diagram?**
   A   3 newtons
   B   5 newtons
   C   8 newtons
   D   15 newtons

3   **If a person applied the same force to move more books, what effect would it have on acceleration?**
   A   Acceleration would not change.
   B   Acceleration would increase.
   C   Acceleration would decrease.
   D   Acceleration would initially increase and then decrease.

Directions: Questions 4 and 5 are based on the information below.

Newton's third law states that for every action force, there is an equal and opposite reaction force. For example, when a person stands on a floor, the person's weight pushes down on the floor. To hold the weight, the floor pushes up on the person's feet with an equal and opposite force. In the illustration below, the person has a mass of 50 kg. The force he exerts on the floor is equal to his weight. Near Earth's surface, an object's weight in newtons is equal to its mass in kilograms times 9.8. Therefore, the person's weight is 50 kg × 9.8 = 490 N.

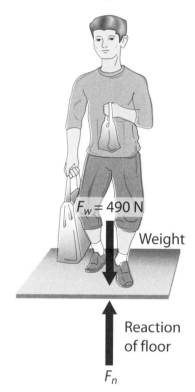

4   **What is the value of F_n?**
   A   9.8 newtons
   B   19.6 newtons
   C   50 newtons
   D   490 newtons

5   **What is the value of F_n for a person who has a mass of 65 kg?**
   A   6.6 newtons
   B   9.8 newtons
   C   65 newtons
   D   637 newtons

Directions: Questions 6 and 7 are based on the information below.

Distance is the amount of space between two positions. Displacement is the difference between the initial position of something and its final position. Displacement does not depend on the path that an object takes.

In the diagrams below, Person 1 and Person 2 each walks from Point A to Point B. Person 1 walks a straight line between the two points. Person 2 walks the long way around the block.

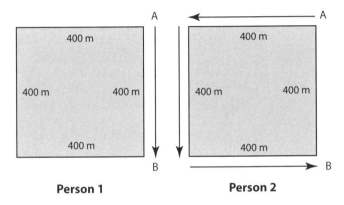

Person 1   **Person 2**

6 What distances do the people walk?
   A Person 1 walks 400 m, and Person 2 walks 800 m.
   B Person 1 and Person 2 both walk exactly 400 m.
   C Person 1 walks 400 m, and Person 2 walks 1200 m.
   D Person 1 and Person 2 both walk 800 m.

7 What is each person's displacement?
   A Person 1 and Person 2 both have displacements of 0 m.
   B Person 1 has a displacement of 400 m, and Person 2 has a displacement of 1200 m.
   C Person 1 and Person 2 both have displacements of 400 m.
   D Person 1 has a displacement of 1200 m, and Person 2 has a displacement of 400 m.

Directions: Questions 8 and 9 are based on the information below.

An object's speed is a measure of how quickly its position is changing. Speed can be calculated by dividing distance traveled by the time required to travel that distance. The direction of travel is unimportant in calculating speed. However, direction of travel is important in calculating velocity. An object's velocity is its total displacement divided by the time required to travel. Therefore, if an object's motion returns it to its starting point, it has an average velocity of 0, even if it was traveling at high speed the whole time.

Velocity can be defined as speed coupled with direction. It is not enough to say that an object is traveling at 60 mi/hr. A description of velocity must include information about direction, such as "The object is traveling 60 mi/hr west." The only exception to this is if velocity is zero. Then you do not need to specify a direction.

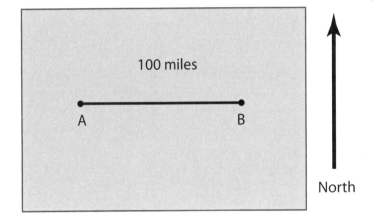

North

8 A bird flies from Point A to Point B in 5 hours. What is its approximate speed and velocity?
   A speed 10 mi/hr; velocity 10 mi/hr east
   B speed 20 mi/hr; velocity 20 mi/hr east
   C speed 50 mi/hr; velocity 50 mi/hr north
   D speed 100 mi/hr; velocity 100 mi/hr east

9 The bird flies directly from Point A to Point B, and then flies from Point B back to Point A. The trip takes 10 hours. What is the bird's average velocity for the whole trip?
   A 20 mi/hr east
   B 0 mi/hr
   C 10 mi/hr north
   D 50 mi/hr east

Directions: Questions 10 and 11 are based on the information below.

The diagram below shows an object in free fall. As time increases, the distance the object travels per second increases, and the object's velocity increases. Due to the force of gravity, when an object is dropped, its acceleration is constant at 9.8 m/s². The velocity of a dropped object increases at a rate proportional to the amount of time it falls. An equation to express this is $V = at$, where V = velocity, a = 9.8 m/s², and t = time.

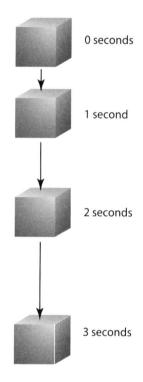

0 seconds

1 second

2 seconds

3 seconds

10 Based on the information, what is the velocity of the block at 3 seconds?
A   3 m/s downward
B   3.26 m/s downward
C   9.8 m/s downward
D   29.4 m/s downward

11 If the block continues to free fall, what will most likely happen to its velocity between 3 seconds and 4 seconds?
A   It will remain the same.
B   It will increase.
C   It will decrease.
D   It will reach 9.8 m/s.

Directions: Questions 12 through 14 are based on the information below.

The diagram below illustrates unbalanced forces on a basketball. They are not balanced, because they are not equal to each other. Because the forces are acting in opposite directions, the combined force equals the difference between the two. As a result of the pressure of the unbalanced forces, the basketball will move in the direction of the strongest force.

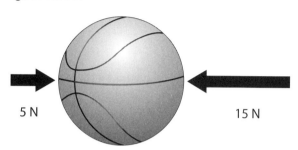

5 N   15 N

12 What is the overall force on the basketball?
A   5 N to the right
B   5 N to the left
C   10 N to the left
D   15 N to the right

13 Which best describes the movement of the basketball?
A   downward
B   upward
C   to the right
D   to the left

14 If the 5 N force doubled in strength, what would the total force on the basketball be?
A   5 N to the left
B   10 N to the right
C   15 N to the left
D   20 N to the right

Directions: Questions 15 and 16 are based on the information below.

Friction is the resistance that results from two pieces of matter rubbing against each other. The force of friction between an object and a surface can be calculated by the equation $F = \mu m$. F is the force caused by friction (expressed in newtons). μ is a constant that varies by substance, and m is the mass of the object.

Before an object will move, the force on the object must be greater than the frictional force between the object and the surface on which it rests.

Frictional force = 31 N   Force needed to push the box

The drawing above shows a wooden box sitting on a concrete floor. The mass of the box is 50 kg and μ is 0.62.

15 **Which of the following forces would allow the box to begin moving across the floor?**

A   10 N
B   30 N
C   31 N
D   32 N

16 **If the floor became wet and caused the value of μ to reduce to 0.2, what would be the result?**

A   More force would be needed to move the box.
B   Less force would be needed to move the box.
C   The mass of the box would decrease.
D   The mass of the box would increase.

Directions: Questions 17 and 18 are based on the diagram below.

The diagram below shows the forces that act on a wagon.

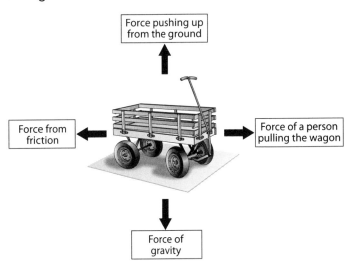

Force pushing up from the ground

Force from friction

Force of a person pulling the wagon

Force of gravity

17 **Which best describes the force pushing on the wagon from the ground and the force of gravity?**

A   They are balanced forces.
B   They are unbalanced forces.
C   The force pushing on the wagon from the ground is stronger.
D   The force of gravity is stronger.

18 **Suppose the wagon is moving to the right. Which of the following could be the force of friction on the wagon and the pulling force that the person is applying to the wagon?**

A   force of friction = 10 N; pulling force = 5 N
B   force of friction = 25 N; pulling force = 15 N
C   force of friction = 25 N; pulling force = 20 N
D   force of friction = 15 N; pulling force = 20 N

Draw Conclusions from Multiple Sources

① Learn the Skill

You make an inference by using facts, evidence, experience, and reasoning to make an educated guess. Then you can draw a **conclusion**, or an explanation or a judgment usually based on inferences. You can **draw conclusions from multiple sources** by using the information in charts, diagrams, tables, and text to make a statement that explains all of your observations and the facts that are presented.

② Practice the Skill

By mastering the skill of drawing conclusions from multiple sources, you will improve your study and test-taking skills, especially as they relate to science high school equivalency tests. Examine the paragraph, illustration, and strategies below. Use the information to answer question 1.

Ⓐ Pay attention to both the given information and any information that is left out. The phrase "six basic tools called simple machines" tells you that there are six types of simple machines. However, you are only given specific information about one—the lever. Inferences and conclusions you make about the lever may not apply to all simple machines.

In science, work is done only when a force moves an object. No work is done if an object does not move when a force is applied. Machines make work easier by changing the size or direction of the force needed to do work. <u>All machines are made up of six basic tools called simple machines. The lever is one type of simple machine.</u> The diagram shows how a lever can be used to lift a box.

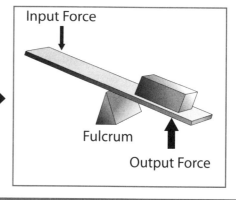

Ⓑ Carefully examine diagrams and other visuals for clues about the content. Notice that the lever turns around the part called the fulcrum. The input force arrow is smaller than the output force arrow. So, you can infer that the input force is smaller than the output force.

🧩 MAKING ASSUMPTIONS

In analyzing information from multiple sources, assume that information from one source complements information from another source. For example, diagrams can help show how a topic discussed in the text works.

1 Based on the information above, what conclusion can you draw?

   A Levers are the only simple machines that can increase the size of the force.

   B Levers make work easier by changing the direction of the applied force.

   C Levers are the only type of simple machine.

   D Levers apply force to the fulcrum.

Directions: Questions 2 through 5 are based on the information below.

A pulley is a simple machine that is used to lift objects. A pulley has two main parts—a grooved wheel and a rope. The rope fits into the groove of the wheel. Pulleys may change the direction of the applied force or the amount of applied force required to lift an object. Pulleys do not change the amount of work that is done. The size of applied force needed to lift an object with a moveable pulley is less because the force is applied over a longer distance. The table below shows the advantages of the three main types of pulleys. A block-and-tackle pulley contains at least one fixed pulley and one movable pulley, as the diagram shows.

TYPE OF PULLEY	CHANGE IN DIRECTION OF FORCE	CHANGE IN SIZE OF FORCE
Single, fixed	Yes	No
Movable	No	Yes
Block and tackle	Yes	Yes

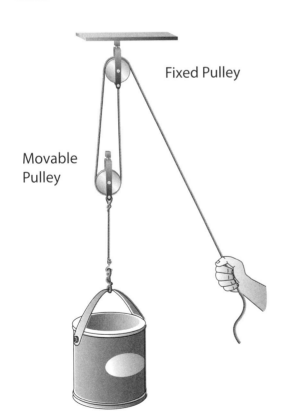

Fixed Pulley

Movable Pulley

2 **Based on the information, what can you conclude about using a single, fixed pulley?**
  A Less force is applied over a longer distance.
  B Single, fixed pulleys are only used as a part of the block and tackle.
  C A force of 10 N must be applied to the pulley to lift an object that weighs 10 N.
  D Pulling up on the rope lifts the object.

3 **Based on the information in the diagram and the table, the user of a block and tackle**
  A pulls down on the rope to make the object move down.
  B uses less force to lift an object than would be needed without the pulley.
  C pulls the rope a shorter distance than the object will move.
  D does more work to lift the object with the pulley than without the pulley.

4 **Based on the information above, what conclusion can you draw about the benefit of pulleys?**
  A They always decrease the size of the applied force that is needed.
  B Block-and-tackle pulleys can be combined to make movable pulleys.
  C They never change the direction of the applied force.
  D Some pulleys allow you to use your own weight to pull an object upward.

5 **Suppose 30 joules (J) of work is done to lift the paint can without a machine. Based on the information, how much work is done when using a single pulley to lift the same can?**
  A 30 J
  B 45 J
  C 90 J
  D 120 J

UNIT 2

Directions: Questions 6 and 7 are based on the information below.

An inclined plane is a type of simple machine. You might infer what an inclined plane is from its name; it is a flat, sloped surface. A ramp is an example of an inclined plane. Pushing a heavy object up a ramp is easier than picking up the object because less force is needed. However, the force must be applied over a longer distance. Ramps do not change the amount of work done. Work is equal to force times distance ($W = Fd$), where W = work (in newton-meters), F = force (in newtons), and d = distance (in meters). When an object is pushed up a ramp, less force is applied over a longer distance.

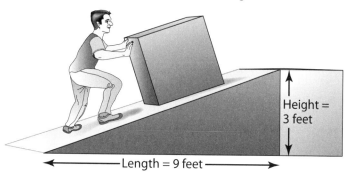

Height = 3 feet
Length = 9 feet

6 Based on the information, what can you infer about ramps?
  A Pushing objects up shorter ramps is easier than pushing objects up longer ramps.
  B Ramps can be used to elevate objects that are too heavy to lift straight up.
  C All simple machines are similar to ramps.
  D Pushing an object up a ramp requires less work than lifting the object straight up.

7 Based on the information, what can you conclude will happen if the length of the ramp shown in the illustration is shortened by two feet?
  A More force will be needed to move the box up the ramp.
  B Less force will be needed to move the box up the ramp.
  C More work will be done when the box is moved.
  D Less work will be done when the box is moved.

Directions: Question 8 is based on the information below.

A wedge is made of two inclined planes. The head of an axe is a wedge. The input force that is applied at the base of a wedge is distributed along its angled sides. When a force is applied to the axe, the sides of the axe blade push outward on the wood. The outward force causes the wood to split.

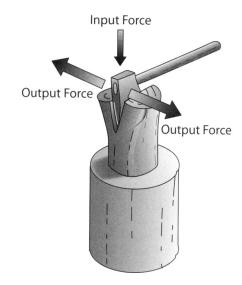

Input Force
Output Force
Output Force

8 Splitting an object with a wedge
  A is more difficult than without a wedge.
  B requires a person to use more force.
  C allows a person to use less force.
  D can only be done by using an axe.

Directions: Question 9 is based on the passage below.

A screw is an inclined plane wrapped in a spiral around a cylinder. When a screw is turned, a small force is applied over a long distance along the inclined plane. Meanwhile, the screw applies a large force through the short distance it is pushed.

9 When you turn a screw, you apply a small input force over a large distance, and the screw exerts
  A a large output force over a small distance.
  B a large output force over a large distance.
  C a small output force over a small distance.
  D a small output force over a large distance.

Directions: Questions 10 and 11 are based on the information below.

Screwdrivers make putting in screws easier. A screwdriver is a type of simple machine known as a wheel and axle. A wheel and axle is made up of two circular objects of different sizes. The larger object is the wheel; the smaller is the axle. The wheel and the axle turn at the same time. Because the wheel has a larger radius than the axle, it moves a greater distance than the axle. A small force applied to the wheel becomes a larger force on the axle.

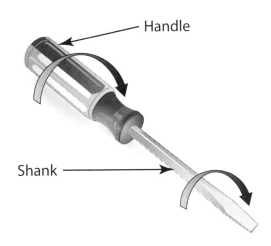

Handle

Shank

10 **Based on the information, what can you infer about a screwdriver?**
  A When the shank rotates, it moves a smaller distance than the handle.
  B A large force must be applied to drive in a screw.
  C The handle is the axle.
  D The shank is the wheel.

11 **Based on the information, what conclusion can you draw about wheels and axles?**
  A Wheels and axles are all screwdrivers.
  B Wheels and axles work only when force is applied to the wheel.
  C Wheels and axles work only when force is applied to the axle.
  D Wheels and axles are used when a force is applied to rotate an object.

Directions: Question 12 is based on the information below.

Simple machines, such as levers, wedges, and inclined planes, make work easier. Mechanical advantage is a measure of how much easier a machine makes work. More specifically, it is the amount by which a machine multiplies the applied force. If a machine has a mechanical advantage of two, it multiplies the applied force by a factor of two.

A student did an experiment to determine how the length of an inclined plane affects the mechanical advantage. The student set the height of the inclined plane to one meter and varied its length. The graph below shows the results of the experiment.

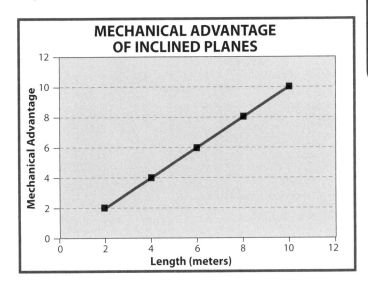

12 **Based on the above information, what can you conclude about mechanical advantage?**
  A Mechanical advantage depends only on the height of an inclined plane.
  B Longer inclined planes have a greater mechanical advantage.
  C Mechanical advantage is not affected by the length of an inclined plane.
  D In the experiment, the inclined plane with a length of six meters multiplied the applied force by a factor of two.

Directions: Questions 13 and 14 are based on the information below.

Inclined planes, wedges, screws, pulleys, wheels and axles, and levers are the six types of simple machines. However, most machines are not simple machines. Most machines are compound machines, because they contain two or more simple machines. A bicycle is a compound machine. Wheels and axles turn force into motion. Bicycle wheels and pedals are both examples of wheels and axles. The chain and gears make up a pulley system. The brake handles and the cranks attached to the pedals are levers.

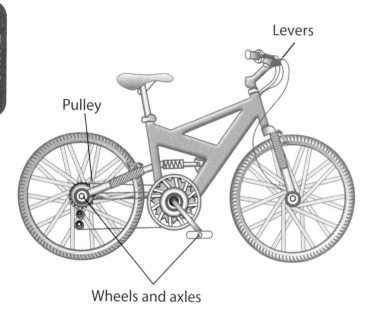

Levers

Pulley

Wheels and axles

13 Based on the information, what can you conclude are the types of simple machines involved in making a bike move?
  A gears and chains
  B pulleys and wheels and axles
  C pulleys and gears
  D pulleys, levers, and wheels and axles

14 Based on the information, which tool can you infer is a compound machine?
  A a bicycle wheel
  B a ramp
  C a lever
  D a pair of scissors

Directions: Questions 15 and 16 are based on the information below.

The amount by which a machine makes work easier is the mechanical advantage of that machine. The larger the value of the mechanical advantage, the easier that a machine makes doing work. The table below shows the mechanical advantage for four machines.

MECHANICAL ADVANTAGE OF DIFFERENT MACHINES	
MACHINE	**MECHANICAL ADVANTAGE**
Wedge A	1.5
Wedge B	5.0
Pulley	3.0
Ramp	2.5

15 Based on the information, what can you infer?
  A All simple machines have a mechanical advantage of at least 2.0.
  B All pulleys have a mechanical advantage of 3.0.
  C Pulleys make work easier than wedges.
  D All of the machines in the table make doing work easier.

16 Based on the information above, what can you conclude about using a wedge to split wood?
  A The work will be easier if Wedge A is used.
  B The work will be easier if Wedge B is used.
  C The work will be easier if Wedge A is combined with a pulley.
  D The work will be easier if Wedge B is combined with a ramp.

Interpret Graphs

1 Learn the Skill

As you have learned, graphs present data in a visual way. Line graphs can be used to show change over time. Bar graphs can be used to show the relationship of various items. Pictographs use symbols instead of lines or bars to represent numerical data. Knowing how to **interpret graphs** will enable you to answer questions about information contained in them.

2 Practice the Skill

By mastering the skill of interpreting graphs, you will improve your study and test-taking skills, especially as they relate to science high school equivalency tests. Study the information and strategies below. Use the information to answer question 1.

A Read the paragraph before trying to interpret the graph. The explanatory text usually provides information about data contained in the graph. In this case, the text tells you how the two data sets (kinetic energy and potential energy) are related.

B Graphs do not always contain legends or keys. This graph identifies the data sets next to the lines. Bar graphs may identify the data sets in the bars.

The law of conservation of energy states that energy cannot be created or destroyed. Energy only can change forms. Potential energy is stored energy. Kinetic energy is the energy of motion. The total amount of energy is always equal to the sum of the kinetic energy and the potential energy. The graph below shows how energy changes in a model rocket that is launched. The rocket has the most kinetic energy when it is launched and immediately before it hits the ground.

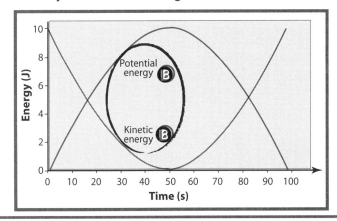

USING LOGIC

Questions about graphs often will require you to interpret the trends shown in the graphs. In multi-line graphs, it is helpful to look at the trend of each individual data set before comparing them.

1 **Based on the graph, what happens to the rocket's kinetic energy at 50 seconds?**
   A It is greater than the total amount of energy.
   B It is equal to the amount of potential energy
   C It changes completely into potential energy.
   D It is the same as when the rocket launched.

Directions: Question 2 is based on the information below.

Many scientists are concerned that an excessive amount of carbon dioxide (CO_2) in Earth's atmosphere is contributing to climate change. Carbon dioxide is produced when fossil fuels are burned in order to change their stored chemical energy into a form of energy that people can use. The graph below shows the projected carbon dioxide emissions for both developed countries and developing countries.

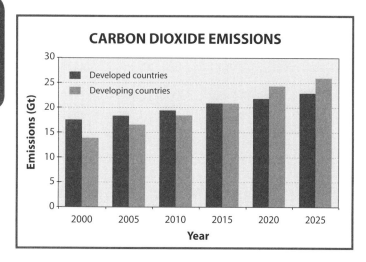

Directions: Questions 3 and 4 are based on the information below.

An incandescent light bulb costs about 75 cents, but uses more electricity than a compact fluorescent light bulb (CFL) and doesn't last nearly as long. However, if the CFL bulb costs about $20, consumers have to decide whether to pay the higher price for the CFL bulb or to instead opt for the cheaper incandescent bulb. The following pictograph shows what happens over the next 10,000 hours of bulb operation for each case.

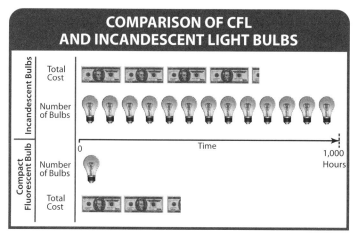

2 Based on the information in the graph, the amount of CO_2 released by developing countries

A is currently greater than the amount released by developed countries.

B is projected to decrease.

C will be equal to the amount released by developed countries in 2015.

D is expected to increase much more slowly than the amount released by developed countries.

3 Based on the information, incandescent bulbs

A are cheaper to use in the long run than CFLs.

B don't burn out as quickly as CFLs.

C have a much shorter lifetime than CFLs.

D cost half as much to operate as CFLs.

4 Based on the information, which of the following statements is most likely true?

A One CFL lasts as long as about 10 incandescent bulbs.

B One incandescent bulb costs about twice as much as one CFL.

C About four CFLs would be required to produce light for 500 hours.

D About 26 incandescent bulbs would be required to produce light for 2,000 hours.

Directions: Questions 5 and 6 are based on the information below.

With human populations on the rise, more and more energy will be needed every year to meet society's needs. Past and projected sources of electricity generation are shown in the following pictograph.

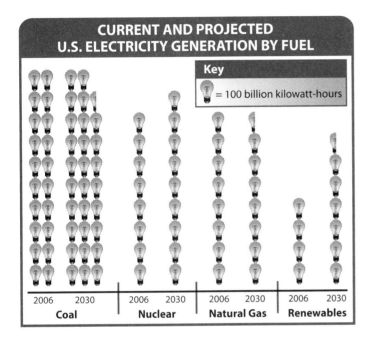

5 **Which fuel is expected to dominate in 2030?**
- **A** renewable fuels
- **B** coal
- **C** natural gas
- **D** nuclear fuels

6 **How much change is expected in the use of nuclear power by 2030?**
- **A** Nuclear power is expected to double.
- **B** Nuclear power is expected to triple.
- **C** Nuclear power is expected to increase slightly.
- **D** Nuclear power is expected to decrease by half.

Directions: Questions 7 and 8 are based on the information below.

Coal is fossil fuel that forms underground over millions of years from decayed swamp plants subjected to high temperatures and pressure. Coal is present in large quantities across the globe. However, like other forms of nonrenewable energy, its supply is finite. At some point in the future, coal reserves will be depleted if we continue to use coal at current rates.

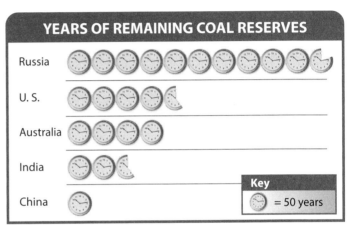

7 **Based on the information, what will happen to coal reserves in about 50 years?**
- **A** China will run out of coal.
- **B** The United States will have more coal reserves than Russia.
- **C** India will have twice as many coal reserves as Australia.
- **D** Russia will have used up half its present coal reserves.

8 **If the data above hold true, when will Russia become the only country with coal reserves?**
- **A** about 500 years from now
- **B** about 230 years from now
- **C** about 200 years from now
- **D** about 130 years from now

Directions: Question 9 is based on the information below.

According to the law of conservation of energy, energy cannot be created or destroyed. A group of students decided to test the law of conservation of energy by measuring the potential energy and kinetic energy of a toy car rolling down a ramp. The graph shows the results of their experiment. At the top of the ramp, the car has only potential energy. The potential energy changes into kinetic energy as the car rolls down the ramp. At the bottom of the ramp, all of the potential energy should be changed into kinetic energy. However, forces such as friction change some energy into thermal energy.

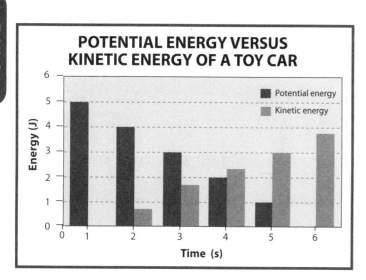

POTENTIAL ENERGY VERSUS KINETIC ENERGY OF A TOY CAR

Directions: Question 10 is based on the information below.

Most of the energy on Earth originally comes from the electromagnetic energy of the sun. Plants can change light energy from the sun into chemical energy. Fossil fuels contain energy from the sun that was stored by ancient organisms. Today, people can use solar cells to change the sun's light energy into electrical energy. The efficiency of a solar cell describes the amount of the light energy that is turned into electrical energy. The graph below shows how the efficiency of three types of solar cell systems has changed and is expected to change.

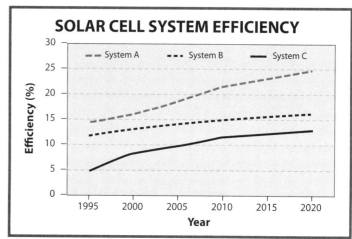

SOLAR CELL SYSTEM EFFICIENCY

9 **Based on the information, what conclusion can you draw about the experiment?**
   A The students did not measure the kinetic energy correctly.
   B About 1.5 J of energy was destroyed during the experiment.
   C The students proved that the law of conservation of energy is incorrect.
   D About 1.5 J of energy changed into thermal energy during the experiment.

10 **Based on the information, what can you conclude about the efficiency of the solar cell systems?**
   A By 2020, the efficiency of the three solar cells will stop improving.
   B The efficiency of System B is expected to improve the most.
   C System A is more efficient than the other two systems.
   D The combined efficiency of the three systems must be 100%.

Directions: Questions 11 through 16 are based on the information below.

Energy from the sun causes wind. Because wind is moving air, it has kinetic energy. For more than 1,000 years, humans have used windmills to change wind energy into mechanical energy that can be used to do work. Wind energy is also used to generate electricity. A wind turbine is a windmill that converts the kinetic energy of the wind into electrical energy. Smaller turbines can be used to provide power to single homes, and larger turbines can be used in wind farms run by electric companies. The graph shows the total amount of energy used during a five-day period by a business that gets some of its energy from a wind turbine.

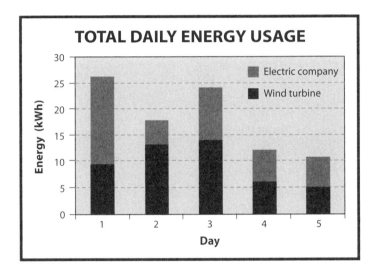

11 Which of the following statements explains why each of the bars shown in the graph is divided into two sections?

  A The sections show the amount of energy used at night and the amount used during the day.

  B The sections show the amount of energy used by the company and used to generate wind.

  C The sections show the amount of kinetic energy in the wind and the amount of electrical energy produced from it.

  D The sections show the portion of the total daily energy that both comes from the wind turbine and also from the electric company.

12 On which day was the greatest amount of wind-generated energy used?

  A day 1

  B day 2

  C day 3

  D day 4

13 The cost of electricity from the electric company was the smallest on

  A day 1.

  B day 2.

  C day 3.

  D day 4.

14 Based on the information, about how much electrical energy was produced from wind energy on day 1?

  A 9 kWh

  B 17.5 kWh

  C 27 kWh

  D 50%

15 Based on the information, what can you conclude about wind energy?

  A Wind energy can provide a significant amount of electrical energy to some people.

  B Wind energy is an unreliable source of energy.

  C Wind energy is only provided by electric companies.

  D Wind energy depends on the amount of energy supplied by the electric company.

16 Suppose the business adds a second wind turbine. What is likely to happen to total daily energy use?

  A Less of the daily energy use will come from energy harnessed by the turbines.

  B More of the daily energy use will come from energy harnessed by the turbines.

  C The amount of energy supplied daily by the electric company will increase.

  D The amount of energy harvested by each of the two turbines will be half as much as the energy harvested by the single turbine in use now.

Relate Text and Figures

① Learn the Skill

As you know, illustrations, graphs, and tables present information in a visual way. Text can help you understand information in these graphics. In this way, text and graphics support one another. Knowing how to **relate text and figures** will allow you to fully understand the information being presented.

② Practice the Skill

By mastering the skill of relating text and figures, you will improve your study and test-taking skills, especially as they relate to science high school equivalency tests. Study the paragraph, diagram, and strategies below. Use the information to answer question 1.

A When you see labels in a diagram, also look for those words in the text. The text may offer additional explanations that can help clarify the labels.

B When text and a graphic occur together, both are usually required to answer the question. Here, read the text carefully. Notice that the text only discusses transverse waves and the diagram shows a transverse wave. Other types of waves are not discussed.

When waves travel through substances, they cause the particles in substances to vibrate. In transverse waves, **B** the particles vibrate perpendicular to the direction in which the wave is moving. The diagram shows how the particles move away from their resting position when a transverse wave passes through a substance. Crests **A** and troughs are the points where particles are farthest from their resting point. The distance from any one point to the next identical point is known as the wavelength.

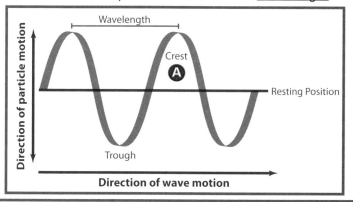

MAKING ASSUMPTIONS

Whenever a graphic accompanies text, you can assume the two pieces of information are related. You also should assume that you need both pieces of information to answer the questions.

1   **Which statement can be derived from the information in the text and diagram?**

   A The wavelength can only be measured from crest to crest.
   B The larger the crest of a wave, the farther the particles move from their resting point.
   C Transverse waves cause particles to move in the same direction as the wave motion.
   D The wavelength measures how far the particles move from their resting point.

③ Apply the Skill

Directions: Questions 2 through 4 are based on the information below.

Sound waves are mechanical waves because they can only move through substances, such as air. They are longitudinal waves because they cause substances to vibrate back and forth parallel to the direction in which the wave is moving. When a sound wave travels through air, it causes the particles in air to move back and forth.

The amplitude of a mechanical wave is the point at which the particles move the farthest from their resting point. Loud sounds have large amplitudes. The wavelength of a sound wave determines the pitch. High-pitched sounds have short wavelengths.

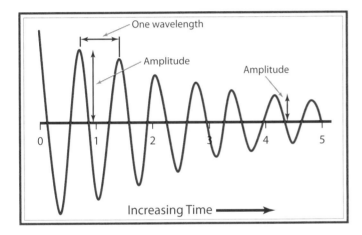

2 Based on the information, you can conclude that the sound represented in the diagram
   A   becomes higher pitched over time.
   B   becomes lower pitched over time.
   C   remains at a constant pitch.
   D   has no pitch.

3 Based on the information, a sound wave that has a small amplitude will produce a sound that
   A   has a high pitch.
   B   has a low pitch.
   C   is loud.
   D   is soft.

4 What is true of the sound that is represented by the diagram?
   A   Its pitch increase over time.
   B   Its loudness is constant.
   C   It becomes softer over time.
   D   It can travel in the absence of air.

Directions: Questions 5 and 6 are based on the information below.

The volume of sound is related to wave amplitude. The larger the amplitude, the greater the volume. Volume is measured in decibels (dB). Hearing damage begins at about the 85 dB level. The table lists the decibel levels of some sounds.

VOLUME OF SOUND	
SOUND	**DECIBEL LEVEL (dB)**
Conversation	50–65
Vacuum cleaner	70
Lawn mower	85–90
Jackhammer	110
Jet engine	140

5 Based on the information in the paragraph and table, which sounds can cause hearing damage?
   A   a conversation, a vacuum cleaner, and a lawn mower
   B   a vacuum cleaner and a lawn mower
   C   a lawn mower, a jackhammer, and a jet engine
   D   a vacuum cleaner, a jackhammer, and a jet engine

6 Based on the information, sound waves from which source have the smallest amplitude?
   A   conversation
   B   vacuum cleaner
   C   jackhammer
   D   jet engine

Directions: Questions 7 through 9 are based on the information below.

When waves pass through a substance, they cause the particles in the substance to vibrate. Waves are classified by the direction in which they make the particles vibrate. The diagram shows the two main types of waves.

A longitudinal wave causes particles to vibrate in the direction that the wave moves. A transverse wave causes particles to vibrate perpendicular to the direction of the wave. A longitudinal wave is similar to a spring that is vibrating back and forth. Shaking a rope up and down can make a transverse wave in the rope.

Sound waves are longitudinal, and light waves are transverse. Longitudinal waves are made up of a repeating pattern of areas where the particles are squished together and areas where they are spread out. Transverse waves are made up of a repeating pattern of high and low points.

NO WAVE

LONGITUDINAL WAVE

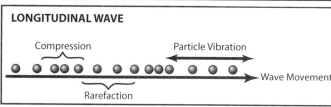

TRANSVERSE WAVE

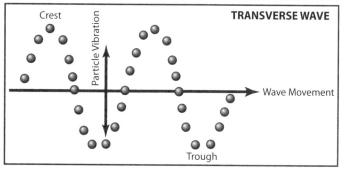

7 Which statement can be derived from the information in the text and diagram?
A Rarefactions are only found in transverse waves.
B The vibrating particles in sound waves form compressions and rarefactions.
C Compressions are the areas in longitudinal waves where the particles are the farthest apart.
D Sound waves can be characterized by their crests and troughs.

8 When a speaker produces a sound wave, what happens to the particles in air as the sound wave passes through?
A Crests and compressions are formed in the air.
B The particles in air form troughs where the particles are pressed together.
C The particles move back and forth perpendicular to the wave's direction.
D The particles move back and forth in the same direction that the wave is moving.

9 Based on the information, what can you conclude about light waves?
A Light waves are made up of compressions and rarefactions.
B Light waves cause the particles in air to vibrate in the same way as sound waves.
C Light waves contain crests and troughs.
D Light waves are similar to a vibrating spring.

UNIT 2

Directions: Questions 10 and 11 are based on the information below.

Surface waves move along the boundary between two different substances. Water waves are surface waves that move at the boundary between air and water. Earthquakes also produce surface waves, known as Rayleigh waves, that travel along the boundary between Earth's crust and the atmosphere. Surface waves have both transverse and longitudinal characteristics. The diagram shows how a Rayleigh wave moves the crust.

Directions: Question 12 is based on the information below.

Electromagnetic waves differ from other types of waves because they can travel through empty space. These types of waves have different properties because they have different energies. The diagram shows the electromagnetic spectrum, which is made up of every type of electromagnetic wave. The waves in the spectrum are arranged in order of increasing energy. Their energy depends on their wavelength. Waves with longer wavelengths have less energy than waves with shorter wavelengths.

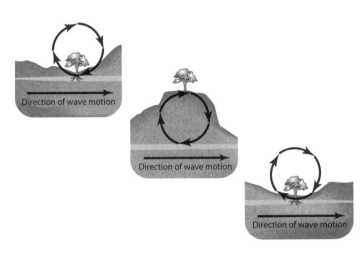

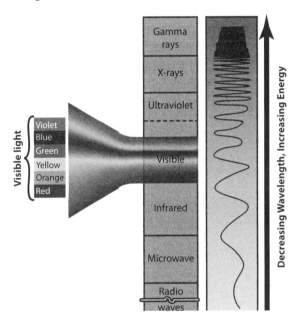

10 **Water waves affect objects floating in the water in a similar way to how Rayleigh waves affect objects on Earth's surface. What would happen to a leaf floating on a lake as a chain of water waves passed it?**
A The leaf would move away from the shore.
B The leaf would move up and down along a circular path.
C The leaf would move parallel to the shore.
D The leaf would move side to side in straight lines.

11 **Why does the Rayleigh wave demonstrated by the diagram affect the tree?**
A It travels along the boundary between Earth's crust and air.
B It moves in two directions at once.
C It travels deep beneath Earth's surface.
D It moves along the boundary between water and air.

12 **Which conclusion is supported by the information presented?**
A Radio waves cannot travel through empty space.
B All electromagnetic waves have identical properties.
C Visible light makes up the largest part of the electromagnetic spectrum.
D Microwaves have less energy than infrared waves.

Directions: Questions 13 through 15 are based on the information below.

The waves in the electromagnetic spectrum have a large range of frequencies and wavelengths, but humans can only see a small portion of the spectrum. The part of the spectrum that humans can see is called visible light. The diagram shows the visible portion of the electromagnetic spectrum. The main colors in the visible spectrum are red, orange, yellow, green, blue, and violet.

In a vacuum, all electromagnetic waves travel at the speed of light. However, the waves have different frequencies and wavelengths. Frequency, measured in Hertz (Hz or s⁻¹), and wavelength, measured in nanometers (nm), are related to speed. Because the speed of all light waves is the same, waves with higher frequencies have shorter wavelengths. Wavelength and frequency are also related to energy. Waves with higher frequencies and shorter wavelengths have more energy than waves with lower frequencies and longer wavelengths.

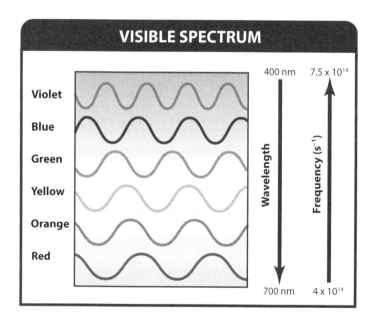

13 Based on the information, which color of light has the longest wavelength?
A   violet
B   green
C   orange
D   red

14 Which statement describes blue and orange light?
A   Blue light has a shorter wavelength and more energy than orange light.
B   Blue light has a shorter wavelength and less energy than orange light.
C   Blue light has a shorter wavelength and lower frequency than orange light.
D   Blue light has a longer wavelength and more energy than orange light.

15 White light, such as the light from the sun, is made up of waves of every color of light. What can you conclude about white light?
A   White light travels six times faster than any one color of light.
B   The wavelengths of the waves that make up white light have a range of 400 nm to 700 nm.
C   All of the waves that make up white light have the same frequency.
D   White light has a short wavelength and high frequency.

Directions: Question 16 is based on the information below.

The speed of a wave is equal to its frequency multiplied by its wavelength. The table shows the speed of sound waves in various substances.

THE SPEED OF SOUND WAVES IN DIFFERENT SUBSTANCES	
SUBSTANCE	**SPEED OF SOUND WAVES (M/S)**
Water	1,490
Seawater	1,530
Lead	1,320
Rubber	1,600

16 Suppose sound waves traveling in each listed substance have the same wavelength. In which substance do they have the highest frequency?
A   water
B   seawater
C   lead
D   rubber

Analyze Results

① Learn the Skill

The process known as the scientific method usually begins with a question. Using what they already know, scientists attempt to answer the question with a hypothesis, or an educated guess. Scientists then try and prove their hypothesis by conducting tests and gathering data. After the testing is complete, the scientists subject their data to analysis. **Analyzing results** helps scientists determine whether their initial hypothesis is correct.

② Practice the Skill

By mastering the skill of analyzing results, you will improve your study and test-taking skills, especially as they relate to science high school equivalency tests. Examine the graphic and paragraph below. Use the information to answer question 1.

A Once a working hypothesis has been formulated, a scientist should make a plan to test that hypothesis.

B Even when a hypothesis seems to prove correct, additional testing may be done to further confirm it.

After conducting tests as part of the scientific method, a researcher must decide whether the initial hypothesis has been proved. To do this, the researcher must collect and analyze data from the tests. If the researcher's analysis proves the hypothesis incorrect or only partially correct, the hypothesis may be modified. More testing is then performed on the updated hypothesis. This process continues until tests that can be duplicated by others prove that the modified hypothesis is correct.

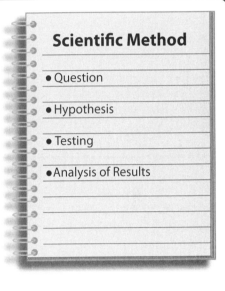

Scientific Method

- Question
- Hypothesis
- Testing
- Analysis of Results

USING LOGIC

The scientific method is based on logic. If results are not analyzed logically, conclusions will not be valid.

1 When a hypothesis is proved incorrect by analyzing test data, what should a researcher plan to do next?

   A change the results to match the hypothesis
   B modify the hypothesis
   C develop a new test
   D analyze the data again

③ Apply the Skill

Directions: Questions 2 through 6 are based on the information below.

A scientist wants to know whether certain common liquids have the acidic potential to kill some varieties of aquatic life. The scientist forms a hypothesis stating that five common liquids are acidic enough to be toxic to fish and young frogs. While conducting background research, the scientist learns that U.S. government researchers had previously studied the effects of various pH levels on some common forms of aquatic life.

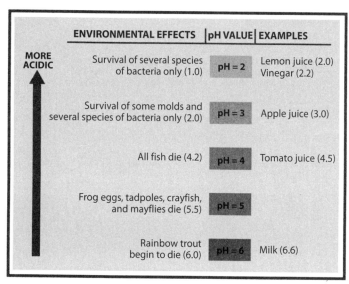

2 Which of the following conclusions is a logical analysis of the test data?

  A None of the tested liquids threatens aquatic life.

  B All of the tested liquids except lemon juice threaten aquatic life.

  C All of the tested liquids threaten aquatic life.

  D All of the tested liquids except milk threaten aquatic life.

3 To which of the following further studies would this data be most relevant?

  A the effects of acid rain on food chains

  B the effects of high acidity on the human digestive system

  C an analysis of food preferences of tadpoles

  D an analysis of predator-prey relationships in pond ecosystems

4 Does analysis of the test data support the hypothesis?

  A Yes, it completely supports the hypothesis.

  B No, it completely refutes the hypothesis, and a new hypothesis must be formed.

  C It demonstrates a flaw in the hypothesis, so the hypothesis must be modified.

  D The data are not sufficient to confirm or refute the hypothesis.

5 Based on the analysis of the test results, what should the researcher do next?

  A Modify her hypothesis and repeat her tests.

  B Develop an entirely new hypothesis and repeat the same tests.

  C Develop an entirely new hypothesis and conduct entirely new tests.

  D Discontinue her research.

6 Based on the data, which organisms are least tolerant of acidity?

  A tadpoles

  B crayfish

  C mayflies

  D rainbow trout

Directions: Questions 7 and 8 are based on the information below.

The scientific method is the established means of discovering facts about the physical world. Scientists in many different fields base their research on this procedure. It has proved consistently reliable as a way to separate facts from mistakes or from wishful thinking.

Before the scientific method, science was largely a matter of guesswork and argument. As a result, scientific knowledge often was indistinguishable from opinion. The scientific method allowed scientists to show that their ideas were clearly supported by observations and data. Following the scientific method also allows scientists to identify incorrect ideas and to objectively show that they are incorrect. The diagram below shows the steps in the scientific method.

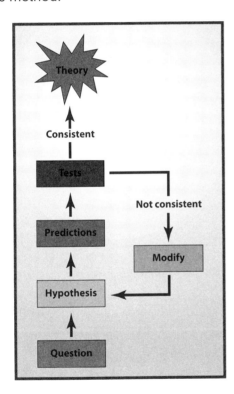

7 How can someone who doubts a scientific assumption prove it to be incorrect?
  A by arguing against it
  B by applying the steps of the scientific method and producing different results
  C by altering test results and publishing the work in a respected journal
  D by encouraging others to ignore it

8 Which of the following should be done when a new fact contradicts a long-established hypothesis?
  A The new fact should be ignored.
  B The new fact should be modified to fit the hypothesis.
  C An entirely new hypothesis should be formed and tested.
  D The original hypothesis should be modified and retested.

Directions: Question 9 is based on the information below.

Observations and questions form the basis of the scientific method. There is a famous story about Sir Isaac Newton sitting beneath an apple tree. As the story goes, an apple fell from the tree and hit Newton on the head. This made him ask himself, "What makes things fall?" and led to his development of the law of gravity. While this story is probably not historically accurate, it illustrates the process of observation that can prompt the scientific method.

9 What is the connection between a hypothesis, an observation, and a question?
  A All three apply exclusively to academic scientific investigation.
  B Hypotheses prompt questions, which are answered by observations.
  C Hypotheses and observations lead to questions.
  D Observations prompt questions, which lead to the formation of hypotheses.

UNIT 2

Directions: Questions 10 through 12 are based on the information below.

A hypothesis is a tentative prediction based on a question. It gives a researcher a starting point from which to begin testing and analysis. When analysis of test results does not produce facts that confirm a hypothesis, the hypothesis may be modified or even abandoned.

A hypothesis is a possible explanation for a specific observation. In contrast, a scientific theory is an explanation for a large number of related observations. A valid scientific theory is supported by all available data, explains all available observations, and can be used to make predictions about the results of future investigations.

10 How is a hypothesis formed?
A as a likely answer to a scientific question
B as an alternative to be abandoned
C as a substitute for analysis of scientific data
D as a scientific theory to be tested

11 Modern atomic theory is considered a valid scientific theory in part because
A many people think atoms exist.
B everybody knows about it.
C it can be used to make accurate predictions.
D prominent scientists believe in it.

12 Which of the following best describes the difference between a hypothesis and a theory?
A A hypothesis explains observations, but a theory does not.
B A theory is always true, but a hypothesis is not.
C A theory explains a wider range of observations than a hypothesis does.
D A hypothesis relies on more accurate data than a theory does.

Directions: Questions 13 and 14 are based on the information below.

An important characteristic of all valid scientific hypotheses and theories is that they are falsifiable. In other words, there must be a situation which, if it occurred, would prove the hypothesis or theory false. Another important characteristic of a hypothesis or theory is that it can never be proven absolutely true. This is because it is impossible to test every situation. It's always possible that the next test will prove the hypothesis or theory false. However, the more tests that support the hypothesis or theory, the more likely it is to be correct.

This is one reason that a statement such as "Leprechauns exist, but they are invisible and impossible to catch" cannot be considered a theory. There is no test you could do that could prove it false. In contrast, the statement "Leprechauns do not exist" could be considered a valid hypothesis, because all available evidence supports it, and it could be proven false if a leprechaun were ever spotted.

13 For a statement to be a theory, there must be a possibility that it
A cannot be tested.
B can be proved false.
C cannot be analyzed.
D cannot be modified.

14 Before the modern atomic theory was accepted, many scientists thought that Dalton's atomic theory was accurate. According to Dalton's theory, atoms were solid spheres that could not be broken down into smaller particles. Which of the following factors most likely caused scientists to reject Dalton's theory?
A Dalton's experiments could be carried out using inexpensive equipment.
B They were able to replicate all of Dalton's experimental results.
C Dalton was unable to publish his ideas in popular newspapers.
D Dalton's theory could not explain some of the new observations that scientists were making.

Directions: Questions 15 through 17 are based on the information below.

When preparing to test a hypothesis, it is important for researchers to be organized. Testing procedures should be planned beforehand. Everything needed for the testing should be within easy reach. Any safety concerns should be discussed and planned for.

During testing, researchers should plan to record data in one location, such as in a notebook. Any measurements should be made carefully and accurately. Researchers should record results as soon as they happen. Anything unexpected, as well as any insights, should be recorded at the time that they occur. This will be important when it is time to analyze and interpret results.

15 **Which of these methods would be best for researchers producing a record of testing and results?**

A paying close attention and writing everything down afterward

B recording the test with a camera as the team narrates results and insights

C designating a person to write down everything that supports the hypothesis

D taking no notes but repeating the same procedures the following day

16 **Which step in the scientific process follows testing?**

A deciding on a hypothesis

B forming a new question and analyzing data

C analyzing and interpreting the results

D making a prediction

17 **When conducting an experiment, which of the following steps should a scientist do first?**

A record observations accurately and precisely

B identify all equipment and materials required for the experiment

C determine whether the results support the hypothesis

D set up the equipment for the experiment

Directions: Questions 18 and 19 are based on the information below.

The table contains the results of an experiment to test how impurities affect the freezing point of water. The hypothesis was, "The more impurities that water contains, the lower its freezing point becomes." Following the table is the analysis of the results, as written by the researcher.

FREEZING POINTS OF DIFFERENT SOLUTIONS	
1 QUART PURE WATER	**FREEZING POINT (°C)**
With 1 tsp sugar	0
With 10 tsp sugar	0
With 25 tsp sugar	−2
With 50 tsp sugar	−5

"According to the testing, one quart of pure water freezes at 0°C. When one teaspoon of sugar was added to one quart of pure water, the freezing point remained at 0°C. Adding 10 teaspoons of sugar to one quart of pure water produced the same result.

"At 25 teaspoons per quart the freezing point began to drop. It was at this point that the sugar did not remain dissolved in the water during the freezing process.

"My hypothesis is that the freezing point of pure water drops as more impurities are added to it. The results support my hypothesis."

18 **What might account for the similar results until the sugar reached a certain concentration?**

A Sugar turns into water at low concentrations.

B Sugar evaporates at low concentrations.

C Sugar gives off heat when mixed with water.

D Differences in freezing points at lower sugar levels were too small to detect.

19 **Which of the following would be a good modification of the hypothesis?**

A replace the word *water* with *impurities*

B replace the word *impurities* with *sugar*

C replace the word *water* with *liquid*

D replace the word *pure* with *freezing*

UNIT 2

Apply Scientific Concepts

① Learn the Skill

A **concept** is a model based on general knowledge of a subject. Concepts can be useful in determining answers to new questions or in finding solutions to new problems. Researchers often interpret new information by relying on concepts with which they are already familiar. Knowing how to **apply scientific concepts** is valuable to research and discovery.

② Practice the Skill

By mastering the skill of applying scientific concepts, you will improve your study and test-taking skills, especially as they relate to science high school equivalency tests. Examine the paragraph and diagram below. Use the information to answer question 1.

A Illustrations and diagrams can visually demonstrate a concept in such a way that it helps you to better understand that concept.

B Text in a question often gives background information about a concept. It may also give some details about the concept.

Magnetism is a fundamental property of matter. Objects that are magnetic produce magnetic fields. A magnetic field exerts a force on objects within the field. The illustration shows how iron filings are affected by the magnetic field around a bar magnet.

Ⓐ
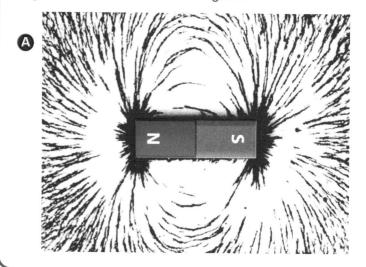

🧩 MAKING ASSUMPTIONS

You can assume that processes and forces described in one situation apply to other similar situations. Making this assumption allows you to apply known concepts to new situations.

1 Based on the information, where is the bar magnet's **Ⓑ** magnetic field most likely strongest?
   A in the center of the magnet
   B several inches away from the magnet
   C along a circle through the center of the magnet
   D at the magnet's north and south poles

Directions: Questions 2 through 6 are based on the information below.

Magnets are surrounded by invisible lines of force. These lines result from the property of bipolarity. Bipolarity means that a magnet has two poles where the lines of force are most concentrated. These poles are designated "north" and "south." Force lines moving from north to south produce a magnet's field. When two magnets are brought close to each other, their magnetic fields interact. The directions of their force lines result in predictable patterns of attraction and repulsion.

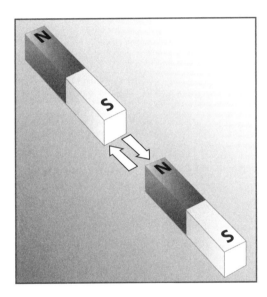

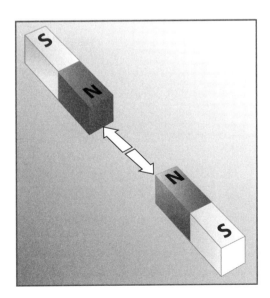

2 The illustration demonstrates that
   A opposite magnetic poles repel each other, while like poles attract each other.
   B opposite magnetic poles attract each other, while like poles repel each other.
   C all magnets always attract each other.
   D all magnets always repel each other.

3 Which of the following concepts is supported by the text and illustrations?
   A Magnetic forces are variable.
   B Magnetic forces have a great deal of strength.
   C Magnetic forces do not affect solid objects.
   D Magnetic lines of force are directional.

4 The reaction of two magnets placed side by side depends on
   A the metal of which each magnet is made.
   B the temperature of the surrounding air.
   C which of the magnets is placed on the left side.
   D how the magnets' poles are aligned.

5 Which of the following would be the best way to see the range of a magnet's field?
   A sprinkle sand on and around it
   B sprinkle iron filings on and around it
   C place a piece of metal near it
   D place another magnet near it

6 How does the saying "opposites attract" apply to magnets?
   A Opposite magnetic poles attract each other.
   B Opposite magnetic poles repel each other.
   C Magnets painted different colors attract each other.
   D Magnets of extremely different temperatures attract each other.

UNIT 2

Directions: Questions 7 through 9 are based on the information below.

Some natural substances have magnetic properties. The best known of these is the mineral magnetite, an iron oxide commonly called lodestone. Pieces of lodestone were used in compasses as early as 200 B.C.E. Magnetite does not have magnetic properties when it is first formed. It acquires them and keeps them when exposed to magnetism through lightning or other sources.

Tiny pieces of this mineral are found in many rocks. Because of its magnetic properties, it tends to align with Earth's magnetic field. By examining the arrangements of lodestone bits in ancient rocks, geologists are able to learn about past changes in our planet's magnetic field.

7 **Who most likely made the earliest use of lodestone?**

   A geologists

   B astronomers

   C engineers

   D navigators

8 **Geological examination of magnetite arrangements could most likely be used to support which of the following ideas?**

   A black holes

   B relativity

   C continental drift

   D gravity

9 **Scientists think that Earth's magnetic poles have switched places many times over Earth's long history. Which observations did scientists most likely make to help them come up with this idea?**

   A Lodestone in old rocks is aligned opposite that of younger rocks.

   B Some samples of lodestone are older than others.

   C Ancient sailors used lodestone to stay on course.

   D Lodestone is much denser than non-magnetic rocks.

Directions: Questions 10 and 11 are based on the information below.

Any material's electrons will be affected if it is placed in a magnetic field, regardless of whether that effect is noticeable. Materials can be sorted into one of three categories based on how they react to magnetic forces.

Diamagnetic: These materials are slightly repelled by magnetic forces. They do not retain any magnetic effects when removed from those forces. Most elements are diamagnetic. Carbon is an example of a diamagnetic material.

Paramagnetic: These materials are slightly attracted to magnetic forces. They do not retain any magnetic effects when removed from those forces. Magnesium is paramagnetic.

Ferromagnetic: These materials are strongly attracted to magnetic forces. They retain magnetic properties after being removed from these forces. Iron is the most common ferromagnetic element.

10 **Which statement can be inferred from the information provided?**

   A Most compass needles are made of diamagnetic materials.

   B The steel used in most refrigerators is diamagnetic.

   C Substances used to produce magnetic surfaces contain ferromagnetic materials.

   D Paramagnetic materials are found only in Earth's core.

11 **Steel is an alloy of iron and several other elements, such as chromium. A piece of steel that was placed in a strong magnetic field would likely be**

   A repelled by the field, and have no magnetic properties after it was removed from the field.

   B slightly attracted to the field, and have strong magnetic properties after it was removed from the field.

   C neither attracted to nor repelled by the field, and have no magnetic properties after it was removed from the field.

   D strongly attracted to the field, and have magnetic properties after it was removed from the field.

Directions: Questions 12 through 14 are based on the information below.

An electrical circuit is a device that uses electricity to perform a task, such as power a lamp. The circuit is a closed loop formed by a power source, wires, a load, and a switch. The switch allows you to stop or start the flow of electricity through a circuit. A load is any device on the circuit powered by electricity.

There are two main types of circuits. A series circuit has only one possible path that the electrical current may flow. If the electrical circuit is broken, none of the devices on the circuit will work. Parallel circuits contain more than one path for electricity to flow. Thus, if one path is broken, the other paths will continue to work.

12 Which is a device that opens or closes a circuit?
A   switch
B   series
C   load
D   parallel

13 A conductor is a material that allows electricity to flow easily. Resistors impede the flow of electricity. A researcher wants to test a new material to determine whether it is a conductor or a resistor. Which part of a circuit would be best for the researcher to replace?
A   the load
B   the switch
C   the power source
D   the wires that connect all parts of the circuit

14 A homeowner is purchasing strings of holiday lights. If the homeowner wants to ensure that the the strings stay lit, even if a bulb burns out, what should he look for?
A   strings wired in series
B   strings wired in parallel
C   strings that contain a switch
D   strings that have no load

Directions: Questions 15 and 16 are based on the information below.

HOW BATTERIES WORK

Potential energy is stored as chemical energy in a non-rechargeable battery. Chemical reactions inside the battery cause electrons to collect on the zinc shell. That potential energy changes to electrical energy once a circuit is completed between the (positive) carbon rod and (negative) zinc shell. The resulting electrical energy can be changed into other forms of energy, as shown in the diagram. As the chemical paste in the battery reacts with the metals in the battery, the metals eventually decompose and the battery "dies."

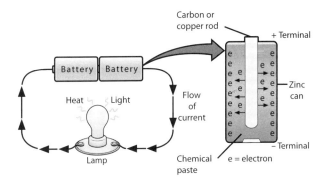

15 Which statement describes what happens to the battery's stored energy in this system?
A   It changes from electrical, heat, and light energy to chemical energy.
B   It changes from chemical energy to electrical, light, and heat energy.
C   It changes from light and heat energy to chemical and electrical energy.
D   It changes from electrical energy to heat, light, and chemical energy.

16 What would happen to the energy in this system if the wire were disconnected from one terminal of the battery?
A   The electrical energy would change to potential energy.
B   The light and heat energy would change to chemical energy.
C   Energy would stop changing from potential chemical energy into other forms.
D   Energy would stop changing from kinetic chemical energy into other forms.

Directions: Questions 17 through 20 are based on the information below.

Electricity and magnetism are closely related. When an electric current runs through a wire, it produces a magnetic field around the wire. By running electricity through a wire, a magnetic field is generated. Engineers and scientists often rely on tools that use electricity to generate a magnetic field. These tools are called electromagnets. Electromagnets are quite useful. You can find them in many everyday objects, from cars to computers.

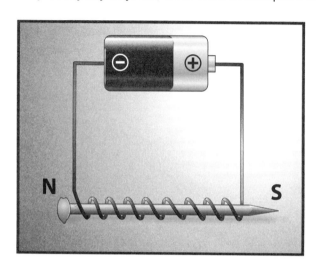

A simple electromagnet can be made from a battery, some copper wire, and a nail. By wrapping the wire around the nail and attaching each end of the wire to opposite poles of the battery, a path of electron flow is created. This generates flux lines and produces a magnetic field.

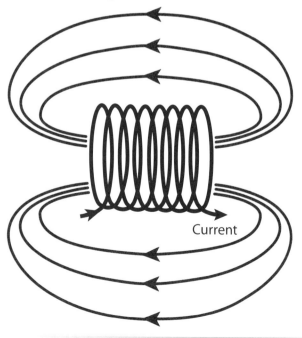

Current

Flux lines travel from the electromagnet's north pole to its south pole, just as they do in an ordinary magnet. A battery used as an electromagnetic source drains quickly. Most electromagnets are attached to more reliable sources of power.

17 **Which of the following is a practical advantage of an electromagnet over an ordinary magnet?**
  A Electromagnets cost less money.
  B Magnets have fewer uses.
  C Electromagnets produce magnetic fields.
  D Electromagnets can be switched off.

18 **What is similar about the flux lines of an electromagnet and those of an ordinary magnet?**
  A They are both produced by charged particles.
  B They both run from a south pole to a north pole.
  C They cannot exist in a vacuum.
  D They form concentric circles around their poles.

19 **What would most likely happen if you reversed the battery in the figure, so that the positive and negative terminals were switched?**
  A The north and south poles of the electromagnet would become reversed.
  B The nail would heat up.
  C The battery would lose energy more quickly.
  D The electromagnet would no longer have a north pole.

20 **Based on the information, what would most likely happen to a ferromagnetic material that is placed near a strong electromagnet?**
  A It would melt quickly.
  B It would remain unchanged.
  C It would lose its magnetic charge.
  D It would become magnetized.

Unit 2 Review

The Unit Review is structured to resemble science high school equivalency tests. Be sure to read each question and all possible answers very carefully before choosing your answer.

To record your answers, fill in the numbered circle that corresponds to the answer you select for each question in the Unit Review.

Do not rest your pencil on the answer area while considering your answer. Make no stray or unnecessary marks. If you change an answer, erase your first mark completely.

Mark only one answer space for each question; multiple answers will be scored as incorrect.

Sample Question

In which of the following examples would a pictograph provide the best visual representation of information?
  A when showing the concentration of water molecules in different states
  B when showing ionization reactions
  C when showing energy consumption of people in the United States
  D when showing change over time in energy consumption in the United States

---

Directions: Questions 1 and 2 are based on the information below.

The function of a machine is to transfer or change a force. Any machine is made up of one or more of the six simple machines. Simple machines can be characterized by the mechanical advantage that they provide. Mechanical advantage (MA) is a ratio of the size of the output force to the size of the input force.

$$MA = \frac{\text{output force}}{\text{input force}}$$

MECHANICAL ADVANTAGE		
MACHINE	**INPUT FORCE (N)**	**OUTPUT FORCE (N)**
A	300	900
B	15	150
C	5	10
D	800	1000
E	10	40

1 Which machine provides the greatest mechanical advantage?
  A A
  B B
  C C
  D D

Ⓐ Ⓑ Ⓒ Ⓓ

2 The output force of a particular simple machine is 100 N. The machine provides a mechanical advantage of 4. What is the input force?
  A 4 N
  B 25 N
  C 100 N
  D 200 N

Ⓐ Ⓑ Ⓒ Ⓓ

Directions: Questions 3 and 4 are based on the information below.

The everyday meanings of the words *hypothesis* and *theory* are different from their scientific meanings. When reading and evaluating scientific information, it is important to understand what scientists mean when they use these words.

In science, a hypothesis is an educated guess that is based on observations and knowledge. It is a possible answer to a scientific question. A hypothesis can be proved false, but it can never be proved true, because there is no way to test every possible situation to see whether the hypothesis holds true in all of them. A hypothesis generally applies only to a very specific situation.

A scientific theory is a well-supported explanation for many different observations. For a scientific theory to be accepted, all available observations and evidence must support it. A valid scientific theory, like a hypothesis, can be proved false if enough observations contradict it. An important characteristic of both hypotheses and theories is that they *must* be disprovable. In other words, a statement is not a valid scientific hypothesis or theory if there is no possible way to prove that it is not true.

3 Consider the following statement:

"The force of gravity can be explained by the presence of invisible rays that objects create. The rays interact with one another, producing gravity. Because the rays are neither matter nor energy, there can be no way to detect them."

Which of the following statements best explains why the statement above is not a valid scientific hypothesis?
A   It does not explain observable events.
B   There is no way to test it in all situations.
C   There is no test that could prove it is false.
D   No scientists accept it as true.

ⒶⒷⒸⒹ

4 The modern atomic theory was developed in the late 1800s and early 1900s. It replaced earlier atomic theories. What was the most likely reason scientists accepted the modern atomic theory and rejected older atomic theories?
A   The modern atomic theory explains new observations that older theories could not.
B   The scientists who proposed the modern atomic theory were better respected than those who supported older theories.
C   Scientists knew that newer theories are always more accurate than older theories.
D   Most of the general public thought that the atomic theory was correct.

ⒶⒷⒸⒹ

Directions: Question 5 is based on the information below.

According to Newton's second law of motion, the motion of an object can change only if unbalanced forces are acting on it.

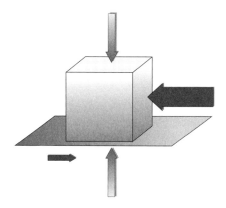

5 Based on the information, which statement describes the motion of the box when the forces represented in the diagram act on it?
A   The box will move far to the left.
B   The box will move slightly left.
C   The box will move far to the right.
D   The box will move slightly right.

ⒶⒷⒸⒹ

Directions: Questions 6 and 7 are based on the information below.

A child's toy is rolling from the top of a steep ramp (point 25) to the bottom (point 0). The graph represents the potential and kinetic energy at various points on the ramp.

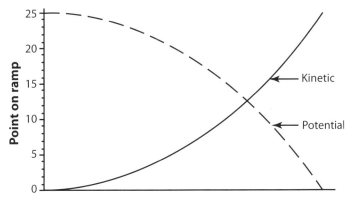

6 At which point is the potential energy of the toy at its greatest?

A point 0
B point 5
C point 10
D point 25

ⒶⒷⒸⒹ

7 Which of the following conclusions is best supported by data in the graph?

A As potential energy decreases, kinetic energy increases.
B An object can have potential energy or kinetic energy, but not both.
C An increase in potential energy causes an increase in kinetic energy.
D Kinetic energy is lowest when an object is in motion.

ⒶⒷⒸⒹ

Directions: Question 8 is based on the information below.

Although many people don't realize it, electricity and magnetism are closely related. A magnet spinning inside a coil of wire produces an electric current in the wire. Similarly, running electric current through a wire produces a magnetic field around the wire. The direction in which the current flows determines where the north and south poles of the magnetic field lie.

This relationship is very important to many aspects of modern life. For example, most of the electricity we use is generated by moving magnets. Electric power plants use different forms of energy—such as moving water or steam— to spin large magnets. The spinning magnets produce electric current, which is transmitted through wires to homes and businesses.

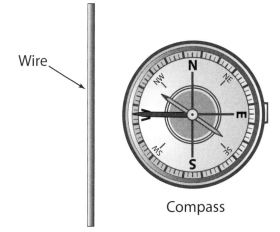

Wire

Compass

8 There is an electric current in the wire shown in the illustration. If the direction of that electric current were reversed, what would most likely happen to the needle on the compass?

A The compass needle would spin around quickly.
B The compass needle would point to the left.
C The compass needle would point to the right.
D The compass needle would point downward.

ⒶⒷⒸⒹ

Directions: Questions 9 and 10 are based on the information below.

Most waves can be classified into one of two types: transverse waves or longitudinal waves. Transverse waves are the waves that come to mind when many people think of waves. When a transverse wave passes through matter, it moves the matter up and down or side to side. The matter moves in a direction perpendicular to the direction that the wave is traveling. Part A of the diagram below shows the parts of a transverse wave.

When a longitudinal wave passes through matter, it causes the matter to expand and contract. The matter moves in a direction parallel to the direction that the wave is traveling. Part B of the diagram shows a longitudinal wave.

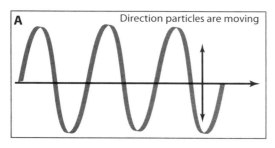

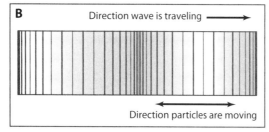

9 Based on the information, in what direction is the transverse wave in Part A of the diagram most likely moving?

A outward from a central point
B upward
C from the edge of the wave to its center
D from left to right

Ⓐ Ⓑ Ⓒ Ⓓ

10 Sound waves are longitudinal waves. If a sound wave passes through an object from top to bottom, what type of motion do the particles in the object probably experience?

A up and down
B left and right
C front to back
D along a circular path

Ⓐ Ⓑ Ⓒ Ⓓ

Directions: Question 11 is based on the information below.

Organic chemistry is the study of compounds that contain chains of carbon atoms. Prefixes are commonly used in the names of organic compounds to indicate the number of carbon atoms in the main carbon chain. A group of organic compounds called alcohols all contain an −OH group attached somewhere along the main (longest) carbon chain. The models below represent molecules of two alcohols.

PREFIXES AND THE NUMBERS THEY REPRESENT			
PREFIX	**NUMBER**	**PREFIX**	**NUMBER**
Meth-	1	But-	4
Eth-	2	Pent-	5
Prop-	3	Hex-	6

Molecule A   Molecule B

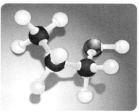

11 Based on the information, what is the name of Molecule B?

A ethanol
B propanol
C butanol
D pentanol

Ⓐ Ⓑ Ⓒ Ⓓ

The process in which atoms and molecules are arranged into new combinations is called a chemical reaction. The table below identifies several different types of chemical reactions.

REACTION TYPE	MODEL EQUATION
Synthesis	$A + B \rightarrow AB$
Decomposition	$AB \rightarrow A + B$
Single displacement	$AX + B \rightarrow BX + A$
Double displacement	$AX + BY \rightarrow AY + BX$
Neutralization	$AOH + HB \rightarrow AB + H_2O$

12 **Which of the following reactions would be classified as a single-displacement reaction? (Note: The equations given below are not balanced.)**

A $CuCl_2 + Al \rightarrow AlCl_3 + Cu$
B $Na + Cl_2 \rightarrow NaCl$
C $HCl + NaOH \rightarrow NaCl + H_2O$
D $S_8 + O_2 \rightarrow SO_2$

Ⓐ Ⓑ Ⓒ Ⓓ

13 **Which kind of reaction is represented by the chemical equation below?**

$$Pb(NO_3)_2 + KI \rightarrow KNO_3 + PbI_2$$

A synthesis
B decomposition
C single displacement
D double displacement

Ⓐ Ⓑ Ⓒ Ⓓ

Directions: Question 14 is based on the information below.

The melting point of pure water is 0°C. The boiling point of pure water is 100°C.

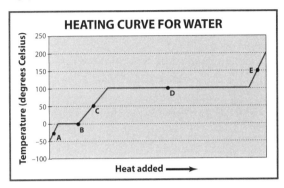

HEATING CURVE FOR WATER

14 **Based on the information, which state(s) of water would you expect to have in a sample that is at Point D on the heating curve?**

A solid
B liquid
C gas
D liquid and gas

Ⓐ Ⓑ Ⓒ Ⓓ

Directions: Question 15 is based on the information below.

The pH of a solution describes the concentration of certain ions. The greater the concentration of hydronium ions, the more acidic a solution becomes. The greater the concentration of hydroxide ions, the more basic a solution becomes.

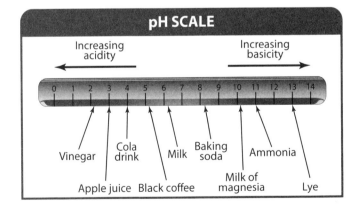

pH SCALE

15 **Which of the following solutions has the lowest concentration of hydronium ions?**

A black coffee
B ammonia
C cola drink
D vinegar

UNIT 2

Unit 3

Unit Overview

Every day, whether or not you realize it, you study Earth science. Weather forecasts, reports on climate change, stories about renewable energy—all these provide information about the world around us, how the world affects us, and how we affect that world.

Earth and space science also plays an important part in high school equivalency tests, comprising about 25 percent of the science questions. As with other areas of the science test, Earth and space science questions will test your ability to read and analyze different types of text and graphics. Unit 3 spotlights the introduction and interpretation of various diagrams, maps, flowcharts, and other core science concepts that will help you prepare for high school equivalency tests in science.

Table of Contents

Key Earth/Space Science Terms

asthenosphere: the soft layer of the mantle on which pieces of the lithosphere move

continental drift: the hypothesis that continents can drift apart from one another and have done so in the past

core: the central, spherical part of Earth below the mantle

crust: the thin, outermost layer of Earth, or the uppermost part of the lithosphere

delta: a fan-shaped deposit of sediment at the mouth of a stream, where the stream empties into a large body of water

deposition: the process by which material is dropped or settles

epicenter: the point on Earth's surface directly above an earthquake's starting point

erosion: the removal or transport of sediment by gravity, wind, water, or ice

focus: the point inside Earth where an earthquake begins

igneous rock: rock made from the cooling of magma

inner core: the solid, dense center of Earth

lava: magma that flows onto Earth's surface

lithosphere: the outermost, rigid layer of Earth that consists of the crust and the rigid upper part of the mantle

magma: the hot liquid that forms when rock partially or completely melts

mantle: the layer of Earth between the crust and the core

mesosphere: the strong lower part of the mantle between the asthenosphere and the outer core

metamorphic rock: rock that forms when the texture and composition of preexisting rock changes due to heat or pressure

outer core: the liquid layer of Earth's core that lies beneath the mantle and surrounds the inner core

plate tectonics: the theory that Earth's lithosphere is divided into tectonic plates that move around on top of the asthenosphere

revolution: the elliptical motion of a body as it orbits another body in space

rotation: the spinning motion of a body on its axis

seafloor spreading: the process by which new oceanic lithosphere is formed at mid-ocean ridges as older materials are pulled away from the ridge

sedimentary rock: rock that forms when sediments are compacted and cemented together

solar nebula: a large cloud of rotating gases and dust from which the solar system formed

tectonic plate: a piece of the lithosphere that moves around on top of the asthenosphere

water cycle: the continuous movement of water from water sources into the air, onto land, into and over the ground, and back to the water sources

watershed: the land drained by a river system, which includes the main river and all of its tributaries

Analyze and Evaluate a Hypothesis

① Learn the Skill

In everyday speech, people often use the terms *hypothesis* and *theory* to mean "a guess." A **hypothesis** is a guess, but one based on evidence and logic. In science, however, a theory is definitely not a guess. A **theory** is a unifying explanation for a broad range of hypotheses and observations that have been supported by testing. To **understand and evaluate a hypothesis**, you need to make sure there is evidence to support the guess. You will also need to be sure that a hypothesis can be restated in the form of a question that could be tested by a scientific investigation.

② Practice the Skill

By mastering the skill of understanding and evaluating a hypothesis, you will improve your study and test-taking skills, especially as they relate to science high school equivalency tests. Read the paragraph and strategies below. Then use that information to answer question 1.

A Scientists must reject a hypothesis if evidence from scientific investigations shows that the hypothesis is incorrect.

B A theory is an explanation of observations. The last sentences of the paragraph are descriptions. Because they are not explanations of how the continents move, the ideas do not make up a theory.

USING LOGIC

Identifying a hypothesis requires similar skills to identifying and making inferences. In fact, a hypothesis could be thought of as an extended inference. When you evaluate a hypothesis, look for the evidence given to support the inference, and make sure that the inference is a logical one based on the available evidence.

CONTINENTAL DRIFT

Up until the early 1900s, most scientists thought Earth's continents and oceans were fixed in their positions. Alfred Wegener did not agree. <u>Based on observations he made, Wegener proposed a new hypothesis of continental drift</u>. According to Wegener's hypothesis, all of Earth's land hundreds of millions of years ago was part of one large land mass that he called Pangaea. *Pangaea* is a Greek word that means "all Earth." According to Wegener, about 250 million years ago, Pangaea started to break apart. Over millions of years, the pieces drifted to new locations. They became the continents that we see today.

1   If Wegener's continental drift hypothesis is correct, which of the following most likely will happen?
   A   The continents will remain fixed in their current positions.
   B   The oceans will slowly disappear.
   C   The continents will be in different positions millions of years from now.
   D   Pangaea will reform.

Directions: Questions 2 and 3 are based on the information below.

Wegener based his ideas about Earth's continents on several pieces of evidence. One piece of evidence involved the shapes of South America and Africa. Wegener wrote:

"It is just as if we were to refit the torn pieces of a newspaper by matching their edges and then check whether the lines of print ran smoothly across. If they do, there is nothing left but to conclude that the pieces were in fact joined in this way."

From Wegener's *The Origin of Oceans and Continents*

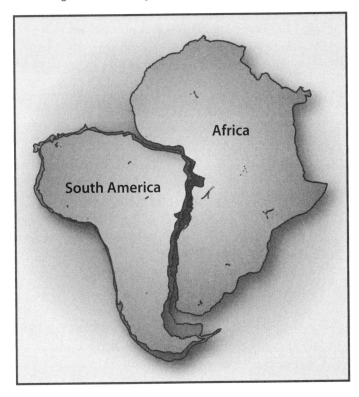

2 Which statement best explains the importance of Wegener's observation about the "fit" of the coasts of South America and Africa?

A It provided evidence for the idea that continents move.

B It showed how the continents moved to their current positions.

C It was based on reasoning instead of data.

D It proved that Africa and South America share many similarities today.

3 Which additional piece of evidence would support Wegener's hypothesis that Africa and South America once had been joined?

A different plant and animals species found on the two continents

B a lack of fossils on both continents

C the presence of similar fossils on both continents

D a map drawn by another scientist showing how the continents might have looked

Directions: Questions 4 and 5 are based on the information below.

Until the 1960s, scientists still did not know the mechanism that allows continents to "drift," or move. With the development of new technologies and the collection of more data, scientists got a clearer picture not only of how continents move but of how this movement is related to other Earth processes and features. According to the theory of plate tectonics, Earth's crust is broken up into several large plates as well as many smaller ones, and the plates move on a solid (but flowing) Earth layer. This theory explains not only how continents moved to their present locations but also the formation of land features, such as mountains, and geological events, such as volcanic eruptions.

4 Which statement best explains why plate tectonics is a theory and not a hypothesis?

A Plate tectonics explains many observations.

B Plate tectonics is a guess about how the continents moved.

C Plate tectonics developed from the continental drift hypothesis.

D Plate tectonics can never be disproven.

5 What does plate tectonic theory explain?

A the composition of each of Earth's layers

B how many land features form

C the density of Earth's crust

D how water formed on Earth

UNIT 3

Directions: Questions 6 through 9 are based on the information below.

Geologists have discovered fossils of an ancient animal called *Mesosaurus* in just two places on Earth: eastern South America and southwestern Africa. Evidence from fossil-dating techniques indicates that *Mesosaurus* lived during the Permian period, about 300 to 270 million years ago. The animal was about 1 meter long and lived in freshwater habitats, where it fed on small crustaceans.

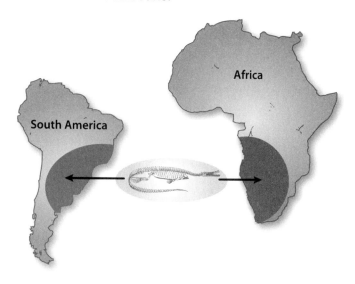

6 Which discovery would further strengthen the *Mesosaurus* fossil evidence for continental drift?
   A *Mesosaurus* fossils are equally common all over the world.
   B *Mesosaurus* was a poor long-distance swimmer.
   C A species exists today that descended from *Mesosaurus*.
   D The *Mesosaurus* fossils on the two continents actually came from different species.

7 Some scientists did not accept *Mesosaurus* fossils as evidence that South America and Africa once were joined. They hypothesized that the animals might have moved between the continents on a land bridge. What evidence would have supported the land bridge hypothesis?
   A maps from Wegener's day showing the hypothesized land bridge
   B the presence of land bridges between continents today
   C remnants of the land bridge on the seafloor today
   D signed statements from other scientists expressing the same idea

8 Fossils of an ancient seed fern called *Glossopteris* also have been cited as evidence supporting continental drift. Where have these fossils most likely been found?
   A South Africa and Antarctica
   B South America and North America
   C Asia and Europe
   D Africa and South America

9 Which of the following is a valid hypothesis about the relationship between the *Mesosaurus* fossils and continental drift?
   A *Mesosaurus* fossils provide the best evidence of continental drift.
   B *Mesosaurus* was an ancient animal whose fossils have only been discovered on two continents.
   C *Mesosaurus* fossils are only found in South America and Africa because both places once were joined.
   D *Mesosaurus* fossils have convinced many scientists that continental drift is a valid scientific theory.

Lesson 1 | Analyze and Evaluate a Hypothesis

Directions: Questions 10 and 11 are based on the information below.

A.

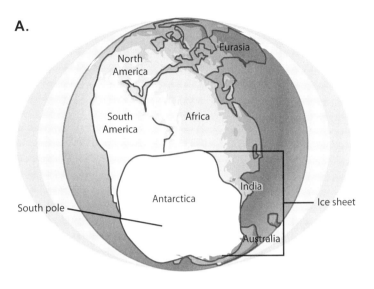

Hypothesized positions of the continents
300 million years ago

B.

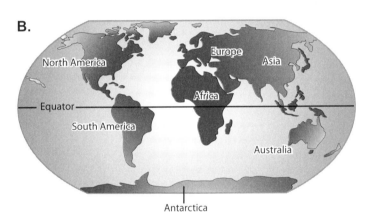

Positions of the continents today

10 **Diagram A shows a hypothesized position of the continents relative to the South Pole 300 million years ago. Which of the following would be evidence to support that hypothesis?**
  A a close fit between parts of the coast of North America and the coast of Africa
  B fossils of tropical marine organisms in India today
  C remnants of land bridges between India and Africa
  D marks on rocks in Africa indicating they once were covered by large ice sheets

11 **Based on the diagrams, what can you infer?**
  A Climates were roughly the same today as they were 300 million years ago.
  B The climate of Antarctica was colder 300 million years ago.
  C Parts of Africa and South America were once much colder than they are today.
  D Africa and South America were once much closer to the equator than they are today.

Directions: Questions 12 and 13 are based on the table below.

SOME MAJOR EVIDENCE FOR PLATE TECTONIC THEORY	
GENERAL EVIDENCE	**EXAMPLES**
A. Shapes of coastlines	Africa and South America
B. Fossil evidence	*Mesosaurus, Glossopteris* (fern)
C. Similarities in rock layers on separate continents	Appalachian Mountains in North America and mountains in Europe
D. Young ocean floor	Most of it is less than 150 million years old
E. Geologic processes (earthquakes, volcanic eruptions)	Most common near plate boundaries

12 **Plate tectonic theory developed out of many lines of evidence. Which pieces of evidence for continental drift contributed to plate tectonic theory?**
  A A, B, and C
  B A and D
  C D and E
  D B only

13 **Which pieces of evidence were observed long after Wegener proposed his hypothesis?**
  A A, B, and C
  B D and E
  C A only
  D E only

SEAFLOOR SPREADING

In the 1950s and 1960s, scientists developed the seafloor-spreading hypothesis. New discoveries showed that seafloor forms from magma that pushes up through cracks in the crust at mid-ocean ridges. The magma cools and hardens to become new seafloor. As the process continues over time, seafloor spreads outward from the ridges.

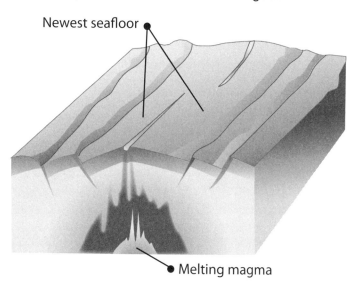

14 **Which piece of evidence would support the seafloor-spreading hypothesis?**
   A Continents on either side of a mid-ocean ridge are moving closer together over time.
   B Rocks on one side of a mid-ocean ridge are older than the rocks on the other side.
   C The age of rocks increases as you move away from a mid-ocean ridge.
   D Different rock types are found on opposite side of a mid-ocean ridge.

15 **How does evidence for seafloor spreading support Wegener's older continental drift hypothesis?**
   A It shows that continents can be pushed apart.
   B It shows continents float on the oceans.
   C It shows that there was once a landmass called Pangaea.
   D It shows that oceans move but continents do not.

The theory of plate tectonics explains not only how the continents moved to their present positions but also how many of Earth's features, such as mountains, formed. It also explains many geologic processes, such as volcanic eruptions and earthquakes. The map below shows the locations of earthquakes around the world.

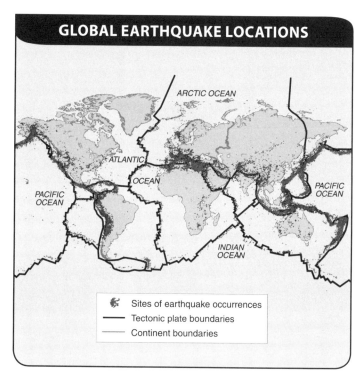

16 **Which hypothesis is best supported by the information in the map?**
   A Earthquakes happen on the edges of continents, not the interiors.
   B The boundaries of continents represent plate boundaries.
   C Earthquakes are most dangerous in the Pacific Ocean.
   D Earthquakes are most common at plate boundaries.

Interpret 3-Dimensional Diagrams

① Learn the Skill

Many **3-dimensional (3-D) diagrams** show part of an object or structure cut away so that the inside of the object is visible. To **interpret 3-dimensional diagrams**, pay attention to how the outside of the object is related to the inside features shown in the diagram.

② Practice the Skill

Examine the diagram and read the strategies below. Use the information to answer question 1.

Ⓐ Labels identify and describe the parts of the object that are shown in the diagram.

Ⓑ Callouts are blocks of text that describe part of a figure in detail. They may describe how the parts of an object work. Leader lines point from labels and callouts to the parts of the diagram that they identify or describe.

There are two different characteristics scientists use to divide Earth into layers: composition and physical strength. Scientists divide Earth into three layers based on composition. The crust is made of rock that is not very dense. The mantle is made of denser, hotter solid rock. The core is made of iron and nickel. The diagram shows the division of layers based on physical strength.

Lithosphere
The lithosphere consists of the crust and the upper part of the mantle. It is cooler than the asthenosphere, is brittle, and cannot flow.

Asthenosphere
The asthenosphere is made of hot, soft mantle rock. It is solid, but it can flow under pressure.

Mesosphere
The mesosphere is made of hot, solid rock that is under high pressure.

Outer Core
The outer core is made of melted iron and nickel.

Inner Core
The inner core is made of solid iron and nickel.

Core Ⓐ

Ⓑ

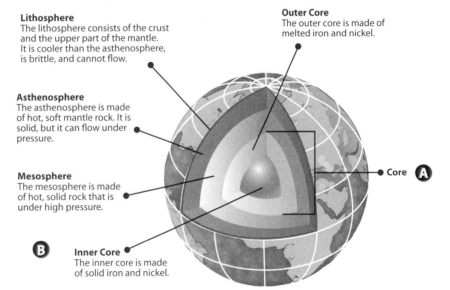

🧩 MAKING ASSUMPTIONS

Although a 3-D diagram represents what the actual object looks like, they are not always to scale. A scale diagram is one in which the relative sizes of the parts of the diagram are the same as they are in real life. Unless specifically stated, assume that diagrams are not to scale.

1 Based on the diagram, what can you conclude?

A The lithosphere is thicker than the crust.

B All layers have the same composition.

C The mantle and outer core are completely liquid.

D All of Earth's layers are equally thick.

Directions: Questions 2 and 3 are based on the information below.

Earth's crust is broken up into several large pieces called tectonic plates. The tectonic plates move slowly—about as fast as fingernails grow. As the plates move, they collide, pull apart, or scrape past each other. These movements and interactions of tectonic plates are responsible for the formation of many landforms, such as mountains, and for most earthquakes and volcanic eruptions.

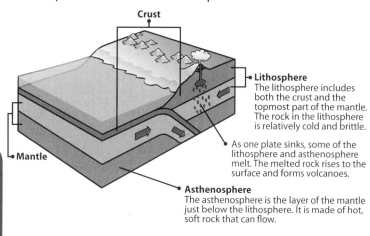

Crust

Lithosphere
The lithosphere includes both the crust and the topmost part of the mantle. The rock in the lithosphere is relatively cold and brittle.

As one plate sinks, some of the lithosphere and asthenosphere melt. The melted rock rises to the surface and forms volcanoes.

Mantle

Asthenosphere
The asthenosphere is the layer of the mantle just below the lithosphere. It is made of hot, soft rock that can flow.

2   Based on the diagram, where does melting of rock happen?

   A   on Earth's surface
   B   within the crust
   C   in the mantle
   D   at the surface of an oceanic plate

3   Based on the information, what can you conclude about volcanoes?

   A   Volcanoes are common where two plates collide.
   B   Most volcanoes are far from the ocean.
   C   The rock in a volcano comes mainly from the lowest part of the mantle.
   D   The tallest volcanoes are found beneath the oceans.

Directions: Questions 4 and 5 are based on the information below.

Water is a powerful force in shaping Earth's surface. Flowing water can pick up and carry rock and soil from one place to another. This process is called erosion. Fast-moving water causes more erosion than slow-moving water, because fast-moving water can carry more rock and soil than can slow-moving water.

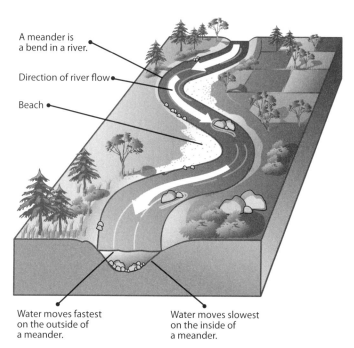

A meander is a bend in a river.

Direction of river flow

Beach

Water moves fastest on the outside of a meander.

Water moves slowest on the inside of a meander.

4   Based on the information, at which point does the most erosion probably occur?

   A   on the outside of a meander
   B   on the inside of a meander
   C   in the shallowest parts of the river
   D   at the river's surface

5   Based on the information, what can you infer about where rock and soil are laid down?

   A   Rock and soil are laid down where the water flows slowest.
   B   Rock and soil are laid down where the water is cleanest.
   C   Rock and soil are laid down where the water speeds up.
   D   Rock and soil are laid down where the water is turbulent.

Directions: Questions 6 through 8 are based on the information below.

An earthquake happens when rock beneath Earth's surface moves suddenly. This movement produces waves of energy that travel away from the break. The shaking we think of as an earthquake occurs when the waves reach Earth's surface. The diagram below shows how an earthquake occurs.

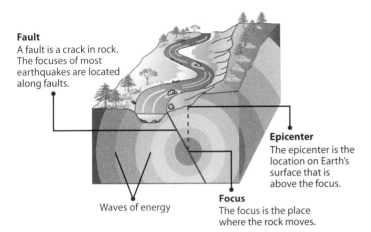

Fault
A fault is a crack in rock. The focuses of most earthquakes are located along faults.

Epicenter
The epicenter is the location on Earth's surface that is above the focus.

Waves of energy

Focus
The focus is the place where the rock moves.

6 **Which of the following statements correctly describes the epicenter and the focus?**
  A They are in the same place.
  B They are both on the surface.
  C They both lie directly on the fault.
  D The focus is directly below the epicenter.

7 **Based on the information, how do the waves produced by a break in rock travel?**
  A The waves travel outward from the focus.
  B The waves travel along the fault until they reach the surface.
  C The waves travel from the epicenter to the fault.
  D The waves travel directly from the focus to the epicenter.

8 **When does an earthquake occur?**
  A when waves of energy reach Earth's surface
  B when rock beneath the surface suddenly moves
  C when the focus and the epicenter are aligned
  D when waves of energy move away from the epicenter

Directions: Questions 9 and 10 are based on the information below.

A volcano is a crack in Earth's surface that allows materials to escape from beneath the surface. Many volcanoes erupt melted rock, or lava. They also may give off gases and ash.

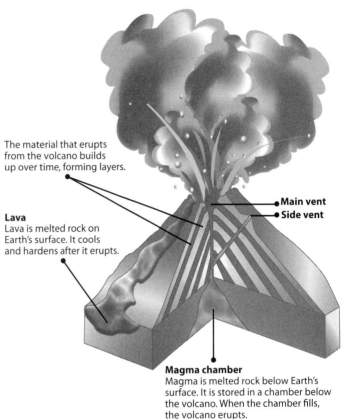

The material that erupts from the volcano builds up over time, forming layers.

Lava
Lava is melted rock on Earth's surface. It cools and hardens after it erupts.

Main vent
Side vent

Magma chamber
Magma is melted rock below Earth's surface. It is stored in a chamber below the volcano. When the chamber fills, the volcano erupts.

9 **What are the layers of the volcano in the diagram made of?**
  A lava and magma
  B ash and cooled lava
  C gas and ash
  D magma and cooled gas

10 **Based on the information, what can you infer about volcanoes?**
  A Lava always erupts from the center of a volcano.
  B Most volcanoes erupt continuously.
  C Most volcanoes are small when they first form.
  D Volcanoes cannot erupt ash and lava at the same time.

Directions: Questions 11 and 12 are based on the information below.

Mount Saint Helens is a large volcano in the state of Washington. Mount Saint Helens was inactive for many years. Then, in 1980, it erupted. The diagrams show the structure of Mount Saint Helens before and after it erupted. Since 1980, Mount Saint Helens generally has been quiet, but it is considered one of the most dangerous volcanoes in the United States.

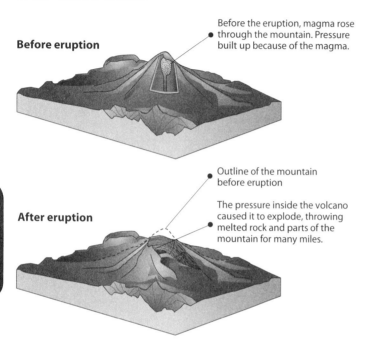

Before eruption

Before the eruption, magma rose through the mountain. Pressure built up because of the magma.

After eruption

Outline of the mountain before eruption

The pressure inside the volcano caused it to explode, throwing melted rock and parts of the mountain for many miles.

11 **Based on the information, how did the eruption in 1980 change Mount Saint Helens?**

  A   It made the volcano narrower.

  B   It made the volcano shorter.

  C   It prevented the volcano from ever erupting again.

  D   It made the volcano larger.

12 **Based on the information, what type of material did Mount Saint Helens give off when it erupted?**

  A   a mixture of melted rock from below the surface and rock from the mountain

  B   only rock from below the surface

  C   mainly liquid rock mixed with ash

  D   mainly crushed rock from inside the magma chamber

Directions: Questions 13 through 15 are based on the information below.

Earth's crust is broken up into several large pieces called tectonic plates. There are about 12 large plates and several smaller plates. These plates are constantly moving in different directions.

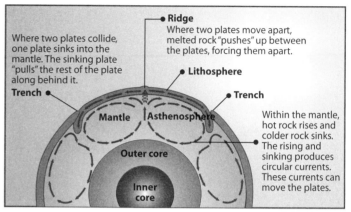

Where two plates collide, one plate sinks into the mantle. The sinking plate "pulls" the rest of the plate along behind it.

● **Ridge**
Where two plates move apart, melted rock "pushes" up between the plates, forcing them apart.

● **Lithosphere**

● **Trench**

Trench ●

Mantle   **Asthenosphere**

Outer core

Within the mantle, hot rock rises and colder rock sinks. The rising and sinking produces circular currents. These currents can move the plates.

Inner core

13 **Based on the information, what causes tectonic plates to move?**

  A   motions of rock in the mantle

  B   melted rock rising from the core

  C   the pressure of ocean water on the crust

  D   earthquakes that occur where plates collide

14 **Based on the information, tectonic plates are located in which of Earth's layers?**

  A   the lithosphere

  B   the lower mantle

  C   the asthenosphere

  D   the outer core

15 **Based on the information, what is a trench?**

  A   the edge of a tectonic plate

  B   the surface of a tectonic plate

  C   the area where one plate moves under another

  D   the area where two plates move apart

UNIT 3

Directions: Questions 16 and 17 are based on the diagrams below.

Upstream

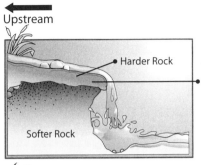

The waterfall flows over a ledge of harder rock. The rock below the ledge is softer.

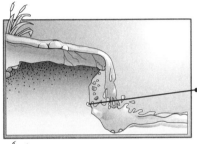

The water at the bottom of the waterfall wears away the softer rock under the ledge.

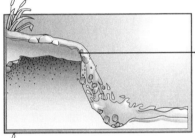

The ledge collapses when too much rock has been worn away.

16 Based on the diagrams, how do waterfalls change over time?

A Over time, waterfalls become taller.

B Over time, waterfalls slow down.

C Over time, waterfalls become narrower.

D Over time, waterfalls move upstream.

17 Based on the diagrams, why does a waterfall change over time?

A The water in the river wears away the banks.

B The amount of water moving over the waterfall increases.

C Falling water wears away rock under the waterfall.

D Large rocks build up at the bottom of the waterfall.

Directions: Question 18 is based on the information below.

In some areas, tectonic plates move apart. Most of these areas are below the oceans, so they are called mid-ocean ridges. At a mid-ocean ridge, new crust forms. The diagram shows how new crust forms at a mid-ocean ridge.

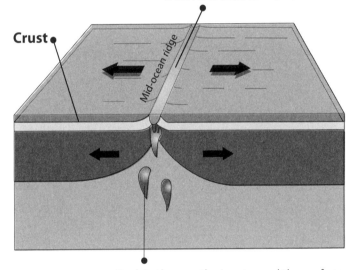

The melted rock rises to the surface and erupts. When it cools, it forms new crust.

Crust

Mid-ocean ridge

Rock in the mantle rises toward the surface. As it rises, the pressure on it decreases. That causes the rock to melt.

18 Based on the information, where does the rock that becomes new crust originate?

A deep within the core

B less dense parts of the plate

C in the crust

D within the mantle

Interpret Flowcharts

① Learn the Skill

Flowcharts are diagrams that show the steps in a process. Many flowcharts use boxes and arrows to show the relationship between each step. When you **interpret flowcharts**, you study the steps in a process, such as how a recycling program works or how to fix a problem with your computer.

② Practice the Skill

By mastering the skill of interpreting flowcharts, you will improve your study and test-taking skills, especially as they relate to science high school equivalency tests. Examine the flowchart and strategies below. Use the information to answer question 1.

Ⓐ Each rectangle in the flowchart represents a different step in the process of coal formation. As you can see in the first box, the first step in the formation of coal is that plants die and pile up in swamps.

Ⓑ The arrows between the boxes point from one step to the next, in sequence. This arrow points from the first step, in which plants die, to the next step, in which sediment quickly buries the plants.

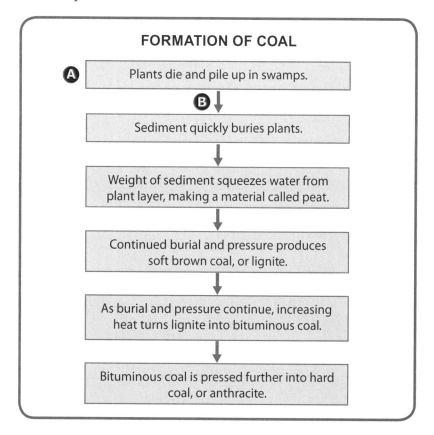

FORMATION OF COAL

Ⓐ Plants die and pile up in swamps.

Ⓑ Sediment quickly buries plants.

Weight of sediment squeezes water from plant layer, making a material called peat.

Continued burial and pressure produces soft brown coal, or lignite.

As burial and pressure continue, increasing heat turns lignite into bituminous coal.

Bituminous coal is pressed further into hard coal, or anthracite.

USING LOGIC

When reading flowcharts, use logic to understand that each subsequent step depends on the one before it. In this flowchart, peat will not form unless sediment quickly buries plant material.

1 Based on the flowchart, what is the second step in the formation of coal?

   A Bituminous coal forms from lignite.
   B Water gets squeezed out, creating peat.
   C Sediment quickly buries plant matter.
   D Huge amounts of plant matter accumulate.

UNIT 3

③ Apply the Skill

Directions: Questions 2 through 6 are based on the information below.

The flowchart below shows the rock cycle. A cycle is a series of steps that repeats again and again. In the rock cycle, the conditions surrounding rocks, such as exposure to weather or location beneath Earth's surface, can change one type of rock into another type of rock. For example, if an igneous rock is weathered into sediment, and that sediment is then subjected to compaction and cementation, it may eventually become a sedimentary rock. Similarly, if an igneous rock is exposed to high heat and pressure beneath Earth's surface, it may change into a metamorphic rock.

THE ROCK CYCLE

2 **Based on the paragraph and flowchart, what turns igneous rock into metamorphic rock?**
   A compaction and cementation
   B weathering and erosion
   C heat and pressure
   D cooling

3 **The paragraph and flowchart describe a process that is a cycle. What does this tell you about the process of rock formation?**
   A The process has a beginning and an end.
   B It is an ongoing process.
   C The process happened millions of years ago.
   D It is a process that flows in one direction.

4 **Which of the following statements can be derived from the flowchart?**
   A Sedimentary rock can never become metamorphic rock.
   B Rock never gets hot enough to melt.
   C Igneous rock always becomes metamorphic rock.
   D Each type of rock can become any other type of rock.

5 **Based on the flowchart, which of the following processes results in the formation of magma?**
   A heat and pressure on metamorphic rock
   B melting of various forms of rock
   C heat and pressure on sedimentary rock
   D weathering of igneous rock

6 **Which of the following statements best describes why metamorphic rocks are most commonly found in mountain ranges?**
   A Mountain ranges contain large amounts of magma.
   B Sediment builds up quickly at the base of a mountain range.
   C Melting occurs deep within most mountain ranges.
   D The processes that produce mountains generate considerable heat and pressure.

Directions: Questions 7 through 10 are based on the information below.

FORMATION OF IGNEOUS ROCK

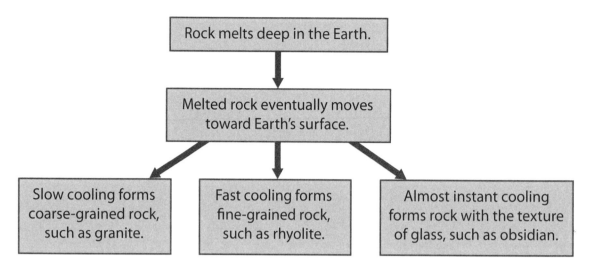

Igneous rock forms when melted rock cools. Melted rock below Earth's surface is called magma. If magma remains below Earth's surface, it eventually cools and becomes igneous rock. Magma also can rise to the surface through cracks in the crust. Melted rock that reaches Earth's surface is called lava. Lava generally erupts from volcanoes. When lava erupts, it cools very quickly and becomes igneous rock.

7   What are two types of igneous rock?
   A   lava and magma
   B   metamorphic and sedimentary
   C   coarse-grained and fine-grained
   D   cool-grained and hot-grained

8   Which type of rock would you most likely find at a volcano?
   A   coarse-grained rock only
   B   fine-grained rock and glassy rock
   C   a mixture of coarse-grained rock and fine-grained rock
   D   glassy rock only

9   What causes different types of igneous rock to form?
   A   different types of rock that make up magma and lava
   B   the rate at which magma or lava cools
   C   the size of the grains that make up magma and lava
   D   the location of the source of magma beneath Earth's surface

10 Granite is an igneous rock with large, coarse grains. Based on the information, how does granite form?
   A   slowly, deep underground in cooling magma that moves upward in a volcano
   B   quickly, from volcanic lava that is shot into the air and cooled
   C   quickly, in magma pouring over the ground from an erupting volcano
   D   slowly, from lava that flowed over the surface

Directions: Questions 11 through 16 are based on the information below.

Earth has a limited supply of water, and living organisms have used the same supply over and over for millions of years. The water cycle makes that possible. The water cycle purifies and recycles Earth's water continuously, so the supply never runs out.

WATER CYCLE

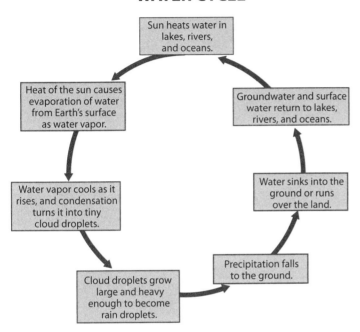

11 Which process sends water from ground sources into the air?

  A condensation
  B precipitation
  C surface runoff
  D evaporation

12 What is the main difference between droplets in clouds and rain droplets?

  A Rain droplets are larger.
  B Cloud droplets are more concentrated.
  C Rain droplets contain less water.
  D Cloud droplets form closer to the ground.

13 Based on the flowchart, why is cloud formation an important part of the water cycle?

  A Cloud formation produces new water to cycle through the system.
  B Cloud formation helps form precipitation, which falls to the ground to continue the cycle.
  C Cloud formation produces shade and coolness that helps water condense.
  D Cloud formation helps water from the ground heat and evaporate.

14 Based on the flowchart, what would happen if water did not evaporate from the ground?

  A The water cycle would end.
  B There would be more water cycling between the air and the ground.
  C Surface runoff would increase.
  D There would be more water in rivers.

15 Which water cycle process is directly responsible for cloud formation?

  A evaporation
  B condensation
  C runoff of surface waters
  D precipitation

16 Scientists find that ocean waters are saltier at a particular time of year. Which process is probably the direct cause of the increased ocean saltiness?

  A greater evaporation during periods of high temperatures
  B greater condensation due to cooler temperatures in the atmosphere
  C increased runoff of surface waters due to heavy rainfall
  D increased precipitation during warmer parts of the year

Directions: Questions 17 and 18 are based on the information below.

Deltas are sediment that rivers deposit at their mouths. A river's mouth is the place where it empties into a larger body of water, such as a lake or ocean.

Directions: Questions 19 and 20 are based on the information below.

The process of erosion carries away rock from an area. Continuous erosion by ocean waves causes the shapes of coastlines to change over time. This flowchart shows the steps in the collapse of a coastal cliff through erosion.

FORMATION OF A DELTA

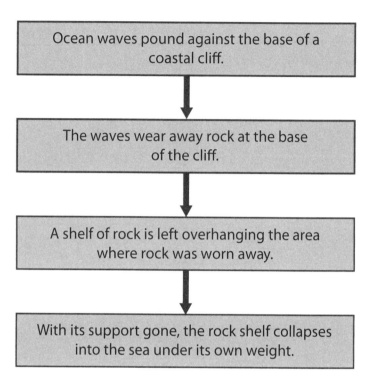

17 **Based on the paragraph and flowchart, which of the following events would increase the size of a delta?**

A   an increase in the speed of the river

B   an increase in the amount of sediment in the river water

C   a decrease in the width of the river

D   a decrease in the amount of evaporation in the river

18 **Which of the following could stop the formation of a delta?**

A   a dam that prevents sediment from flowing downstream

B   pollution of surface water

C   a bridge that crosses over the river near its mouth

D   increased sediment in the river

19 **Based on the flowchart, what role does gravity play in the collapse of a coastal cliff?**

A   Gravity produces ocean waves that smash into the cliff.

B   Gravity pulls down on shelves of overhanging rock.

C   Gravity wears away rock at the cliff's base.

D   Gravity produces wind that smashes sediment into the cliff.

20 **Which of the following most likely would be the next step in the flowchart?**

A   A shelf of rock reforms on the cliff.

B   Waves pound at the shortened cliff.

C   The shortened cliff collapses into the ocean.

D   Fallen rock rebuilds the old cliff.

LESSON 4

Compare and Contrast Visuals

① Learn the Skill

When you compare and contrast, you look for similarities and differences among objects, processes, events, and ideas. When you **compare and contrast visuals**, you identify the similarities and differences in tables, charts, graphs, diagrams, and illustrations.

② Practice the Skill

By mastering the skill of comparing and contrasting visuals, you will improve your study and test-taking skills, especially as they relate to science high school equivalency tests. Examine the information, diagrams, and strategies below. Use the information to answer question 1.

A To compare and contrast two visuals, look for parts of the images that are the same. That will help you see how the pictures are related and identify how they are different.

B When you contrast two visuals, look for the ways in which they are different. Note that these two illustrations are labeled "Before" and "After." In a case such as this, look for what has changed between the two images.

This set of illustrations shows the power of streams to erode, or wear away, their channels. At first, the stream meanders over an area of flat land in a series of wide curves. The land over which the stream flows slowly rises due to tectonic forces. After many years, the stream has carved a deep and curved canyon.

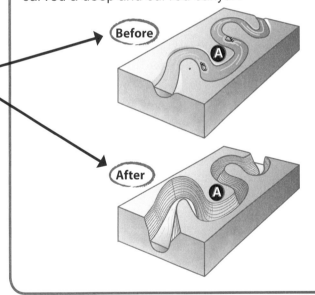

MAKING ASSUMPTIONS

You might assume that a river doesn't change much over time, but it does. If the land over which a river flows changes in some way, then the river will flow differently.

1 **Contrast the two illustrations. In the second illustration, the stream**
   A flows in the opposite direction.
   B has disappeared.
   C is surrounded by flatter land.
   D has cut a deep canyon.

UNIT 3

Directions: Questions 2 and 3 are based on the information below.

Longshore currents run parallel to the shoreline. These currents carry sediment as they move. Wherever they deposit sediment, they can produce new landforms.

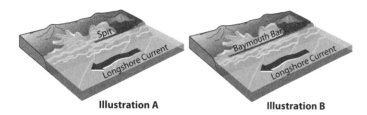

Illustration A   Illustration B

2   **Illustrations A and B show the same area at two different times. Illustration A occurred before Illustration B. What did the area most likely look like before Illustration A?**
   A   The spit was larger.
   B   The spit did not exist.
   C   The longshore current ran in the opposite direction.
   D   The baymouth bar was larger.

3   **Compare what occurred in Illustration B to what occurred in Illustration A.**
   A   The current has continued to build the spit until it has become a baymouth bar.
   B   The current has washed away the spit and built a baymouth bar in its place.
   C   The current has reversed direction and built a baymouth bar.
   D   The current has built a spit where a baymouth bar used to be.

Directions: Questions 4 and 5 are based on the information below.

When it rains, some water falls into bodies of water. Water that falls on land becomes runoff in a watershed. A watershed is the land drained by a river system, which includes the main river and all of its tributaries. The speed of runoff depends on many things, including the slope of the land, the size of the channels, and the landforms and features of the watershed. Soil quality also affects runoff. Permeable surfaces, such as healthy soil and wetlands, can absorb water, while impermeable surfaces, such as asphalt and compacted soil, do not allow runoff to soak into the ground. The two graphs show different streams' water volumes after a storm.

RUNOFF IN TWO STREAMS AFTER A STORM

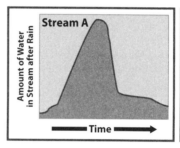 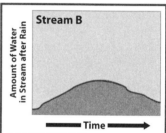

4   **Which of the following can you conclude based on the information?**
   A   Stream A is part of a different watershed than Stream B.
   B   Stream A absorbs rainwater more easily than Stream B.
   C   Stream A discharges into a different river than Stream B.
   D   Stream A is part of a watershed with less absorbent soil than Stream B.

5   **In which way do streams A and B differ?**
   A   Stream B is probably next to a parking lot.
   B   Stream A is probably beside a wetland.
   C   Stream B has an overall larger volume of water.
   D   Stream A accumulated more runoff during the storm.

Directions: Questions 6 and 7 are based on the information below.

Sediment carried by ocean waves and wind often strikes coastal cliffs. As the sediment smashes against the rock, it can wear away softer rock. The diagram below shows the formation of a sea stack.

Time A: Headland

Time B: Sea cave

Time C: Sea stack

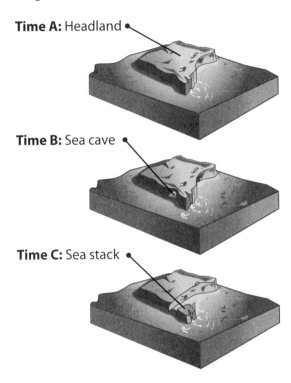

6 How did the sea change this landform?
  A The sea lifted it.
  B The sea lowered it.
  C The sea extended it.
  D The sea cut through it.

7 Based on the diagram, what did the landform most likely look like between Time A and Time B?
  A The sea cave was shallower.
  B The headland was shorter.
  C The sea stack was connected to the headland by an arch of rock.
  D The sea stack was worn away by sediment in the waves.

Directions: Questions 8 and 9 are based on the diagrams below.

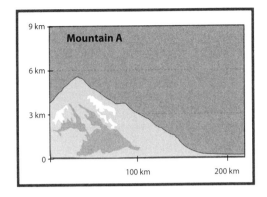

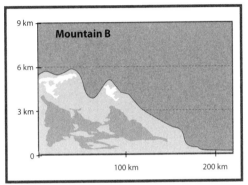

8 Based on the diagrams, how does Mountain B differ from Mountain A?
  A Mountain B is less steep.
  B Mountain B is taller.
  C Mountain B is narrower.
  D Mountain B is shorter.

9 As water runs down mountainsides, it erodes rock and soil. In general, the steeper the mountainside, the greater the erosion. Based on this information, which landform will change faster?
  A Mountain A, because it is higher and soil has farther to fall
  B Mountain A, because it is steeper and there will be more erosion
  C Mountain B, because its slope is less steep and will cause faster erosion
  D Mountain B, because its flatter slope means rain will remain on it longer

Directions: Questions 10 and 11 are based on the information below.

Glaciers are huge, heavy sheets of slow-moving ice. As glaciers move, they change the landforms under them. Rock and sediment stuck in the bottom of a glacier scrape the ground, wearing away rock and soil under the ice. Glaciers also act like huge bulldozers, pushing rock and soil in front of them.

Before Glaciation

A. V-shaped valley

During Glaciation

B. Main glacier

After Glaciation

C. U-shaped valley

10 At one point, a glacier filled this valley. Then it retreated when the climate warmed. Based on the diagram, how has the glacier changed the land?
  A The river is now wider and deeper.
  B The mountains nearby are taller.
  C The valley contains more soil.
  D The valley is now wider.

11 Suppose figures A and C were extended so that you could see the end of the valley. How would the end of the valley in Figure A most likely differ from the end of the valley in Figure C?
  A There would be more rock and soil at the end of the valley in Figure C.
  B The end of the valley would be narrower in Figure A.
  C The end of the valley would be steeper in Figure C.
  D There would be glacial ice at the end of the valley in Figure A.

Directions: Questions ⁊ ⁊ the information below.

Weathering and erosⁱ s to Earth's surface. Other changes. Krakatoa is a vⁱ the volcano erupted in one of sions ever on Earth's surface. T profile of Krakatoa before

KRAKATOA BEFOⁱ

4 km

KRAKATOA AFTER 1883 ERUPTION

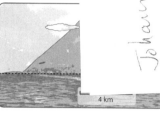

Sea level

4 km

12 Based on the diagrams, what was the main change due to the eruption?
  A The sea level changed.
  B Krakatoa was not as wide.
  C The ice atop Krakatoa melted away.
  D Most of the island was destroyed.

13 If Krakatoa had not erupted since 1883, what would it most likely look like today compared to what it looked like immediately after the 1883 eruption?
  A Today, Krakatoa would be as tall as it was just before the 1883 eruption.
  B Today, Krakatoa would be narrower than it was just before the 1883 eruption.
  C Today, Krakatoa would be even shorter than it was just after the 1883 eruption.
  D Today, Krakatoa would be taller than it was after the 1883 eruption, but not as tall as it was before the 1883 eruption.

Directions: Questions 14 through 17 are based on the information below.

The Cascades are a line of volcanic mountains in Washington, Oregon, and California. Eleven of them have erupted during the past 4,000 years, with a few erupting much more frequently than others.

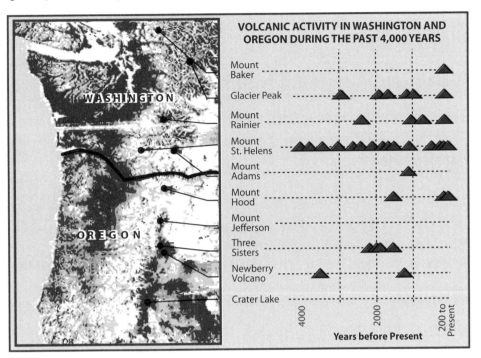

14 Which volcano has been most active in the last 4,000 years?

A Mount Hood

B Mount Jefferson

C Mount Rainier

D Mount St. Helens

15 Based on the diagram, which of these statements is true?

A The Washington and Oregon volcanoes are in a relatively linear formation.

B The Oregon volcanoes are much more dangerous than the Washington volcanoes.

C The Washington volcanoes form along lakes, while the Oregon volcanoes form on mountains.

D The Washington volcanoes are mostly dormant right now.

16 Which of the following is a volcano in Oregon that has erupted within the last 200 years?

A Mount Rainier

B Mount Hood

C Three Sisters

D Crater Lake

17 Based on the diagram, the Washington volcanoes

A are more numerous than the Oregon volcanoes.

B are smaller in size than the Oregon volcanoes.

C have erupted more frequently in the last 200 years.

D erupted less frequently than the Oregon volcanoes more than 3,000 years ago.

Determine Fact and Opinion

① Learn the Skill

When you read text or the captions on photographs, illustrations, diagrams, or cartoons, you need to know how to evaluate them. That's why it is important to know how to **determine fact and opinion**. A **fact** is something that can be proved true or false. An **opinion** is a point of view that cannot be proved or supported with facts. Sometimes, text that is opinion appears to be fact. Determining the difference can be useful.

② Practice the Skill

By mastering the skill of determining fact and opinion, you will improve your study and test-taking skills, especially as they relate to science high school equivalency tests. Read the excerpt and strategies below. Use the information to answer question 1.

> **A** Never trust any writing based solely on its quality. Terms such as *postulate* and *pervade* may sound impressive, but they do not prove that the text is entirely factual. Always check the source.

> **B** To answer the question, first ask yourself, "What would make readers trust this writing?" Then look at the source of the writing. In this case, you can find the source in the credit line. The credit line signifies that the material comes from the National Aeronautics and Space Administration, which is an official, trusted source of information.

"The Big Bang Model ... postulates that 12 to 14 billion years ago, the portion of the universe we can see today was only a few millimeters across. It has since expanded from this hot dense state into the vast and much cooler cosmos we currently inhabit. We can see remnants of this hot dense matter as the now very cold cosmic microwave background radiation which still pervades the universe and is visible to microwave detectors as a uniform glow across the entire sky."

From *The National Aeronautics and Space Administration (NASA.gov)*

MAKING ASSUMPTIONS

Never assume that a report is unbiased and only contains facts just because it comes from an official source. Look closely at the source to determine whether there might be a political motive for the report or whether the organization behind the report is promoting a certain point of view.

1 Why is this excerpt easy to accept as fact?

   A The writing is intelligent.

   B The passage is from a respected organization that uses valid research.

   C Everyone agrees with the Big-Bang Model.

   D The passage contains many specific details.

Directions: Questions 2 and 3 are based on the paragraph below.

Scientists have evidence that our solar system was formed by a solar nebula. A solar nebula is a large cloud of rotating gases and dust from which the solar system formed about 4.6 billion years ago. Research shows that the gases and dust cooled over time, causing the cloud to condense. Eventually, the cloud collapsed and flattened into a disk. Matter inside the disk collected to form the planets and the sun.

From *The National Aeronautics and Space Administration (NASA.gov)*

2 **Which of the following word or words indicates that the passage is mostly fact?**
   A "4.6 billion years"
   B "over time"
   C "research shows"
   D "eventually"

3 **Which of the following is an opinion based on this paragraph?**
   A The solar nebula theory is the best explanation for how the solar system formed.
   B Our solar system formed more than four billion years ago.
   C The sun formed from a collection of matter inside the solar nebula.
   D Our solar system is a disk-like shape.

Directions: Questions 4 through 6 are based on the timeline below.

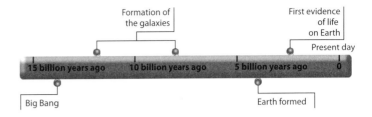

4 **Which statement below is a fact based on the timeline?**
   A Galaxies began to form approximately 1 billion years after the Big Bang.
   B The next step on the timeline will be a second Big Bang.
   C More events should be added to the timeline.
   D The Earth formed before galaxies did.

5 **Which of the following information would be most reliable to use in constructing a timeline like the one above?**
   A dates taken from journals written by early scientists
   B observations from astronauts who have explored space
   C data based on research performed by respected astronomers
   D information collected from interviewing astronomy students

6 **Which of the following is an opinion based on the timeline?**
   A The Big Bang is an unimportant event in the history of the universe.
   B The formation of galaxies occurred over billions of years.
   C Earth formed less than 5 billion years ago.
   D When compared with the age of the universe, life on Earth appeared relatively recently.

UNIT 3

Directions: Question 7 is based on the paragraph below.

> In the spiral arms of every galaxy are dense clouds of gas. It is in these clouds where stars are born. Stars, including our sun, shine from nuclear reactions deep in their center. These reactions change lighter elements into heavier ones—specifically the fusion of hydrogen to form helium—which releases energy. The outflow of energy from the center of the star provides pressure, keeping the star from collapsing under its own weight. A star collapses when energy stops flowing from its core.

7 Which statement is an opinion?

A Stars are formed in dense clouds of gas.

B Scientific research has discovered all the information about stars in our universe.

C When energy stops flowing from the sun's core, the sun will collapse.

D The fusion of hydrogen elements to make helium allows a star to release energy.

Directions: Question 8 is based on the flowchart below.

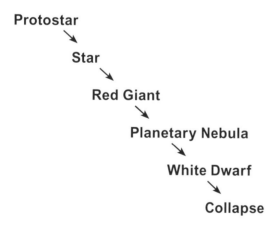

8 Evidence shows that sun has enough energy to last another 5 billion years. Based on the flowchart, what is a fact about our sun's life cycle?

A Before its collapse, the sun will become a white dwarf star.

B Our sun will last longer than similar stars.

C Research should track the sun's energy.

D More people should know that the sun will collapse in about 5 billion years.

Directions: Questions 9 and 10 are based on the passage below.

> Radioactive isotopes are unstable, causing them to release energy at a relatively constant rate. Scientists use these isotopes as natural "clocks." This is because their decay can be measured at this constant rate, which is not influenced by external forces. Through radiometric or isotope dating, scientists have discovered that the oldest known fossils are about 3.8 billion years old.

9 What is an opinion based on the passage?

A Radioactive isotopes can be used to measure time.

B Geologists used isotopic dating to date the oldest known fossils.

C There are better ways of determining fossil age than through radiometric dating.

D Radioactive isotopes release energy at a constant rate.

10 Some scientists think that life existed even before 3.8 billion years ago. Which of the following would provide evidence to support this hypothesis?

A a museum of natural history with an extensive display of plant fossils

B an article in a science-fiction magazine

C a thorough study of extinct species

D the discovery of fossils that are 4 billion years old

UNIT 3

Directions: Questions 11 through 13 are based on the passage below.

> The telescope is the most important instrument used in astronomy. It was invented in the early 1600s by Hans Lippershey, but it was Galileo who first used telescopes to study the sky. Before the use of the telescope, astronomy focused on the positions of the sun and planets, mostly for purposes of creating the yearly calendar. Since Galileo's revolutionizing work, the research of extraterrestrial objects has changed. Astronomy now focuses on a number of broad topics such as the solar system, the makeup of stars, and other, more distant galaxies.

11 Which phrase in the passage indicates an opinion?

A "most important instrument"
B "Galileo's revolutionizing work"
C "more distant galaxies"
D "a number of broad topics"

12 Which of the following is a fact based on this passage?

A Astronomy has changed since the discovery of the telescope.
B Hans Lippershey's work was less significant than Galileo's.
C Galileo was more intelligent than Hans Lippershey.
D Studying our solar system is less important to astronomers today than it was in the 1600s.

13 Which of the following sources would indicate that the information presented in the passage is probably reliable?

A data from Hans Lippershey's journals
B data collected from science-fiction movies
C an op-ed piece written by an amateur astronomer
D an essay in a scientific journal

Directions: Questions 14 and 15 are based on the information below.

Discussion about developing the Space Shuttle program first began in the late 1960s. The program officially began several years later as a goal to provide less-expensive, reusable means of travel to space. Since 1981, NASA's fleet of shuttles has flown 135 missions into space, carrying large satellites into orbit, conducting scientific experiments, and building the International Space Station. The Space Shuttle program ended in 2011.

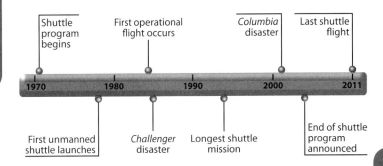

14 Which of the following is an opinion based on the information?

A NASA launched the shuttle program in the early 1970s.
B The *Challenger* disaster marked the beginning of the end of the shuttle program.
C Unmanned shuttle missions were used following the *Challenger* and *Columbia* disasters.
D The shuttle program aided in construction of the International Space Station.

15 What is a fact based on the information?

A NASA announced the end of the shuttle program shortly after the *Columbia* disaster.
B Continuing the shuttle program likely would lead to additional accidents.
C The shuttle program experienced its heyday in the early 1980s.
D Most people believe that the shuttle program should continue beyond 2011.

UNIT 3

Directions: Questions 16 through 18 are based on the passages below.

"Returning to the moon is an important step for our space program. Establishing an extended human presence on the moon could vastly reduce the costs of further space exploration, making possible ever more ambitious missions. Lifting heavy spacecraft and fuel out of the Earth's gravity is expensive. Spacecraft assembled and provisioned on the moon could escape its far lower gravity using far less energy, and thus, far less cost. Also, the moon is home to abundant resources. Its soil contains raw materials that might be harvested and processed into rocket fuel or breathable air. We can use our time on the moon to develop and test new approaches and technologies and systems that will allow us to function in other, more challenging environments. The moon is a logical step toward further progress and achievement."

From a speech by President George W. Bush, January 14, 2004

NASA recently developed a strategy that concentrates on six areas in moon exploration. These areas include preparing for future exploration to Mars and other bodies within our solar system, gaining scientific knowledge, expanding human civilization beyond Earth, expanding economic opportunities, developing partnerships with other countries, and educating the public on space exploration. While on the moon, astronauts will conduct scientific studies and test technologies for future missions that will travel further into space.

From the NASA Web site

16 Which of the following statements from the first passage is a fact?
A "Returning to the moon is an important step for our space program."
B "Establishing an extended human presence on the moon could vastly reduce the costs of further space exploration …"
C "Spacecraft assembled … on the moon could escape its far lower gravity using far less energy …"
D "Lifting heavy spacecraft and fuel out of the Earth's gravity is expensive."

17 Which of the following phrases best indicates that the first passage is mainly opinion?
A "establishing an extended human presence"
B "important step for our space program"
C "develop and test new approaches"
D "function in other more challenging environments"

18 Why is the second passage more likely to contain factual information than the first passage?
A Its data is more current than that from President Bush's speech.
B It includes ideas from leaders in the scientific community.
C The second passage includes strategies, which always contain factual information.
D NASA is the source of the passage and it created the strategy for lunar exploration.

Judge the Reliability of Sources

① Learn the Skill

When you **judge the reliability of a source**, you evaluate it in several ways. You assess its effectiveness in communicating a main idea, data, or a point of view. You also assess the source as well as the quality and accuracy of the data incorporated. Judging information can help you get the most from a variety of sources.

② Practice the Skill

By mastering the skill of judging the reliability of sources, you will improve your study and test-taking skills, especially as they relate to science high school equivalency tests. Read the excerpt and strategies below. Use the information to answer question 1.

A Note that there is little opinion about Pluto's demotion in the article. The author neither agrees nor disagrees with the decision to call Pluto a dwarf planet. However, there is strong opinion about the emotion involved in the debate. Pay attention to any opinion that seems to slip into an article or essay. Too much opinion can indicate that a source is unreliable.

B Information is only as good as its source. Certain newspapers and magazines, such as *The New York Times*, *Scientific American*, and *Science*, have a strong, well-earned reputation for fair and accurate reporting.

PLUTO IS DEMOTED TO 'DWARF PLANET'

"After years of wrangling and a week of bitter debate, astronomers voted on a sweeping reclassification of the solar system. In what many of them described as a triumph of science over sentiment, Pluto was demoted to the status of 'dwarf planet.' . . .

"It has long been clear that Pluto . . . stood apart from the previously discovered planets. Not only was it much smaller . . . but its elongated orbit tilted with respect to the other planets and it goes inside the orbit of Neptune part of its 248-year journey around the Sun. . . .

"Two years ago, the International Astronomical Union appointed a working group of astronomers to come up with a definition that would resolve the tension. . . ."

From *The New York Times*, August 24, 2006

☑ TEST-TAKING TIPS

If you are trying to judge the reliability of sources, it helps to be familiar with newspapers, magazines, and Web sites known for being good and reliable sources of news and information. You also should be familiar with those sources that have a political slant or bias.

1 **Which characteristic of this article helps you evaluate it as a valid source of information?**
   A It reports on an important event.
   B It mentions the International Astronomical Union (IAU).
   C It is about a subject often discussed in the news.
   D It is printed in a respected newspaper.

Directions: Questions 2 and 3 are based on the excerpt below.

"The International Astronomical Union (IAU) Resolution means that the Solar System consists of eight planets: Mercury, Venus, Earth, Mars, Jupiter, Saturn, Uranus, and Neptune. A new distinct class of objects called dwarf planets was also decided on. It was agreed that planets and dwarf planets are two distinct classes of objects. The first members of the dwarf planet category are Ceres, Pluto, and Eris. . . ."

From the International Astronomical Union's Web site

2 **Why would the International Astronomical Union be a good source for information about the reclassification of Pluto?**
   A Astronomers are experts when it comes to the solar system.
   B As an international organization, it would not have local bias.
   C The IAU made the decision.
   D The IAU is probably the only organization with updated information about Pluto.

3 **There were many stories about the change in the status of Pluto when it occurred. Which of the following would be the most reliable source for a story about Pluto?**
   A *Science Fiction Weekly*
   B the Hayden Planetarium
   C a newsletter published by the Museum of the American Indian
   D the Web site of the U.S. Environmental Protection Agency

Directions: Questions 4 and 5 are based on excerpts A and B below.

A. From *Harold Kinder, Ph.D. candidate, posted at superplanetguy.blogspot.com, December 2006*

"Oh, I just heard that the IAU demoted Pluto. Good for them! It should never have been a planet in the first place. They made the right decision as far as I'm concerned. It's a rock out in space—basically a wayward asteroid. I could pluck out about 20 such rocks in the belt and call them planets too."

B. From *The Encyclopedia of Science,* 1988

"Pluto is the ninth planet in the solar system, and the only rocky planet of the outer planets. This makes it different from the gas giants beyond the asteroid belt. It has an orbit of 248 years, and its orbit swoops out of alignment with the other planets. Pluto's moon, Charon, was discovered in 1978."

4 **Suppose you are writing a report about the characteristics of Pluto. Which of the following statements best explains why Excerpt A would not be an appropriate source?**
   A It is not written by a professor.
   B It gives mainly opinions.
   C It was published online.
   D There is no information about the writer's qualifications.

5 **Which of the following statements best explains why Excerpt B would not be an appropriate source for the report?**
   A It gives information about Pluto's moons.
   B It compares Pluto to gas giants.
   C It was written more than 25 years ago.
   D It does not give information about the scientist who discovered Pluto.

Directions: Questions 6 through 9 are based on the excerpts below.

ASTRONOMERS RELEGATE PLUTO TO DWARF STATUS

"After a week of contentious public and private debate a small cluster of astronomers has voted to demote Pluto from its planetary status. Rejecting an expansive definition proposed by a special committee, the astronomers of the International Astronomical Union (IAU) defined a planet as: a celestial body that orbits around the sun; has sufficient mass to become round; and has 'cleared the neighborhood around its orbit.' On the strength of puny Pluto's inability to dominate nearby Neptune, whose orbit it crosses, as well as to clear out the Kuiper belt of many Pluto-size objects, it fails to qualify as a planet under the new definition."

From *Scientific American,* August 24, 2006

PLUTO

"Once known as the smallest, coldest, and most distant planet from the Sun, Pluto has a dual identity, not to mention being enshrouded in controversy since its discovery in 1930. On August 24, 2006, the International Astronomical Union (IAU) formally downgraded Pluto from an official planet to a dwarf planet. According to the new rules a planet meets three criteria: It must orbit the Sun, it must be big enough for gravity to squash it into a round ball, and it must have cleared other things out of the way in its orbital neighborhood. The latter measure knocks out Pluto. . . . No crewed spacecraft have yet visited Pluto. However NASA launched a mission called New Horizons that will explore both Pluto and the Kuiper belt region starting in 2014."

From NASA Web site

6   One of the sources to the left is from a science magazine. The other is from the U.S. space agency, NASA. Both are valid sources for information on Pluto because
A   Pluto is a big news story.
B   few articles are written about Pluto.
C   they are both major publishers.
D   both have expertise in science.

7   Sometimes a source of information has both facts and opinion. Which of the following is an opinion expressed in one of these sources?
A   "astronomers . . . defined a planet as: a celestial body that orbits around the sun"
B   "On the strength of puny Pluto's inability to dominate nearby Neptune . . ."
C   "[Pluto] fails to qualify as a planet under the new definition."
D   "the smallest, coldest, and most distant planet from the Sun . . ."

8   Both sources communicate their information effectively. What information does the NASA source add that would be expected from a space agency?
A   information about astronauts
B   the year in which Pluto was discovered
C   information on space missions to Pluto
D   the definition of a dwarf planet

9   What do both sources provide to justify the decision to downgrade Pluto to a dwarf planet?
A   the new definition of a planet
B   the names of other planets that were reclassified as dwarf planets
C   quotes from astronomers who agree and disagree with the decision
D   descriptions of Pluto's size and distance from the Sun

Directions: Questions 10 and 11 are based on the excerpt below.

Directions: Questions 12 and 13 are based on the excerpt and timeline below.

PLUTO

"Pluto, formally designated (134340) Pluto, is the second-largest known dwarf planet in the solar system (after Eris) and the tenth-largest body observed directly orbiting the sun. Originally classified as a planet, Pluto is now considered the largest member of a distinct region called the Kuiper belt.

"Like other members of the Kuiper belt, Pluto is composed primarily of rock and ice and is relatively small: approximately a fifth the mass of Earth's moon and a third its volume. It has a highly eccentric and highly inclined orbit."

From *Wikipedia*, Updated July 16, 2014

from STAR SAND

Jennifer looked out her window. It had been the same for the last three months: cold and black. The wind whipped past the thick silicon glass, and she knew she would be housebound for another five months, unable to venture out into the frozen wastes near her home. She thought of Louis and Frank, stuck in their homes. If only this part of Pluto could get phone service, but the scientists had not found a way to keep the lines from freezing. Jennifer's parents tried to keep her spirits up. "How about another game of gin rummy?" her mom asked. But Jennifer wasn't feeling like cards today. She just wanted to play outside like a normal kid on Earth.

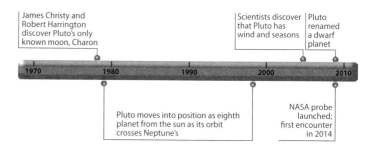

10 This entry on Pluto comes from an online encyclopedia that anyone with an Internet connection can update. One benefit of this source is that

  A the encyclopedia lacks valid information about Pluto.

  B the article has factual errors.

  C the writers can only write about one subject.

  D the information about Pluto is constantly reviewed.

11 Because the public writes the articles in this encyclopedia, what might be a problem with using this source?

  A The articles are too long.

  B It covers only certain subjects.

  C It is difficult to use an online encyclopedia.

  D The information may be incorrect.

12 What information is the same in both of these sources?

  A Charon, Pluto's only known moon, was discovered.

  B Pluto has seasons and wind.

  C Pluto was renamed a dwarf planet.

  D It is too cold for life on Pluto.

13 Which source would you most likely consult for information about Pluto, and why?

  A the first source, because it is science fiction

  B both sources, because they both give specific details

  C the second source, because it provides objective information

  D neither source, because neither provides reliable information about Pluto

UNIT 3

Directions: Questions 14 through 18 are based on the table below.

PLANETS OF THE SOLAR SYSTEM									
	Mercury	Venus	Earth	Mars	Jupiter	Saturn	Uranus	Neptune	Pluto
Distance from Sun (millions of miles)	36	67	95	142	483	886	1783	2794	3666
Diameter (miles)	3,000	7,500	7,920	4,200	88,700	75,000	29,000	28,900	~2,300
Rotation	59 days	244 days	24 hrs	24.5 hrs	10 hrs	10 hrs	17 hrs	16 hrs	6 days
Revolution	88 days	225 days	365 days	687 days	12 yrs	30 yrs	84 yrs	165 yrs	248 yrs
Known Moons	0	0	1	2	63	56	27	13	1+

14 The table contains data on Pluto as the ninth planet of the solar system. What does this tell you about the information in the table?

A All of the data in the table are wrong.

B The information in the table does not come from a valid source.

C Some of the information is out of date.

D The table was created before the year 2000.

15 Why should a student carefully examine the source and date of the information in the table before using the table as a reference?

A New discoveries may change some of the data in the table.

B The table contains mostly opinions.

C Planets enter and leave the solar system frequently.

D The data in the table are probably not based on measurements.

16 Which of the following rows would be most appropriate to add to this table?

A Mass of Planet

B Appearance of Planet

C Life on Planet

D Quotes about Planet

17 A revision of this table changes the row heading "Distance from Sun" to "Average Distance from Sun." What is the most likely reason for this change?

A A planet's distance from the sun never changes.

B Some planets are only thousands of miles away from the sun.

C A planet's distance from the sun changes as it orbits the sun.

D Some planets are too far from the sun to measure the distance in miles.

18 What would be the most valid source to use to corroborate the information in this table?

A a NASA Web site

B a Web site that displays students' reports on the solar system

C a scientist's Web log

D a geology Web site

UNIT 3

Identify Problem and Solution

① Learn the Skill

Sometimes, an author may organize a subject around a problem and the way in which it was solved. When you **identify problem and solution**, you locate the problems presented in the text and evaluate the possible solutions that are outlined by the author. This will help you understand more about the subject and its history.

② Practice the Skill

By mastering the skill of identifying problem and solution, you will improve your study and test-taking skills, especially as they relate to science high school equivalency tests. Read the paragraph and strategies below. Use that information to answer questions 1 and 2.

> **A** One problem is clearly identified in both the article's title and the paragraph's first two sentences. However, there are other problems mentioned in the paragraph. You must decide which is the main problem.

> **B** There is a solution presented in this paragraph, but it doesn't solve all the problems. The paragraph explains how it solves problems in Asia, but not in Africa.

LACK OF CLEAN WATER HARMS MANY

Clean water is essential for every person. But more than 1 billion people worldwide have no access to clean water, according to the United Nations children's agency, UNICEF. Each year, 1.5 million children under age 5 die from disease due to unsanitary conditions and lack of access to safe drinking water. The problem is especially serious in certain parts of Asia and Africa. However, the UNICEF report calls South Asia a success story, with improvements in sanitation and increased access to clean water over the last couple of decades. Projects in sub-Saharan Africa have met with less success. In some areas, especially those with armed conflicts, only a small percentage of people have access to clean water.

✓ TEST-TAKING TIPS

Try drawing a flowchart to organize problems and solutions. If you identify a problem, write it down. Then read on to see if there is a solution to the specific problem. Sometimes, a text will mention several solutions; sometimes, though, no solution may be mentioned. Solutions should be considered critically so as to avoid causing larger problems or side effects.

1 **Which is the main problem, as stated in the paragraph?**
   A armed conflicts in Africa
   B lack of sanitation and clean water
   C interference from UNICEF
   D an increase in population

2 **What is a possible solution in the paragraph for the situation in sub-Saharan Africa?**
   A a groundbreaking report by UNICEF
   B vaccination against disease
   C improvements in sanitation
   D providing clean water to armies

Directions: Questions 3 and 4 are based on the information below.

Earth's supply of fresh water is an important natural resource. There are freshwater shortages in many parts of the world. As the world's population grows, even greater supplies will be needed. Therefore, it is important that we protect our clean water resources. Cleaning up polluted lakes and rivers is one aspect of protecting freshwater supplies.

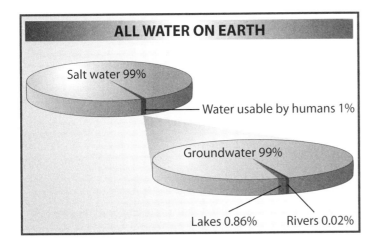

ALL WATER ON EARTH

Salt water 99%

Water usable by humans 1%

Groundwater 99%

Lakes 0.86%   Rivers 0.02%

3 The diagram shows the distribution of Earth's water. All living things on Earth need fresh water. Interpret the diagram to identify the problem with Earth's water supply.

A Earth's water supply does not contain enough salt water.

B Earth's water supply has most of its fresh water in swamps.

C Earth's water supply has more fresh groundwater than salty ocean water.

D Earth's water supply has a relatively small proportion of fresh water.

4 Based on the paragraph and the diagram, which of these is a solution to the problem?

A finding new supplies of fresh water

B protecting scarce supplies of liquid fresh water

C drinking salt water from the ocean instead of fresh water

D drinking fresh water from swamps

Directions: Questions 5 and 6 are based on the passage below.

Most of Earth's water supply is salt water, which people cannot drink. What if we could turn salt water into fresh water? Actually, we can. This process is called desalination, and it provides water to people in some parts of the world where fresh water is scarce. There are various methods of desalination. In one, salt water is heated until the fresh water evaporates, leaving the salt behind. The water vapor then cools and condenses. The fresh water is collected in another chamber. In the United States, a few towns in California and Florida are already using desalination to meet their freshwater needs.

5 Based on the information, what is the main problem?

A lack of fresh water in some places

B towns in California and Florida without salt water

C salt water overheating and causing fresh water

D the relative difficulty of desalination

6 Desalination is given as a potential solution to the problem in the paragraph. Which of the following additional pieces of information would best help you evaluate whether this solution could be widely useful?

A the number of towns currently using desalination

B the history of the invention of desalination

C the costs and efficiency of desalination processes

D the amount of salt water present on Earth

UNIT 3

Directions: Questions 7 through 10 are based on the information below.

The map shows the areas of the world that are "water-stressed." That means they have too many people for the water that occurs naturally there. In developed countries such as the United States, there are large water-stressed areas. However, dams, pipelines, and aqueducts bring water to areas that are naturally dry. In poor, developing countries, this is not the case. People in these areas often have difficulty finding adequate supplies of clean, safe water.

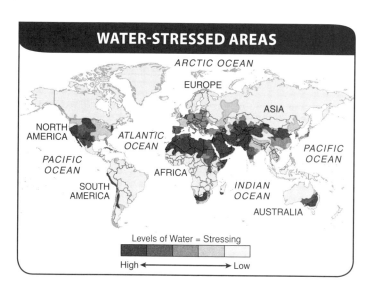

7   **What is the main problem that the passage and map are trying to convey?**
   A   Earth's water supply is stressed.
   B   Some areas of the world don't have enough water.
   C   The United States does not have enough water.
   D   Dams and aqueducts bring in water from far away.

8   **Which statement accurately describes a problem with water availability?**
   A   People in central and southern Africa do not have enough water.
   B   Most of South America is experiencing severe drought.
   C   Water stress is not restricted to desert areas.
   D   People in the world's northern regions need more fresh water.

9   **Based on the map and the paragraph, which of the following is the best *feasible* solution?**
   A   use ocean water as a drinking water source
   B   build a pipeline between Australia and North Africa
   C   use pipelines to transport water from southern Africa to northern Africa
   D   give a great deal of money to Spain and Portugal

10 **Many areas of the world have no freshwater stress. What is the most likely reason for this?**
   A   people there drink more water than people in other areas
   B   there are no people in these areas
   C   they have adequate precipitation or underground water supplies
   D   they recycle water

Directions: Questions 11 and 12 are based on the information below.

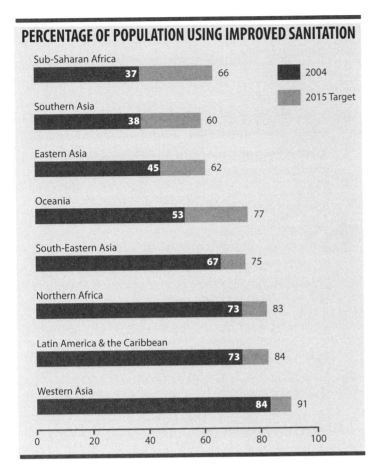

PERCENTAGE OF POPULATION USING IMPROVED SANITATION

Sub-Saharan Africa: 37 | 66
Southern Asia: 38 | 60
Eastern Asia: 45 | 62
Oceania: 53 | 77
South-Eastern Asia: 67 | 75
Northern Africa: 73 | 83
Latin America & the Caribbean: 73 | 84
Western Asia: 84 | 91

■ 2004
□ 2015 Target

The above data are from the United Nations Millenium Development Goals. The main goal that the United Nations hoped to meet was to reduce by half the number of people in the world who lack sustainable access to safe drinking water. The bars show the percentage of people in each area who now have access to basic sanitation and safe water. Pink lines show the targets for improved sanitation by 2015.

11 Which of the following is the main problem suggested by the graph?

A Fewer than 60 people in many of these countries use standard sanitation.

B No progress is being made in improving sanitation in these areas.

C Some countries have not yet made enough progress to meet the 2015 goals.

D By 2004, none of these countries had met its 2015 goal.

12 Which of the following is a *feasible* solution that will help the United Nations meet its goals?

A remove other areas from the target population and focus only on Africa

B identify additional ways to increase access to clean water

C change the 2004 benchmarks so that it appears as though the countries are on-target

D direct regions with access to clean water to use only half as much water as they do now

Directions: Questions 13 and 14 are based on the passage below.

SIMPLE SOLUTIONS

Diseases such as cholera, typhoid, and malaria are waterborne. These diseases are rare in developed countries. However, they are still a problem in developing nations where safe, clean water is rare. In the long term, the goal is to make treated drinking water and sanitation facilities available. In the short term, there are simple solutions: adding chlorine to water to kill bacteria, washing hands often, boiling water before use, and collecting rainwater. These simple actions can clear water of some bacteria, decrease the spread of illnesses, and save lives.

13 What is the main problem that unclean water causes?

A Unclean water can spread disease.

B Unclean water can make your hands dirty.

C Unclean water can kill bacteria.

D Unclean water can have an unpleasant taste.

14 Why are simple solutions proposed for cleaning water in developing countries?

A Leaders of developing countries cannot agree on more complex solutions.

B Developed countries do not want to share their technology.

C It would take too long for countries to build water-treatment plants.

D Developing countries may not have money for expensive water-treatment systems.

Directions: Questions 15 through 19 are based on the passage below.

Agricultural practices can contaminate ground water and other supplies of drinking water. Most modern farms grow only one or two types of plants. These plants, however, use up the nutrients in the soil, so fertilizers must be applied. These crops are more vulnerable to pests and weeds, so chemical pesticides and herbicides are needed. These chemicals can enter drinking water supplies through runoff.

Modern animal farming also contributes to water contamination. In most modern animal farms, large numbers of animals live in a relatively small area. Their wastes build up and can enter groundwater or surface water. Animal wastes can contain disease-causing organisms. Because most animals in modern farms are given drugs to improve their growth, their wastes also can contain these drugs.

Some people think that rotating crops and allowing animals to graze (and spread their wastes) over larger areas can help reduce the negative effects of agriculture on drinking water. However, for these methods to be feasible, they must be able to produce the same volume of food as modern agricultural practices.

15 **What is the main problem identified in the passage?**
- **A** Agriculture uses too much water.
- **B** Some farming practices can pollute drinking water sources.
- **C** Farmers do not use water efficiently.
- **D** Animals produce wastes that pollute the environment.

16 **Which of the following solutions does the passage suggest?**
- **A** banning hormones
- **B** confining animals
- **C** reducing agriculture
- **D** rotating crops

17 **What is another appropriate solution to the main problem?**
- **A** farm only in places with very little rainfall
- **B** discourage animals from open grazing
- **C** use only water-soluble medications
- **D** use non-chemical methods to control weeds and pests

18 **The passage proposes several solutions to water contamination. Which of the following would be a problem that, if true, would limit the feasibility of one of the proposed solutions?**
- **A** Properly disposing of wastes extends the lives of animals.
- **B** Most farmers do not have enough space in which animals may graze.
- **C** Some farms are not near surface water or groundwater sources.
- **D** Using less water means that the farms will not produce as much runoff.

19 **Although the passage identifies some possible solutions to agricultural water contamination, it also points out a possible problem with those solutions. According to the passage, what problem must be overcome if the proposed solutions are to be successful?**
- **A** Alternative farming methods must produce enough food.
- **B** Animals must be allowed to graze on land currently used for crops.
- **C** Farmers must be willing to accept less money for their crops.
- **D** More chemicals must be produced.

Apply Scientific Principles

① Learn the Skill

A **scientific principle** is an idea or model that explains some natural phenomenon. For example, our understanding of why the planets in our solar system remain in orbit around the sun is explained by our concept of gravity. To **apply scientific principles**, you must use all of the skills you have learned in this book, including interpreting and applying data or information, analyzing procedures and results, and evaluating and generalizing to form conclusions and answer questions.

② Practice the Skill

By practicing the skill of applying scientific principles, you will improve your study and test-taking skills, especially as they relate to science high school equivalency tests. Examine the information below. Use the information to answer question 1.

Ⓐ Scientific principles are supported by evidence. For example, the theory that the Big Bang was the start of the universe is supported by Hubble's observation.

Ⓑ A scientific principle is a big idea that can explain a number of related occurrences. Here, the idea of the Big Bang provides a common explanation for several scientific phenomena.

> ### BIG BANG THEORY
>
> **Ⓐ** In 1929, astronomer Edwin Hubble observed that the galaxies in the universe around our galaxy, the Milky Way, are speeding away from us. This model of an expanding universe was important in developing the Big Bang theory.
>
> The Big Bang theory states that all the matter and energy that exists was once inside a hot, dense mass just a few millimeters across. About 14 billion years ago, a huge explosion blasted that material outward in all directions. This blast, known as the Big Bang, was the start of the universe as we know it.
>
> **Ⓑ** Three major pieces of evidence support the Big Bang theory. First, if the universe began with a tiny mass that exploded, the galaxies that formed after that blast would be moving away from each other. This phenomenon appears to exist. Scientists also calculated that, given the way the first atoms formed, 25 percent of the mass in the universe should be helium. They discovered that this circumstance is also true. Finally, in the 1940s, scientists predicted that the Big Bang should have left behind background radiation throughout the universe. Such cosmic background radiation was detected in the 1960s.

💡 USING LOGIC

Compare the answer choices with what you have learned about the evidence that supports the Big Bang theory. Evaluate which choices are consistent with this evidence and which seem to contradict it.

1 **Based on the Big Bang theory, which statement describes an aspect of the universe?**
   A The Milky Way is the center of the universe.
   B Galaxies will soon begin to move toward each other.
   C Galaxies are farther apart now than 50 years ago.
   D A second Big Bang will occur in a few billion years.

UNIT 3

③ Apply the Skill

Directions: Questions 2 through 6 are based on the information below.

A geological time scale shows the major divisions of time in Earth's history. These time divisions generally correspond to a major change in the life-forms on Earth as observed in the fossil record. The table shows major changes to life-forms during two eras and the periods that make up those eras.

ERA	PERIOD (AND TIME IN MILLIONS OF YEARS AGO)	MAJOR LIFE-FORMS AND EVENTS
LIFE-FORMS AND EVENTS THAT CHARACTERIZE THE PALEOZOIC AND MESOZOIC ERAS		
Mesozoic	Cretaceous 145–65	Flowering plants appear; modern birds appear; mass extinction of dinosaurs
Mesozoic	Jurassic 200–145	Primitive birds appear; dinosaurs dominant
Mesozoic	Triassic 251–200	Dinosaurs appear; mammals appear
Paleozoic	Permian 299–251	Mass extinction of most marine species
Paleozoic	Carboniferous 359–299	Reptiles appear; giant dragonflies and cockroaches common
Paleozoic	Devonian 416–359	Amphibians appear; ferns common; fishes dominant
Paleozoic	Silurian 444–416	Land plants and animals appear
Paleozoic	Ordovician 488–444	Echinoderms appear; trilobites decline
Paleozoic	Cambrian 542–500	Trilobites common

2 Based on the table, which event happened most recently?
A Reptiles appeared.
B Amphibians evolved.
C Dinosaurs became extinct.
D Fishes became the dominant animal group.

3 Based on the table, which statement best describes the major change to life-forms during the Mesozoic Era?
A Trilobites were dominant but then declined.
B Dinosaurs evolved, were dominant, and then became extinct.
C Plants and animals first moved onto land.
D Reptiles replaced mammals as the dominant land animals.

4 Which idea is best supported by the table?
A The Paleozoic and Mesozoic eras cover the entire existence of life on Earth.
B The first living things appeared in the Paleozoic Era.
C Mammals caused the extinction of the dinosaurs.
D Echinoderms have a longer history than mammals have.

5 Based on the table, what can you determine about life in the Paleozoic and Mesozoic eras?
A Life on land first began about 145 million years ago.
B A single event led to the extinction of most marine species and all dinosaurs.
C Life began in water and gradually moved onto land.
D Flowering plants appeared before ferns and other land plants.

6 The Cenozoic Era covers the time period from 65 million years ago to present day. Where in the table would you place specific information about the Cenozoic Era?
A in the table heading
B in a new column
C in a new row above the Mesozoic Era
D in the passage

Directions: Questions 7 through 10 are based on the information below.

DETERMINING AGES OF ROCKS

Scientists use observations of rock, radiometric dating, and fossils to determine the ages of rock layers. In an undisturbed column of rock, the oldest layer is at the bottom, and the youngest is at the top. The sequence of geological events, therefore, can be seen in the rock. The times in Earth's history when certain plants or animals lived is also known. Therefore, fossils found in rock, as demonstrated in the diagram, can help approximate the rock's age. Radiometric dating can identify the exact age of rock through the use of radioactive isotopes. Isotopes are forms of an element with the same number of protons but different numbers of neutrons. Isotopes decay, or lose their radioactivity, at different rates. When scientists know the amount of a radioactive isotope in a rock, the known rate of decay for that isotope, and the amount of the isotope and the product of its decay in a rock, they can pinpoint the age of the rock.

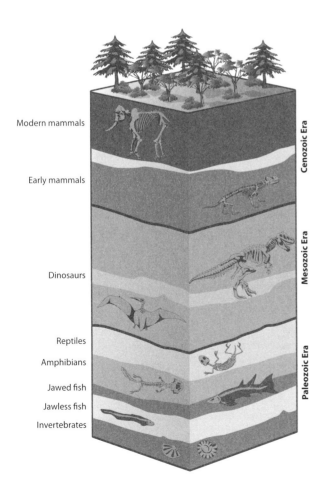

7 **Based on the diagram, when in geologic time did jawed fish likely come into existence?**
   A the middle of the Paleozoic Era
   B the end of the Paleozoic Era
   C the middle of the Mesozoic Era
   D the end of the Cenozoic Era

8 **A scientist measures the amount of the same radioactive isotope and the product of its decay in two different rocks. Based on the passage, what is a reasonable conclusion that the scientist can make based on this evidence?**
   A The rock with the greater amount of decay product is younger.
   B The rock with the greater amount of decay product is older.
   C The older rock formed in the Mesozoic Era.
   D The younger rock contains dinosaur fossils.

9 **Based on the diagram, what conclusion can be drawn about the age of dinosaurs?**
   A The age of dinosaurs coincided with the Mesozoic Era.
   B The age of dinosaurs started during the Paleozoic and extended to the middle of the Cenozoic.
   C Dinosaur fossils have only been found in the Paleozoic.
   D The age of dinosaurs cannot be determined from the diagram.

10 **A scientist studies a rock formation in which fossils of jawless fish are found in rock layers above those of early mammals. What can the scientist conclude?**
   A Fossils are unrelated to the age of the rock in which they are found.
   B Jawless fish evolved after early mammals.
   C The rock layers were disturbed by tectonic forces in the past.
   D The rock layers are undisturbed.

Directions: Questions 11 and 12 are based on the information below.

Americans use more water per person than any other people on Earth. Agriculture uses about 41 percent of our freshwater supply. Power plants use another 38 percent. Industrial processes account for about 11 percent of U.S. water use. Public drinking water systems account for just 10 percent of water use.

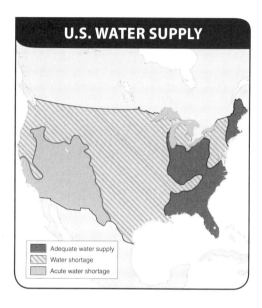

U.S. WATER SUPPLY

- ■ Adequate water supply
- ▨ Water shortage
- □ Acute water shortage

11 **What problem is the author most likely trying to point out?**
- A   Our use of fresh water is not sustainable.
- B   People drink too much water.
- C   Industry does not use enough water.
- D   Fresh water is an unlimited resource.

12 **Which of the following is the best possible solution to this problem?**
- A   encourage industry and agriculture to conserve water
- B   ask people to drink less water
- C   shut down power plants in the United States
- D   prevent people from living in areas that lack fresh water

Directions: Questions 13 and 14 are based on the passage below.

Two scientists moved from the country to a nearby city. They noticed that the temperatures in the city seemed to be much higher than they were in the country. They did some research and learned that the city's temperatures were often higher than the country's temperatures on the same day. After doing more research, they learned that this trend is common in many areas: in general, cities are warmer than the surrounding suburban and rural areas.

13 **One scientist hypothesized that the larger number of people living closer together in the city is what causes city temperatures to be higher than temperatures in surrounding areas. How could the scientists best test this hypothesis?**
- A   Measure the temperature at a busy restaurant and a quiet park and compare the data.
- B   Measure the temperature at a place with many people and then wait until the area is empty to measure it again.
- C   Measure the temperature of two city parks, one with many people and one with few, at the same time of day.
- D   Walk around to different places and see how much the temperature changes.

14 **Which of the following is a valid hypothesis, based on the information provided?**
- A   Parks and areas with trees will have lower temperatures than areas without foliage.
- B   Cities are warmer because the sun shines more brightly on them.
- C   Cars and buses cause lower temperatures in certain areas because of how fast they travel.
- D   Different temperatures prove that certain areas are more populated than others.

Directions: Questions 15 and 16 are based on the information below.

Precipitation that falls from clouds is made up of water that originally came from the ground below. Heat causes the water to flow upward in the form of water vapor. After the water cools, it again falls to the ground.

RAIN FORMATION

```
The sun heats Earth's surface.
        ↓
Water on Earth's surface
evaporates to form
water vapor.
        ↓
Water vapor rises in the
atmosphere.
        ↓
As water vapor rises, it cools and
condenses into tiny water drops
that form clouds.
        ↓
As drops grow, they become
big and heavy enough to fall
back to the ground as rain.
        ↑ (cycle back to sun)
```

15 **Before water vapor forms, liquid water on the ground must**

A freeze and become ice

B cool down and condense

C flow to a large water body such as a lake

D heat up and evaporate

16 **What causes rain to fall from clouds?**

A heat from the sun on the clouds

B evaporation within the clouds

C growth of water droplets within the clouds

D water vapor building up in the clouds

Directions: Questions 17 and 18 are based on the information below.

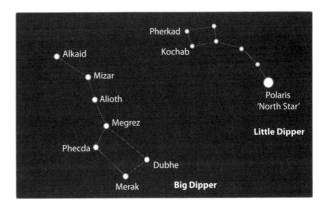

Constellations, such as the Big Dipper and Little Dipper, are patterns that people on Earth saw among the stars in the night sky in ancient times. Some were named for animals or common objects; others were named for mythological people or creatures. Although stars in constellations appear motionless, they are actually streaking around the galaxy, just like our sun. They are just too far away for us to detect their movement. Still, over tens of thousands of years, constellations do change position. The pattern of constellations that is visible to us also changes throughout the year as Earth revolves around the sun.

17 **Based on the information, why do constellations appear to be in different parts of the sky at different times of the year?**

A The constellations change shape throughout the year.

B Constellations exist only for a short period, and then completely new ones form.

C As Earth circles the sun, we see different areas of the sky.

D It is difficult to see constellations during summer when Earth is tilted toward the sun.

18 **How will the Big Dipper most likely look in 100,000 years?**

A It will no longer be recognizable as the Big Dipper.

B It will look the same as it does now.

C It will have the same shape but will be much larger.

D It will be much dimmer than it is today but will retain the same shape.

UNIT 3

The Unit Review is structured to resemble science high school equivalency tests. Be sure to read each question and all possible answers very carefully before choosing your answer.

To record your answers, fill in the numbered circle that corresponds to the answer you select for each question in the Unit Review.

Do not rest your pencil on the answer area while considering your answer. Make no stray or unnecessary marks. If you change an answer, erase your first mark completely.

Mark only one answer space for each question; multiple answers will be scored as incorrect.

Sample Question

In which of the following examples would a flowchart provide the best visual representation of information?

A a representation of temperature and precipitation in different states

B a representation of the internal structure of a mountain range

C a representation of the effects of greenhouse gases around the world

D a representation of how a local recycling program will work

Ⓐ Ⓑ Ⓒ ●

Directions: Questions 1 and 2 are based on the information below.

Sinkholes are depressions that can open up suddenly in the ground. They usually form in areas of soft limestone rock. The process begins when slightly acidic rainfall seeps into the ground. It slowly dissolves the rock, forming caves. Sinkholes then can form, as shown in the diagrams below.

Diagram A: Pre-sinkhole   **Diagram B: Sinkhole**

 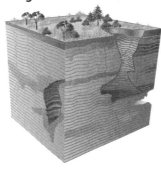

1 **What occurred between Diagram A and Diagram B?**

A Heavy rains collecting on the surface caused the ground to collapse.

B Acidic rainfall eating away rock underground caused the collapse.

C Soft rock collapsed from the weight of the houses built on it.

D Drought caused already dry limestone to become weaker and collapse.

Ⓐ Ⓑ Ⓒ Ⓓ

2 **Areas with which of the following characteristics are most likely to experience sinkholes?**

A hard granite bedrock and dry weather

B limestone bedrock and dry weather

C slate bedrock and wet weather

D limestone bedrock and wet weather

Ⓐ Ⓑ Ⓒ Ⓓ

Directions: Questions 3 and 4 are based on the information below.

You are planning to write an article about the International Astronomical Union's (IAU) decision in August 2006 to change the classification of Pluto from a planet to a dwarf planet. You identify the following sources at the library:

1. **Source A (10/2/2006):** a magazine article explaining the decision using quotes from astronomers who are members of the IAU and were involved in the decision.
2. **Source B (9/26/2006):** a newspaper article that neither quotes astronomers nor mentions the IAU. It does include a diagram of the solar system.
3. **Source C (4/18/2004):** an editorial by a famous geochemist about Pluto's atmosphere.

3 **Which source(s) would you use in your own article?**

A source A, because its information comes from astronomers involved in the decision

B sources A and C, because they include either thoughts or insights from scientists

C source B, because it is from a newspaper rather than a magazine

D sources B and C, because they provide scientific facts about Pluto

Ⓐ Ⓑ Ⓒ Ⓓ

4 **You also find a November 2006 interview with a relative of the scientist who discovered Pluto. She is not an astronomer, but states that she is upset that the IAU changed Pluto's designation. How could this source contribute to your report?**

A It could provide unbiased information about the characteristics of Pluto.

B It could help you understand why some people disagreed with the IAU's decision.

C It could provide details as to why the IAU changed Pluto's designation.

D It could help you convince the IAU that its decision was incorrect.

Ⓐ Ⓑ Ⓒ Ⓓ

Directions: Questions 5 and 6 are based on the diagram below.

COMPOSITE VOLCANO

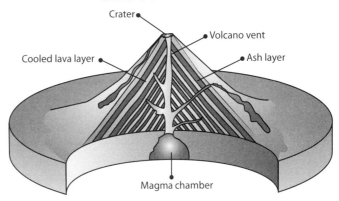

5 **Based on the cross-section diagram, which of the following statements is true?**

A The magma chamber is located on the side of the volcano.

B Lava can spill out the sides of the cone during an eruption.

C The eruptions from a composite volcano would not be deadly.

D Ash and rock are pushed up through the magma chamber in layers.

Ⓐ Ⓑ Ⓒ Ⓓ

6 **Based on the diagram, what can you infer about composite volcano eruptions?**

A Composite volcanoes constantly erupt lava.

B Composite volcanoes can erupt both lava and ash.

C The magma chamber of a composite volcano is not involved in eruptions.

D A composite volcano erupts in a regular, predictable pattern.

Ⓐ Ⓑ Ⓒ Ⓓ

Directions: Questions 7 through 9 are based on the flowchart below.

HOW HAIL FORMS

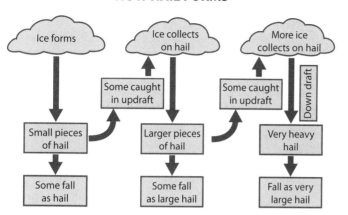

Directions: Questions 10 and 11 are based on the passage below.

> Our solar system consists of eight planets and the sun, which is a star. The planets are organized into two categories based on their densities. The first group of planets—Mercury, Venus, Earth, and Mars—is rocky and dense. The second group of planets—Jupiter, Saturn, Uranus, and Neptune—is large and gaseous. The second group of planets also contains ring systems, which are made up of rock and ice particles. An asteroid belt separates the two groups of planets.

7 **Based on the flowchart, what happens to very large hail?**

  A It is caught in an updraft and returns to the clouds.

  B It falls to Earth in a downdraft.

  C It turns into clouds.

  D More ice collects on it.

Ⓐ Ⓑ Ⓒ Ⓓ

8 **Based on the flowchart, what are you most likely to see during a hailstorm?**

  A snowflakes stuck to large pieces of hail

  B only very large, very heavy hail

  C large and small pieces of hail

  D only very small pieces of hail

Ⓐ Ⓑ Ⓒ Ⓓ

9 **Based on the flowchart, which of the following conditions must be present for hail to form?**

  A clouds that are very close to the ground

  B temperatures high enough to melt ice

  C strong winds parallel to the ground

  D clouds that contain both rising and sinking air

Ⓐ Ⓑ Ⓒ Ⓓ

10 **Which of the following is an opinion?**

  A Because of its similarities to Earth, Mars is likely to contain intelligent life.

  B The solar system contains eight planets.

  C Planets closest to the sun are denser than those that are farther away.

  D Jupiter, Saturn, Uranus, and Neptune all have rings.

Ⓐ Ⓑ Ⓒ Ⓓ

11 **What set of additional information would best support the facts in this passage?**

  A observation from astronauts who have explored space

  B an illustration of Saturn's ring system

  C a diagram of the solar system, showing the locations and orbit patterns of the planets

  D a list of each planet's moons and their sizes

UNIT 3

Directions: Questions 12 through 15 are based on the information below.

Fresh water (water that is not salty) is an important natural resource. It is also limited in supply. Many scientists and conservationists are concerned that if we do not begin to conserve fresh water, we will run out. The graph below shows how people in the United States use fresh water.

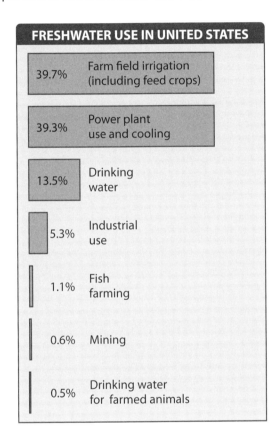

FRESHWATER USE IN UNITED STATES

39.7%	Farm field irrigation (including feed crops)
39.3%	Power plant use and cooling
13.5%	Drinking water
5.3%	Industrial use
1.1%	Fish farming
0.6%	Mining
0.5%	Drinking water for farmed animals

12 Some people think that the use of fresh, drinkable water to irrigate farm crops is a problem because it wastes drinkable water. Which of the following observations would best support this position?

A Undrinkable water can be used to irrigate crops without harming the quality of the crops.

B Many crops on farms do not receive enough water from rain.

C Most farms use the most efficient irrigation systems available.

D Runoff from farm fields can contain contaminants that make it unusable for drinking.

Ⓐ Ⓑ Ⓒ Ⓓ

13 Which of the following actions would probably most reduce the amount of water used in the United States?

A encouraging people to drink less water

B building power plants that do not require as much coolant

C increasing the amount of mining that occurs

D consuming more wild-caught fish

Ⓐ Ⓑ Ⓒ Ⓓ

14 By some estimates, more than 2,000 gallons of water are required to produce one pound of beef. Only about 700 gallons per pound are accounted for by the water that the cow drinks. What is the most likely use of the remaining 1,300 gallons per pound?

A water that evaporates from the cow's breath

B water used to process the beef from the cow

C water used to grow the grains that the cow eats

D water that runs into the ground when the cows drink

Ⓐ Ⓑ Ⓒ Ⓓ

15 Based on the information, which of the following statements is true?

A People in the United States consume most of the world's fresh water for drinking.

B Fish farming and mining account for a majority of the freshwater use in the United States.

C Much more fresh water is used in power plants than is used to irrigate crops.

D Agriculture and power generation account for the vast majority of freshwater consumption in the United States.

Ⓐ Ⓑ Ⓒ Ⓓ

Directions: Questions 16 through 18 refer to the passage below.

Most energy used in the United States for producing electricity and fueling motor vehicles comes from fossil fuels, such as coal, oil, and natural gas. Very little comes from cleaner alternatives such as wind, solar power, and geothermal power. Unlike these alternative sources, combustion of fossil fuels produces waste gases, such as carbon dioxide. Carbon dioxide is naturally present in the atmosphere as part of the carbon cycle. For example, decomposition of plant material releases carbon dioxide to the air. But the combustion of fossil fuels has increased dramatically since the start of the Industrial Revolution in the late 1700s—along with the concentration of atmospheric carbon dioxide. Data suggest that this increase is responsible for changes in climate that could have negative effects on living things.

16 What is the basic problem identified in the passage?

   A People have used fossil fuels since the Industrial Revolution.

   B Excess carbon dioxide is entering Earth's atmosphere.

   C Too much energy is being used to run electric power plants and motor vehicles.

   D Carbon dioxide enters the atmosphere from several natural sources.

Ⓐ Ⓑ Ⓒ Ⓓ

17 Based on information in the passage, what is a possible solution?

   A slowing decomposition of plant material

   B changing the atmosphere to absorb more carbon dioxide

   C using cleaner alternative energy sources instead of fossil fuels

   D using more natural gas instead of coal and oil

Ⓐ Ⓑ Ⓒ Ⓓ

18 What problem must be overcome if the proposed solution is to succeed?

   A Alternative motor vehicles that do not burn fossil fuels must be developed.

   B Scientists must increase the force of the wind.

   C Scientists must find a way to increase the energy output of the sun.

   D Scientists must find a way to increase the amount of heat generated in Earth's interior.

Ⓐ Ⓑ Ⓒ Ⓓ

Directions: Question 19 refers to the passage below.

Glen Canyon Dam blocks the Colorado River in northern Arizona, forming a huge reservoir (Lake Powell) behind it. The waters of the lake rush through the dam, producing hydropower for more than 1 million people. The lake is also a dependable source of water for irrigating arid farmland.

But Glen Canyon Dam has changed the characteristics of the river below it, altering its flow rate and temperature and removing sediment. As a result, several aquatic species below the dam are no longer in the area.

Still, the biggest controversy has been the loss of beautiful Glen Canyon, now deep beneath the waters of Lake Powell. Glen Canyon was especially magnificent, with exquisite rock formations, unique species, and artifacts left behind by the area's ancient peoples. Several groups want to allow the Colorado to flow freely past Glen Canyon Dam again, draining much of Lake Powell and once again exposing Glen Canyon.

19 What are the two opposing arguments about Glen Canyon Dam represented in the passage?

   A hydroelectric power versus the combustion of fossil fuels to produce electricity

   B dryland farming with irrigation versus farming with natural precipitation

   C the value of natural environments versus the needs of a technically advanced society

   D the importance of lakes for producing electric power versus their value for recreation

Ⓐ Ⓑ Ⓒ Ⓓ

Glossary

A

abiotic factors: nonliving physical features of the environment

acid: any compound that increases the number of hydrogen ions when dissolved in water; acids turn blue litmus paper red

adaptation: any characteristic of an organism that makes it better able to survive in its environment

allele: one of a number of different forms of a gene

amplitude: the maximum distance a wave vibrates from its rest position

antibiotics: drugs that kill bacteria, as well as fungi and some parasites; they do not work against viruses

antibody: a protein made by the body in response to a specific antigen

antigens: proteins and chemicals that are foreign to the body

asthenosphere: the soft layer of the mantle on which pieces of the lithosphere move

B

base: any compound that increases the number of hydroxide ions when dissolved in water; bases turn red litmus paper blue

biodiversity: the number, or abundance of different species living within a particular region

biomes: large geographic areas that have similar climates and ecosystems

biotic factors: living organisms in the environment

C

carrying capacity: the largest number of individuals that an environment can support and maintain over time

cell: basic unit of all forms of life

chemical change: a change that occurs when one or more substances are changed into entirely new substances with different properties

chemical reaction: the process by which one or more substances undergo a change to produce one or more different substances

chordates: animals with nerve cords that run along their backs

chromosome: threadlike strands of DNA and protein in a cell nucleus that carry the code for the cell characteristics of an organism

circuit: a complete, closed path through which electric charges flow

commensalism: a symbiotic relationship that benefits one partner, but not the other

community: all the populations of different species that live in the same place at the same time and interact with each other

conclusion: an explanation or judgment based on inferences from data and observations

condensation: the change of state from a gas to a liquid

consumer: an organism that relies on other organisms for its energy and food supply

continental drift: the hypothesis that continents can drift apart from one another and have done so in the past

core: the central, spherical part of Earth below the mantle

covalent bond: the force of attraction between the nuclei of atoms and the electrons shared by the atoms

covalent compound: compound in which two or more atoms share electrons

crest: the highest point of a transverse wave

crust: the thin, outermost layer of Earth, or the uppermost part of the lithosphere

D

delta: a fan-shaped deposit of sediment at the mouth of a stream, where the stream empties into a large body of water

deposition: the process by which material is dropped or settles

displacement: the difference between the initial position of an object and its final position

DNA: *d*eoxyribo*n*ucleic *a*cid; a chemical in the nuclei of cells that codes and stores genetic information

dominant: the form of a genetic trait that appears to mask another form of the same trait

E

ecosystem: a community interacting with the nonliving parts of its environment

electrons: the negatively charged particles found in all atoms

element: a pure substance that cannot be separated or broken down into simpler substances by physical or chemical means

endothermic: term used to describe a physical or chemical change in which energy is absorbed

enzymes: molecules that help chemical reactions occur more quickly

epicenter: the point on Earth's surface directly above an earthquake's starting point

erosion: the removal or transport of sediment by gravity, wind, water, or ice

evaporation: the change of state from a liquid to a gas

evolution: changes that occur over time in the hereditary features of a species of organisms

exothermic: term used to describe a chemical or physical change in which energy is released or removed

F

focus: the point inside Earth where an earthquake begins

food chain: a model used to show how energy from food passes from one organism to another

food web: a model used to describe a series of overlapping food chains

frequency: the number of waves produced in a given amount of time

friction: a force that opposes motion between two surfaces that are touching

fulcrum: the fixed point about which a lever pivots

G

gas: the state in which matter has no definite shape or volume

gene: the segment of DNA of a chromosome that directs the making of a specific protein, thus controlling traits that are passed to offspring

genetics: the science of how traits are inherited through alleles passed from one generation to another

group: a column of elements on the periodic table

H

hydrolysis: a chemical reaction in which an enzyme helps break one substrate into two pieces

hypothesis: a possible explanation or answer to a scientific question

I

igneous rock: rock made from the cooling of magma

indicator: a substance that changes color in the presence of an acid or a base

inner core: the solid, dense center of Earth

invasive species: plants and animals that have migrated to places where they are not native

ionic bond: the force of attraction between oppositely charged ions

ionic compounds: compounds that contain ionic bonds

ions: charged particles that form during chemical changes when one or more electrons transfer from one atom to another

K

kinetic energy: energy of motion

L

lava: magma that flows onto Earth's surface

law of conservation of energy: energy can neither be created nor destroyed; it can only change forms

lever: a simple machine consisting of a bar that pivots at a fixed point, called a fulcrum

life cycle: all the stages an organism goes through from the beginning of one generation to the next

liquid: the state in which matter takes the shape of its container and has a definite volume

lithosphere: the outermost, rigid layer of Earth that consists of the crust and the rigid upper part of the mantle

longitudinal wave: a wave in which the particles of the medium vibrate back and forth along the path that the wave travels

M

machine: a device that helps make work easier by changing the size or direction (or both) of a force

magma: the hot liquid that forms when rock partially or completely melts

magnetic field: the region around a magnet in which magnetic forces can act

mantle: the layer of Earth between the crust and the core

mechanical advantage: a number that tells how may times a machine multiplies force

mesosphere: the strong lower part of the mantle between the asthenosphere and the outer core

metalloids: elements that have properties of both metals and nonmetals; sometimes called semiconductors

metals: elements that are shiny and are good conductors of thermal energy and electric current; most are malleable and ductile

metamorphic rock: rock that forms when the texture and composition of preexisting rock changes due to heat or pressure

metamorphosis: the change in body form during the life cycle—for example: egg, larva, pupa, adult

model: a representation of an object or system

molecule: a neutral group of atoms held together by covalent bonds

mutualism: a symbiotic relationship that benefits both partners

N

NASA: National Aeronautics and Space Administration

Newton's second law: $F = ma$, where F stands for the net force (expressed in newtons), m stands for the object's mass, and a stands for the object's acceleration

Newton's third law: for every action force, there is an equal and opposite reaction force

nitrogen cycle: the continuous movement of nitrogen from the atmosphere, to plants, and back to the atmosphere again

nonmetals: elements that are dull and are poor conductors of thermal energy and electric current

nonvascular plant: a plant lacking vascular tissue; a plant that absorbs water directly through its cell membranes

nucleus: the structure that contains a cell's genetic material and controls the cell's activities; the tiny, extremely dense, positively charged region in the center of an atom made up of protons and neutrons

nutrient: a substance in food that produces energy and materials for life activities

O

osmosis: the movement of water molecules from an area of greater concentration to an area of lower concentration

outer core: the liquid layer of Earth's core that lies beneath the mantle and surrounds the inner core

P

parallel circuit: a circuit in which different loads are on separate branches

parasitism: a symbiotic relationship that benefits the parasite but harms the parasite's partner

period: a horizontal row of elements on the periodic table

physical change: a change that affects one or more physical properties of a substance; no new substances are formed

plate tectonics: the theory that Earth's lithosphere is divided into tectonic plates that move around on top of the asthenosphere

pollutant: any substance that contaminates the environment

population: organisms of one species that live in the same place at the same time and that can produce offspring

potential energy: energy of position or shape

predator: an organism that feeds on another organism

prey: an organism that is eaten by another organism

producer: an organism that can capture energy from sunlight or chemicals and use it to produce food from inorganic compounds

products: the new substances formed as the result of a chemical reaction

protons: the positively charged particles of the nucleus of an atom

pulley: a simple machine consisting of a grooved wheel that holds a rope or cable

Punnett square: a tool that shows how genes can combine; used to predict the probability of types of offspring

R

reactants: the substances initially involved in a chemical reaction

recessive: the form of a genetic trait that seems to disappear in a population but can reappear depending on how the alleles combine

revolution: the elliptical motion of a body as it orbits another body in space

riparian: of or related to the banks of a river

rotation: the spinning motion of a body on its axis

S

scientific principle: an idea or model that explains some natural phenomenon

seafloor spreading: the process by which new oceanic lithosphere is formed at mid-ocean ridges as older materials are pulled away from the ridge

sedimentary rock: rock that forms when sediments are compacted and cemented together

series circuit: a circuit in which all parts are connected in a single loop

simple machines: the six machines from which all other machines are constructed: lever, inclined plane, wedge, screw, wheel and axle, and pulley

solar nebula: a large cloud of rotating gases and dust from which the solar system formed

solid: the state in which matter has a definite shape and volume

speed: a measure of how fast an object moves; $s = d/t$

sublimation: the change of state from a solid directly into a gas

substrate: a molecule that reacts with the help of an enzyme

symbiosis: a close relationship between two organisms from different species that live together

synthesis: a chemical reaction in which an enzyme helps join two substrates together

T

table: a graphic tool used to display complex information in an organized and concise way

tectonic plate: a piece of the lithosphere that moves around on top of the asthenosphere

theory: a description of nature based on many observations; subject to change when evidence changes; a unifying explanation for a broad range of hypotheses and observations that have been supported by testing

transverse wave: a wave in which the particles of the wave's medium vibrate perpendicular to the direction the wave is traveling

trophic level: a step in a food chain or food web

trough: the lowest point of a transverse wave

V

vaccine: a solution made from damaged virus or bacteria particles or from killed or weakened viruses or bacteria; can prevent, but not cure, many viral and bacterial diseases

vascular plant: a plant containing vascular tissue made up of tubelike cells that transport food and water throughout the plant

velocity: the speed of an object in a particular direction

vertebrates: chordates that have backbones that protect the nerve cord and provide the body with support; main groups include fish, amphibians, reptiles, birds, and mammals

W

water cycle: the continuous movement of water from water sources into the air, onto land, into and over the ground, and back to the water sources

watershed: the land drained by a river system, which includes the main river and all of its tributaries

wavelength: the distance between one point on a wave and the corresponding point on an adjacent wave

wetland: ecosystem in which water either covers the soil or is present at or near the surface of the soil for at least part of the year

GLOSSARY

Answer Key

UNIT 1 LIFE SCIENCE

LESSON 1, pp. 2–6
1. C, Earthworms are annelids, and annelids have segments that are all about the same size.
2. D, The table gives information about the defining characteristics of the five main types of chordates.
3. D, All chordates have limbs.
4. D, Both birds and reptiles have lungs and lay eggs with shells.
5. D, Four of the five chordate groups use lungs at some point in their life cycles.
6. C, Information on habitat is the only information not given in the table.
7. D, The number of threatened mammals increased by only 47 between 2006 and 2013.
8. C, The table shows the number of threatened animals in different groups in two different years.
9. A, The table shows that all groups had an increase in number of threatened species.
10. B, Since all groups showed an increase in threatened species between 2006 and 2013, it is reasonable to assume that they will also all increase by 2015.
11. C, The table shows change in numbers of threatened species in different animal groups over time.
12. C, The table describes unique characteristics of amphibians and reptiles.
13. B, Reptiles have characteristics that allow them to survive in drier environments than amphibians can.
14. D, The table gives the chromosome numbers for three different arthropods.
15. B, Removing humans from the table would leave only arthropods.
16. B, The table indicates that only New World monkeys have prehensile tails.
17. C, The paragraph states that primates have opposable thumbs; this information is not presented in the table.
18. D, The table indicates that all primates have hair.
19. D, Each column in the table provides a different piece of information about the various primate groups.

LESSON 2, pp. 7–11
1. D, Eighty-five percent of the bear's diet comes from fruit and plants.
2. B, The graph shows the 1875 hare population to be about 100,000.
3. C, Each lynx population increase was preceded by a hare population increase.
4. A, The data in the table represent the interrelationship of lynx and hare populations.
5. B, The line on the graph corresponding to the year 1935 shows the hare population to be larger than the lynx population.
6. D, Between 1963 and 1966, the reindeer population decreased by about 6,000.

7. A, The reindeer population increased over the course of about 20 years, and then suddenly decreased over about 3 years.
8. D, The carrying capacity of the island was 2,000 reindeer; there were more than 2,000 reindeer on the island in the early 1960s.
9. A, Cattle ranches account for 60% of the deforestation in the Amazon.
10. D, Cattle ranches account for 60% of the deforestation in the Amazon, more than all of the other causes added together.
11. B, The steep slope of the line indicates a rapid decrease in the wolf population between 1980 and 1983.
12. D, Moose populations were largest between around 1983 and 1995, which is when wolf populations were smallest.
13. D, The mass of weeds is smallest when large numbers of wheat plants are planted.
14. C, Wheat plants inhibit the growth of weeds.
15. C, The graph shows that the cheetah population was about 25,000 in 1980.
16. A, The 2007 cheetah population was about 10% of the 1900 cheetah population.
17. C, Circle graphs, like the one referred to in questions 9 and 10, can best describe the causes of certain trends.
18. D, The graph shows the bacteria population at its maximum between 7 hours and 10 hours.
19. Evaluation: (3), The bacteria population leveled off at about 7 hours.
20. D, The bacteria stopped growing because they ran out of nutrients.

LESSON 3, pp. 12–16
1. D, Arrows in a food chain point from prey to predator.
2. D, Caterpillars appear in the overlap between the two circles.
3. A, The diagram shows foods eaten by two desert animals.
4. B, Other mice appear in the circle describing the diet of grasshopper mice.
5. C, Arrows in a food web point from prey to predator.
6. A, The food web shows that many animals in a grassland eat grass.
7 C, The diagram shows the stages in a tomato plant's life cycle.
8. B, Taken together, the diagram and the paragraph indicate that fruit formation follows pollination.
9. C, All of the organisms listed begin life as a fertilized egg.
10. D, Taken together, the diagram and the paragraph indicate that tadpoles and larvae are the second stages of the frog and butterfly life cycles.
11. D, The source of energy, chemicals from inside Earth, is indicated at the base of the diagram.
12. B, The arrows point from prey to predator; thus tubeworms get energy from the bacteria that live inside them.
13. D, Octopuses eat tubeworms, clams, crabs, and mussels.
14. D, The diagram shows that crabs eat the remains of octopuses.
15. A, The diagram shows that foxes and hawks make up the fourth trophic level.
16. D, The diagram shows that hawks are in the fourth trophic level.

UNIT 1 (continued)

17. A, The diagram shows that scorpions, snakes, and lizards are secondary consumers.

18. C, Scorpions are secondary consumers.

LESSON 4, pp. 17–21

1. D, The diagram indicates that ribosomes are involved in protein production.

2. D, The diagram shows the lysosome floating in the cytoplasm.

3. A, The nucleus is responsible for cellular reproduction.

4. D, The electron microscope, invented in the 1950s, allowed scientists to see the internal structures of cells.

5. C, The diagram shows that the axon is involved in transmitting information.

6. D, Dendrites receive information.

7. C, The diagram shows that a neuron has many dendrites, but only one axon.

8. C, The pore is an opening in the nuclear envelope.

9. A, The diagram shows the parts of the nucleus.

10. B, The diagram shows the parts of a mitochondrion.

11. B, The diagram shows that the mitochondrion has two membranes.

12. D, Diagrams can be used to show processes.

13. D, Association neurons in the brain and spinal cord determine the meaning of messages sent from receptors.

14. D, Both the passage and the diagram describe the movement of nerve impulses.

15. A, Motor neurons control muscle movements.

16. B, The diagram shows that carbon dioxide enters and oxygen leaves through the stoma.

17 C, Photosynthesis happens in chloroplasts, which are located in the mesophyll.

18. A, Placing the submerged leaf in sunlight will allow Janelle to see bubbles of gases that are released from the leaf.

19. B, The diagram shows the structure of a leaf.

20. B, The diagram shows a cell membrane—the barrier that surrounds a cell.

LESSON 5, pp. 22–26

1. B, Using bacteria to produce medications is an example of a beneficial use of bacteria.

2. C, The table groups bacteria by shape.

3. D, This statement describes two different effects of different types of bacteria.

4. C, The passage states that bacteria help convert nitrogen to a form plants can use.

5. A, Both the diagram and the passage describe different ways that nitrogen changes form in the environment.

6. B, The table identifies four diseases caused by bacteria.

7. A, The table identifies the disease that each bacterium causes.

8. C, The main idea of both the diagram and the passage is how the Black Death spread.

9. A, Fleas biting people and transmitting the bacteria to them is a supporting detail as to how the Black Death was spread.

10. D, The paragraph is mainly about how water is treated to remove harmful materials and bacteria.

11. A, The diagram shows that aerobic bacteria coat the crushed rock in the tank.

12. D, The paragraph describes primary and secondary treatment.

13. D, The paragraph describes how microorganisms can be used to produce antibiotics.

14. D, The paragraph states that frequent use of antibiotics can make them less effective.

15. C, The rapid reproduction of bacteria allows a mutation to spread quickly through the population.

16. D, The paragraph implies that scientists were expecting to find fewer types of bacteria in the air than what they actually discovered.

LESSON 6, pp. 27–31

1. A, The passage states that there are many different kinds of plants, and that most organisms rely on plants to survive.

2. A, The diagram describes the names and roles of the main organs of a vascular plant.

3. D, The passage describes how vascular and nonvascular plants move materials through their bodies.

4. B, The passage and diagram focus mainly on the movement of substances through plants.

5. B, The passage describes how cactuses differ from many other plants.

6. D, The passage states that most leaves grow either parallel or alternating with one another.

7. C, The passage is about the positions of leaves on plant stems.

8. D, The passage describes the ways in which mosses differ from many other plants.

9. D, The transport of pollen by bees is an important part of plant reproduction.

10. A, The diagram shows the male and female parts of the flower.

11. D, The paragraph describes several ways that seeds can be spread.

12. A, The paragraph describes both living and nonliving things that spread seeds.

13. C, The paragraph and table describe how kudzu, a non-native species, has harmed ecosystems.

14. B, A summary should not include the same wording as the original text.

15. C, The paragraph describes why kudzu is problematic.

LESSON 7, pp. 32–36

1. B, The passage states that fertilizers contribute to algal blooms.

2. C, The diagram shows that riparian areas are located near water, and the passage implies that riparian areas are located near water.

3. A, The EPA is a government agency.

4. A, The passage describes the benefits of wetlands and riparian areas.

5. B, The passage describes the monitoring and control of common pollutants.

6. C, The table describes the water quality of water bodies in Texas.

7. D, Four of the watersheds in the table are listed as having good quality.

UNIT 1 (continued)

8. C, *Stringent* means "rigorous."

9. A, The following paragraph further defines areas with insufficient controls.

10. C, The paragraph mentions creating a ranking of water bodies.

11. D, The paragraph states that growing corn has caused pollution of groundwater.

12. A, *Precipitates* means "falls."

13. B, Acid precipitation is harmful and damaging.

14. C, The paragraph states that acid precipitation is most common downwind of coal-burning power plants.

15. A, *Sustainable* means "able to be self-supporting."

16. D, *Undertaking* and *process* both imply long-term events.

17. B, The paragraph states that the purpose of these efforts is to redirect freshwater back to the Everglades.

18. B, *Ruptured* means "broken open."

19. A, Punitive damages are payments that compensate for damage caused by a person or an organization

20. A, The paragraph states that the oil spill damaged the fisheries.

LESSON 8, pp. 37–41

1. B, Deserts, grasslands, and temperate deciduous forests make up most of the United States; deserts receive an average of 25 cm of rain each year, grasslands receive about 65 cm of rain each year, and temperate deciduous forests receive about 125 cm of rain each year.

2. D, Boreal forest and tundra are the coldest of the biomes.

3. C, Plants and animals have adaptations that allow them to survive in the biome in which they live.

4. C, Animals in boreal forests and tundras must have adaptations for cold weather.

5. A, According to the map, Boston and Paris are located in the same type of biome.

6. D, The graph shows that city E receives less than 25 cm of precipitation per year.

7. C, City C receives about 125 cm of precipitation each year.

8. A, The graph shows that the tundra gets very cold in the winter.

9. B, The graph shows that the rainy season in the savanna occurs at about the same time as the rainy season in the grassland.

10. C, November to February is the driest time in both biomes.

11. D, The paragraph states that soil in the savanna is thinner and less fertile than grassland soil.

12. D, The paragraph states that both biomes have similar plant life.

13. A, Boreal forests and tundras are the coldest biomes, meaning animals must adapt to the cold conditions in order to survive.

14. B, A tropical forest is much warmer than a boreal forest.

15. A, The savanna and the tropical forest have similar temperature ranges.

LESSON 9, pp. 42–46

1. D, The table shows examples of organisms in two different kingdoms.

2. A, Classes are divided into orders, and orders are divided into families; therefore, each class contains at least one family, so there are more families than classes.

3. C, All plants can make their own food.

4. A, Both reptiles and amphibians have a backbone.

5. D, Categories are based on differences among groups.

6. D, Because the characteristics listed are shared by members of both animal groups, there is not enough information provided to definitely classify it as a member of one of the groups.

7. D, Defining characteristics are used to place animals into different orders.

8. B, The members of a class are more similar to one another than they are to members of other classes.

9. D, The table shows tree-dwelling as a defining characteristic of the genus *Tamiasciurus*.

10. A, Giraffes are not rodents.

11. C, Both woodchucks and Douglas squirrels are rodents; the platypus is not.

12. B, Classifications are based on similarities.

13. C, Wolves are more similar to dogs than to cats, bears, or whales.

14. D, The shape of the snout is one of the characteristics that distinguish Alligatoridae from Crocodylidae.

15. C, Members of different genera have different characteristics.

LESSON 10, pp. 47–51

1. D, All mammals have fur or hair.

2. C, The table shows that all three classes of mammals produce milk for their young.

3. D, The table shows that monotremes are the only mammals that lay eggs.

4. B, The table states that lions hunt, but kangaroos do not.

5. C, Both placental mammals and marsupials give birth to live young.

6. A, The central portion of the Venn diagram indicates that all three animals are warm-blooded.

7. C, The echidna lays eggs; the horse gives birth to live young.

8. B, The passage states that early mammals were smaller than many modern mammals.

9. D, Both ancient and modern mammals have all the characteristics listed.

10. D, A term paper about the history of mammals would have to discuss both early and modern mammals.

11. D, The graphs show that the Bactrian camel lives in a climate with lower average temperatures than does the dromedary.

12. C, The paragraph states that marsupial mammals are more common in Australia.

13. A, The passage states that opossums are marsupials, which give birth to undeveloped young.

14. A, The diagram shows that all the limbs have similar bones.

UNIT 1 (*continued*)

15. A, The diagram shows that the humerus (structure A) is longer in humans than in the other animals shown.
16. D, The diagram shows when different primate groups first evolved and their similarities to one another.
17. A, Bar graphs can be used to compare and contrast sets of information.

LESSON 11, *pp. 52–56*

1. D, After the stomach, food passes through the small intestine.
2. C, The sight and smell of food stimulate saliva production.
3. D, Food must enter the mouth and be moved around before it can be chewed.
4. A, The sequence chart shows that bile and pancreatic juices enter the small intestine.
5. B, The sequence chart shows that wastes leave the small intestine, so digestion is mostly complete after food moves through that organ.
6. B, The passage states that esophageal contractions cease when all food has entered the stomach.
7. B, Swallowing and movement through the esophagus occurs before most of the digestive process occurs.
8. C, Waste becomes more compact as it moves through the large intestine and to the rectum.
9. D, Most nutrients are absorbed from food before it enters the large intestine.
10. A, The sequence diagram shows that you should cup your hand over your fist after placing your fist on the person's abdomen.
11. C, The sequence diagram shows that the last step in the Heimlich maneuver is making sure that the food has been dislodged.
12. B, Choking occurs when food that is swallowed blocks the trachea instead of moving down the esophagus.
13. D, Bile helps break down fats.
14. C, The first two steps combined take between 10 and 25 seconds to complete.
15. D, 6 a.m. Saturday is 36 hours after 6 p.m. Thursday.
16. D, Oxygen-poor blood flows through tiny blood vessels in the lungs before it flows through the rest of the body.
17. B, As blood circulates through the body, it loses oxygen and eventually flows back to the heart.

LESSON 12, *pp. 57–61*

1. C, Conservation laws were still being passed after the 1950s.
2. D, All three species became extinct within a ten-year period.
3. D, DDT caused reproductive problems in bald eagles between the 1940s and the 1960s.
4. D, Government mandates in the 1960s and 1970s led to the recovery of bald eagles in the 21st century.
5. C, Roosevelt created the refuge in 1903; the environmentalists asked for help in about 1902.
6. D, Roosevelt created the refuge in 1903; Kroegel started protecting birds in about 1881.
7. B, The refuge celebrated its 100th anniversary long after the other events on the timeline.

8. B, Roosevelt created the refuge only a year or so after environmentalists asked him for help.
9. B, Pelican Island was the first national wildlife refuge, so the creation of other wildlife refuges occurred later.
10. D, Alligator and crocodile populations increased after laws were passed to protect them.
11. D, The crocodile population was 200–300 in the mid-1970s; it reached 1,400–2,100 in the late 2000s.
12. D, The events in the paragraph happen between 1920 and 2013.
13. B, 1973 is about one-third of the way between 1970 and 1980.
14. C, Knowing the original wolf population would help show the number of wolves that were killed.
15. C, People became concerned about buffalo around 1835, and an organization was formed to protect them around 1905.
16. D, A federal law was passed in 1965, and the recovery plan was released in 1985.
17. D, The timeline shows that the birds were captured around 1986.

LESSON 13, *pp. 62–66*

1. C, The diagram shows that fluid and blood cells move into the affected area, which produces swelling.
2. A, Exposure to cowpox produces antibodies to cowpox virus; these antibodies also provide some protection against smallpox.
3. C, Because the causes of disease were not know in the late 1700s, the procedure could not explain why test subjects became immune to the diseases.
4. D, Pasteur's germ theory of disease revolutionized medicine.
5. A, Snake venom causes horses or sheep to make antibodies to the venom.
6. D, Antibodies in the antivenin neutralize the venom.
7. D, The antibody-antigen cluster is more easily recognized by the immune system.
8. A, Clusters form when antibodies recognize and bind to antigens.
9. B, The number of polio cases decreased sharply after 1955.
10. D, Government approval for the vaccine likely made its use more common.
11. A, Live virus vaccines generally give longer-lasting protection than dead virus vaccines.
12. D, The Sabin vaccine provides longer-lasting protection than does the Salk vaccine.
13. C, The diagram shows that the airway narrows and the mucus layer thickens.
14. A, Dust and pollen are typical allergens.
15. D, Tightening of the airways causes shortness of breath.
16. A, The passage states that most AIDS patients die from infections.

LESSON 14, *pp. 67–71*

1. D, Darwin infers that smaller eyes would be less prone to inflammation and therefore would be beneficial to burrowing animals.
2. D, Darwin inferred that the finch species evolved from a single species.

UNIT 1 (*continued*)

3. C, Darwin used his observations to infer how the different beaks may have developed.

4. D, Beak size and shape is related to the type of food that each bird eats; since Bird A and Bird B have different-sized beaks, they probably eat different foods.

5. A, The land on which the mussel beds were found must have been located below the high-tide level prior to the earthquake.

6. D, The observations deal with resource availability and population size.

7. A, Organisms with beneficial traits are more likely to survive and to pass those traits to their offspring; those without such traits are less likely to survive and reproduce.

8. C, Fossils showing the evolution of modern traits support the inference that the fossil record would show the evolution of modern organisms.

9. D, The light moth population decreased from 243 to 150 after the factories were built, and the dark moth population increased from 104 to 227.

10. A, The light moth population was larger when tree trunks were lighter.

11. D, Darwin states that Europe is a relatively small area of the world, and that rock layers represent only small segments of Earth's history.

12. C, The existence of similar species on different continents shows that organisms can exist in different locations and may not be preserved in all of them.

13. D, Darwin's writings indicate that he understood that rock layers in Europe contain only a small fraction of all fossils.

14. B, A larger proportion of damaged shells are dark pink.

15. B, White clams are the same color as the sand on this beach, making them more difficult for seagulls to locate.

16. C, White clams are more likely to survive and reproduce.

17. B, The passage states that the brown coat helps the fox blend into its surroundings. It is a reasonable inference that the winter white coat serves the same purpose.

LESSON 15, *pp. 72–76*

1. B, The white-flower trait is not present in the first generation, but it reappears in the second generation.

2. D, Only plants with two copies of the white-flower trait produce white flowers. Thus, the trait is recessive.

3. B, Although both parent flowers had one copy of the purple-flower trait and one copy of the white-flower trait, they produced flowers that were both purple and white in color.

4. B, A pea plant has white flowers only if both its parents pass on a copy of the white-flower trait.

5. A, The diagram shows that C nucleotides always pair with G nucleotides.

6. D, Nucleotides contain bases, and there are four possible bases.

7. D, Watson and Crick proposed the structure of DNA in 1953.

8. B, The diagram shows that pea plants have two copies of the flower-color gene.

9. D, The forms of a pea plant's seed-color trait determines the color of its seeds.

10. A, The green seeds in the Punnett square have two copies of the green-seed form of the gene; the other seeds are yellow.

11. D, 75% of the offspring of a heterozygous cross are expected to show the dominant trait.

12. C, A cross between homozygous dominant and homozygous recessive plants produces all heterozygous plants.

13. C, An organism with at least one dominant form of a gene will express the dominant trait.

14. B, All pea plants with at least one copy of the smooth-seed form of the gene have smooth seeds.

15. B, A recessive trait appears only in homozygous individuals.

LESSON 16, *pp. 77–81*

1. B, The paragraph states that producers can make their own food, and in most ecosystems, producers are organisms that use energy from sunlight. The generalization that follows is that most producers use sunlight to make food.

2. A, A community is made up of different populations, and each population is made up of a single species.

3. B, Communities in different ecosystems contain different populations.

4. B, Different living things need different amounts of water and sunlight and varying temperature ranges to survive.

5. C, The paragraph states that most organisms survive best under a narrow range of conditions.

6. B, More than half of adults in the United States do not exercise on a regular basis.

7. C, Difference in amount of physical activity can be seen across some racial or ethnic groups.

8. C, Drinking large amounts of alcohol can lead to physical and mental health issues.

9. A, The text clearly indicates that underage drinking is an issue in the U.S.

10. C, Male and female condoms can protect against sexually transmitted diseases.

11. A, None of the birth control types listed can fully protect against pregnancy.

12. B, A healthy relationship between a parent and child can be beneficial to a child's well-being.

13. B, Families with lower incomes often have diets that are not as healthy as families with higher incomes.

14. C, Higher-income families have a longer life expectancy that lower-income families. They also tend to eat healthier diets, so better diet is correlated with longer, healthier lives.

15. D, In exponential population growth, the more time that passes, the faster and larger the population grows.

16. D, A downward curve in the line would represent a population decrease.

LESSON 17, *pp. 82–86*

1. D, In a mutualistic relationship, both species benefit.

2. C, The orchids must benefit for the relationship to be commensal.

3. B, In a mutualistic relationship, both species benefit.

UNIT 1 (continued)

4. B, The graph shows how changes in one population affect the size of the other population.

5. A, If this graph is similar to graphs of other predator-prey relationships, this graph could help you learn more about predator-prey relationships in general.

6. C, To understand why predation and parasitism have similar effects, you first must understand the differences between them.

7. C, In a mutualistic relationship, both species benefit.

8. C, The meaning of the arrows is a key piece of information needed to interpret the diagram.

9. A, Competition is one type of relationship between organisms.

10. C, The diagram shows feeding relationships, so an arrow pointing away from the icefish would be pointing toward an organism that preys on the icefish.

11. B, Water quality changes could cause illness throughout the herd.

12. A, Well water would be more likely to be free of contaminants.

13. D, Dr. Goodall's research focused on learning about chimpanzee society and comparing it to human society.

14. B, The ecologist would be most likely to know how different animal societies work.

15. D, It is assumed that Dr. Goodall's interests motivated her research.

16. D, The paragraph is about colony collapse disorder.

17. D, The graph shows the percentages of various crops that are pollinated by honeybees.

18. D, Scientists would need to know the cause(s) of colony collapse disorder.

19. D, To understand why meerkats cooperate, it is necessary to understand why they do not continually breed.

20. B, As with meerkats, humans spend most of their time raising their young instead of breeding.

UNIT 1 REVIEW, *pp. 87–91*

1. C, At point X, the slope of the curve becomes zero, so the population is no longer growing.

2. A, A limited food supply would restrict the population of a species to a certain level.

3. A, The paragraph describes two types of plant adaptations.

4. C, Denitrifying bacteria convert nitrate into gaseous nitrogen.

5. C, Both parents had one *p* trait.

6. D, Three-quarters of the offspring will have at least one purple-flower trait.

7. B, Kelp make their own food.

8. D, No arrow points from the kelp to the sea star.

9. C, Sea otters eat many of the organisms in the ecosystem.

10. B, Darwin states that the low temperatures of the islands are probably due to the cold polar current.

11. B, The last red wolves were taken from the wild in 1980, and the first pups were born in captivity in 1988.

12. B, The timeline shows that red wolf populations did not recover until both species protection laws and captive breeding programs were implemented.

13. D, Carnivores may eat herbivores, omnivores, or other carnivores.

14. D, The paragraph describes differences between viruses and living things.

15. D, Unlike living things, viruses cannot reproduce themselves.

16. B, The tracking devices can tell scientists whether the bear is still alive.

17. D, Acidic water removes magnesium and calcium from the soil.

UNIT 2 PHYSICAL SCIENCE

LESSON 1, *pp. 94–98*

1. C, The diagram shows that the particles in solids are closer together than those in liquids or gases.

2. D, The diagram shows that the energy change between liquid and gas is much greater than the energy change between solid and liquid.

3. D, The diagram shows that approximately six times as much energy is needed to convert liquid to gas than is needed to convert solid to liquid.

4. D, The diagram shows that the temperature of the system does not change during melting and evaporation.

5. B, A substance's melting and freezing points are the same. Point B represents the temperature at which water begins to melt.

6. C, The diagram shows that fixed shape is a property of solids only.

7. A, The diagram shows that only gases are compressible.

8. C, Sublimation involves a change from a solid to a gas; freezing involves a change from a liquid to a solid. The difference in particle spacing between gases and solids is much larger than that between liquids and solids.

9. D, The freezing point of *tert*-butyl alcohol is approximately 25°C; the boiling point of water is 100°C.

10. C, In the diagram, the range of temperatures that results in solid, liquid, and gaseous states of *tert*-butyl alcohol overlaps with the liquid state of water.

11. D, The melting point of water is higher than –50°C, so it will not melt; the sublimation point of carbon dioxide is between –100°C and –50°C, so it will sublimate.

12. C, Distillation can be used to separate mixtures of liquids; alcohol and gasoline are both liquids.

13. D, The original liquid is heated until it boils and produces vapor. The vapor is then cooled so it condenses back into a liquid.

14. A, The product of a distillation is enriched in the liquid with the lower boiling point, which, in this case, is ethanol.

15. B, The cold water absorbs heat from the vapor, causing it to cool and condense.

16. A, As the difference in boiling points of the two liquids decreases, the degree of enrichment of the distillation product in one of the liquids also decreases.

LESSON 2, *pp. 99–103*

1. B, Elements with larger atomic numbers have greater atomic weights.

UNIT 2 (continued)

2. D, Magnesium fluoride's boiling point is more than 800° C higher than the next highest boiling point.

3. D, The table shows that ionic compounds tend to have higher boiling points than covalent compounds.

4. B, Both hydrogen fluoride and hydrogen sulfide boil below room temperature, so they will exist as gases at room temperature.

5. D, All but two of the noble gases are used in lighting.

6. B, The table's footnote indicates that some noble gases have specific uses in liquid form.

7. D, Of the answer choices, iodine is the only micronutrient.

8. D, Of the answer choices, copper is the only micronutrient; 0.0004 g over a lifetime is much less than 0.1 g per day, so the element in question must be a micronutrient.

9. D, The table shows that calcium is involved in muscle contraction.

10. B, The table shows that sodium is involved in nerve and muscle functioning.

11. B, The table shows that micronutrients and macronutrients are involved in the proper functioning of the muscular, nervous, immune, skeletal, and endocrine systems.

12. B, Atomic mass increases as you move down a column and to the right across a row.

13. C, Atomic number is the number at the top of an element's box on the periodic table.

14. C, Elements in the same column have similar properties.

15. D, Nonmetals are found on the upper right side of the periodic table.

16. D,B, Metalloids have characteristics of both metals and nonmetals.

17. A, Francium has the lowest melting point of the metals listed in the table.

18. A, The heaviest elements have the lowest melting points.

LESSON 3, pp. 104–108

1. A, The text states that each hydrogen atom has one electron, and the model shows that the molecule has two electrons. So the total number of electrons remains the same.

2. A, The paragraph states that the electron is located outside the proton and exists in a cloud around it.

3. B, Showing the atom as an illustrated model allows the location of the electron to be specified.

4. B, A three-dimensional model cannot be shown on two-dimensional paper.

5. C, The left-hand model shows that the hydrogen atoms share two electrons to form a bond.

6. A, The ball-and-stick model can be used to show how the atoms in a molecule are positioned.

7. A, The hydrogen atoms in a water molecule are slightly positively charged, and the oxygen atom is slightly negatively charged.

8. C, The model shows that the atoms in the water molecule form a roughly triangular shape.

9. B, The diagram shows that the two electrons present before bonding are shared between the atoms after bonding.

10. D, The equation shows that two hydrogen molecules and one oxygen molecule are the reactants, and energy and two water molecules are the products.

11. B, The equation shows that two hydrogen molecules and one oxygen molecule are required to produce two water molecules so it would take 100 hydrogen molecules and 50 oxygen molecules to produce 100 molecules of water.

12. D, Electrolysis is the reverse of the formation of water, so the equation representing it should be the reverse of the equation representing the formation of water.

13. B, Water molecules will move from an area of higher concentration to one of lower concentration.

14. D, The enzyme allows the substrates to combine.

15. C, Molecule E forms when the substrates combine.

16. C, The model shows the synthesis of two substrates to form a single product.

17. D, The paragraph states that substrates fit specifically into the reaction sites on an enzyme.

18. D, The model shows the two substrates binding to the enzyme before the reaction occurs.

19. A, If the arrows were reversed, the model would show a substance breaking apart with the help of an enzyme. This process is hydrolysis.

LESSON 4, pp. 109–113

1. C, If the water rose 1/5 of the way up the tube, the volume of gas in the tube must have decreased by 1/5; if only oxygen was removed from the air in the tube, then 1/5 of the air was oxygen.

2. D, The diagram shows that calcium reacted more strongly than zinc, and zinc reacted more strongly than copper.

3. C, Because both calcium and zinc reacted with acid, they must appear above hydrogen in the activity series.

4. B, When paper burns, new substances form.

5. D, During a chemical reaction, new substances form.

6. C, The table shows that the properties of sodium chloride are very different from those of sodium or chlorine.

7. C, The table indicates that the two reactants are a metal and a nonmetal.

8. B, Substances B and C both conduct heat and electricity well; these are characteristics of metals.

9. B, Most metals are not brittle and will bend, not break, when hit with a hammer.

10. C, Ionic compounds generally have higher melting points than covalent compounds.

11. A, Ionic compounds conduct electricity when dissolved in water, but covalent compounds do not.

12. D, Table salt is an ionic compound, and table sugar is a covalent compound. Ionic compounds generally have higher melting points than covalent compounds.

13. A, A brittle substance is not easily stretched into wires.

14. C, The formation of bubbles indicates the formation of a gas.

15. D, Chemical reactions generally involve a change in appearance.

16. A, In an exothermic reaction, the products have less energy than the reactants.

17. D, An endothermic reaction absorbs heat from its surroundings.

UNIT 2 (continued)

LESSON 5, pp. 114–118

1. B, HBr, HI, HCl, and HF are all acids.

2. D, The first equation represents the mixing of two bases, which will probably produce no reaction. The second equation represents the mixing of an acid and a salt, which will probably produce no reaction. The third equation represents the mixing of an acid and a base, which will result in a reaction.

3. C, One molecule of HCl produces one hydrogen ion; one molecule of H_2SO_4 produces two hydrogen ions. Acidity increases as the number of hydrogen ions increases.

4. D, The Li and Cl ions will combine to form the salt. The hydrogen and hydroxide ions will combine to form water.

5. C, The reaction of an acid and a base produces a salt and water.

6. A, The K and Br ions must come from the base and the acid, respectively.

7. D, Acids have pH values less than 7.

8. B, An H^+ concentration of 1×10^{-7} is equivalent to a pH of 7; an H^+ concentration of 1×10^{-6} is equivalent to a pH of 6.

9. C, Only solutions 5, 6, and 7 are bases.

10. B, If pure water is added to an acid, the acid's pH increases.

11. B, Further addition of sodium hydroxide to the solution will continue to make the solution more basic, so the blue litmus paper will remain blue.

12. D, Strong bases have high pH values and will turn red litmus paper blue.

13. C, The resulting pH will be partway between the pH of the acid and the pH of the base.

14. C, One molecule of sodium hydroxide is required to neutralize each molecule of hydrochloric acid.

15. C, When a strong acid completely reacts with a strong base, a neutral solution results.

16. C, The concentration of H^+ ions in a solution of a weak acid is lower than that in a solution of a strong acid.

LESSON 6, pp. 119–123

1. C, The scooter's total displacement is 0 miles, because it returns to its starting point. It travels 8 miles total in 40 minutes, which is equivalent to 12 miles in one hour.

2. D, The product of 3 and 5 is 15.

3. C, If mass increases but force remains constant, acceleration must decrease.

4. D, The force the floor applies to the person is equal in magnitude to the person's weight.

5. D, A person with a mass of 65 kg has a weight of 637 newtons, and the upward force from the floor is equal to the person's weight.

6. C, Each side of the block is 400 m. Person 1 walks one side (400 m); Person 2 walks three sides (3 × 400 m = 1,200 m).

7. C, Displacement is the straight-line distance between two points; it does not depend on the path taken between the points. Person 1 and Person 2 both travel from Point A to Point B; Point A and Point B are 400 m apart.

8. B, Speed is distance (100 mi) divided by time (5 hr), so the bird's speed is 20 mi/hr. Point B is east of Point A, so the bird flies eastward.

9. B, The bird's total displacement is 0 mi, so its total velocity is 0 mi/hr.

10. D, Velocity is equal to the product of acceleration and time (9.8 m/s^2 downward × 3 s = 29.4 m/s downward).

11. B, Gravity will continue to accelerate the object, increasing its velocity.

12. C, The total force is equal to the difference between the two forces (15 N – 5 N = 10 N). It points in the direction of the stronger force (left).

13. D, The ball will move in the direction of the stronger force.

14. A, The total force is equal to the difference between the two forces (15 N – 10 N = 5 N).

15. D, For the box to move, the pushing force on it must be greater than the frictional force on it.

16. B, If μ decreases, frictional force decreases, and less pushing force is required to overcome frictional force.

17. A, The arrows representing the two forces are the same length and point in opposite directions, so they are balanced forces.

18. D, If the wagon is moving to the right, the pulling force must be stronger than the frictional force.

LESSON 7, pp. 124–128

1. B, The diagram shows that the lever transforms a downward force into an upward force.

2. C, A single, fixed pulley does not change the amount of force required.

3. B, A block and tackle reduces the amount of force required to lift an object.

4. D, A pulley system that changes a downward force into an upward force would allow you to pull downward with your weight and use the resulting force to lift an object.

5. A, Single pulleys do not change the amount of work that is done to lift an object.

6. B, A ramp reduces the amount of force needed to lift an object, so it can be used to lift an object that is too heavy to lift straight up.

7. A, Shortening the length of the ramp will make it steeper, so more force will be required to push the box up the ramp.

8. C, The diagram shows that the output force is larger than the input force.

9. A, Less force is needed to turn the screw than the screw exerts on the material through which it is moving.

10. A, The shank is the axle, and the handle is the wheel. A large movement of the wheel translates into a smaller, but more forceful, movement of the axle.

11. D, Wheels and axles transfer rotational motion.

12. B, The graph shows a direct relationship between length and mechanical advantage.

13. D, Pulleys, wheels and axles, and levers are involved in moving a bicycle.

14. D, A pair of scissors contains more than one simple machine.

15. D, All of the machines in the table have mechanical advantages greater than 1.

16. B, Wedge B has a larger mechanical advantage than Wedge A.

UNIT 2 (continued)

LESSON 8, pp. 129–133

1. C, At 50 seconds, the rocket has no kinetic energy.
2. C, The two bars on the graph are at the same length for the 2015 data point.
3. C, Many more incandescent bulbs than CFLs are needed to produce 1,000 hours of light.
4. D, About 13 incandescent bulbs are needed to produce 1,000 hours of light; twice as many would be needed to produce 2,000 hours.
5. B, Many more light bulbs are present in the coal 2030 column than in any of the other 2030 columns.
6. C, The number of light bulbs in the nuclear 2030 column is only about 100 billion kilowatt-hours greater than the number in the nuclear 2006 column.
7. A, The pictograph shows that China has approximately 50 years of coal remaining.
8. B, According to the pictograph, the United States has the second-largest coal reserves, and those reserves will run out in approximately 230 years.
9. D, The graph shows that the total mechanical (kinetic + potential) energy of the car was about 1.5 J lower at the end of the experiment than it was at the beginning, and energy cannot be destroyed.
10. C, The line representing the efficiency of System A is always higher than the lines representing Systems B and C.
11. D, The legend shows that the pink bar represents the amount of energy that comes from the electric company, and the red bar shows the amount of energy that comes from the wind turbine.
12. C, The red bar is largest on day 3.
13. B, The pink bar is smallest on day 2.
14. A, The red bar reaches to approximately 9 on the vertical axis for day 1, and the units on the vertical axis are kilowatt-hours.
15. A, The graph shows that the business got a significant portion of its energy from the wind turbine.
16. B, It is logical to assume that two turbines can harvest twice as much energy from the wind as one turbine, thus reducing the amount of energy needed from the electric company.

LESSON 9, pp. 134–138

1. B, The crest is the distance between the resting position and the highest point on the wave.
2. C, The wavelength remains constant. Thus you can conclude that pitch remains constant.
3. D, As amplitude decreases, loudness decreases.
4. C, The amplitude of the wave is decreasing with time. As amplitude decreases, loudness decreases.
5. C, Lawn mowers, jackhammers, and jet engines produce sounds above 85 dB.
6. A, Conversation has the lowest volume, so its sound waves must have the smallest amplitude.
7. B, Sound waves are longitudinal waves, and longitudinal waves produce compressions and rarefactions.

8. D, Sound waves are longitudinal waves, and particles vibrate parallel to the direction that longitudinal waves travel.
9. C, Light waves are transverse waves, and transverse waves have crests and troughs.
10. B, The diagram shows that Rayleigh waves move the crust in circular paths.
11. A, The paragraph states that Rayleigh waves travel along the boundary between Earth's crust and the atmosphere; trees grow in Earth's crust, so the Rayleigh wave moves the tree as it travels along Earth's crust.
12. D, The diagram shows that microwaves have longer wavelengths than infrared waves.
13. D, The diagram shows that red light has the longest of the wavelengths.
14. A, The diagram shows that blue light has a shorter wavelength than orange light and that energy increases as wavelength decreases.
15. B, The colors of light that make up white light have a wavelength range of 400 nm to 700 nm.
16. D, If the wavelength is the same, the wave with the greatest speed will have the highest frequency.

LESSON 10, pp. 139–143

1. B, If testing shows that a hypothesis is invalid, the hypothesis should be modified.
2. D, The table shows that organisms start to die at pH 6, and milk is the only substance with a pH higher than 6.
3. A, These data can be used to assess the effects of other acids, such as acid rain, on ecosystems.
4. C, The data show that only four of the five liquids are acidic enough to be toxic.
5. A, The data show that the hypothesis is not completely valid, so it must be modified and retested.
6. D, The data show that rainbow trout start to die at the least acidic pH.
7. B, Scientific ideas can be changed or discarded if contradictory evidence is found.
8. D, When new data contradict an established hypothesis, the hypothesis must be modified to account for the new data.
9. D, Most scientific questions stem from observations, and hypotheses are possible answers to scientific questions.
10. A, To form a hypothesis, a scientist uses his or her knowledge to make an educated guess as to the answer to a question.
11. C, A valid scientific theory can be used to make predictions.
12. C, A hypothesis is a possible answer to a single scientific question; a theory is an explanation for a larger range of observations.
13. B, The passage states that a scientific theory must be potentially falsifiable.
14. D, Scientific theories may be replaced if they cannot explain new observations.
15. B, Recording an experiment with a video camera with narration would allow the scientists to record all parts of the experiment accurately.

UNIT 2 (continued)

16. C, Once data have been tested, they must be analyzed before the hypothesis can be evaluated.

17. B, It is important to assemble all necessary equipment and materials before beginning an experiment so that the experiment can proceed smoothly.

18. D, If the freezing point change was small enough, no change would be observed, even though it was present.

19. B, The experiment tested only the effects of sugar, not of impurities in general.

LESSON 11, *pp. 144–148*

1. D, The diagram shows that most of the iron filings are concentrated at the ends of the magnet.

2. B, The diagram shows that a north pole attracts a south pole but repels another north pole.

3. D, The paragraph states that magnetic field lines run in a specific direction.

4. D, If like poles are together, the magnets will repel each other; if opposite poles are together, the magnets will attract each other.

5. B, Iron filings will align themselves with a magnet's magnetic field.

6. A, Magnets attract each other if their opposite poles are facing.

7. D, Ancient navigators used lodestone as a rudimentary compass.

8. C, Because magnetite particles in rock indicate the direction of Earth's magnetic poles at the time that the rock formed, they can be used to infer that continents have moved over time.

9. A, If Earth's magnetic poles switched places in the past, magnetite particles in the rocks that formed at those times would be aligned opposite of particles that form today.

10. C, Substances used to produce magnetic surfaces must be able to maintain a magnetic field.

11. D, Iron is ferromagnetic, and ferromagnetic materials are strongly attracted to magnetic fields and retain magnetic properties after they are exposed to a magnetic field.

12. A, The switch controls the flow of electricity through a circuit.

13. B, Replacing the switch would allow the researcher to test whether the new material would conduct electricity and allow the circuit to close.

14. B, In a parallel circuit, the remaining lights will stay lit if one burns out.

15. B, As long as there are materials in the battery to keep the reaction going, chemical energy will be released and changed to electrical energy and then to heat and light energy as the current passes through the filament of the light bulb.

16. C, Once the circuit is broken, the flow of electricity stops, and the changing of one form of energy to another stops.

17. D, If the electric current in an electromagnet is removed, the electromagnet is no longer magnetic.

18. D, The diagram shows that the flux lines form concentric circles from the north pole to the south pole, just as they do in a normal bar magnet.

19. A, The electric current produces the magnetic field, so reversing the direction of current flow would reverse the direction of the flux lines.

20. D, Ferromagnetic materials retain magnetic properties after they are exposed to a magnetic field.

UNIT 2 REVIEW, *pp. 149–153*

1. B, The mechanical advantage of Machine B is 10; this is the largest mechanical advantage of the machines listed.

2. B, The product of 25 and 4 is 100.

3. C, If the rays are impossible to detect, there is no way to show that they do or do not exist.

4. A, Scientific theories are rejected in favor of new theories if the new theories can explain new data that the older theories could not.

5. A, The leftward force is much greater than the rightward force.

6. D, Potential energy decreases as the point on the ramp decreases.

7. A, The graph shows that potential energy is highest when kinetic energy is lowest.

8. C, If the direction of the current is reversed, the magnetic field polarity also will reverse.

9. D, The particles in a transverse wave vibrate perpendicular to the wave's direction of travel.

10. A, Longitudinal waves cause particles to vibrate parallel to the wave's direction of motion.

11. B, Molecule B contains three carbon atoms.

12. A, In a single-displacement reaction, a pure element reacts with a compound to form a new compound and a different pure element.

13. D, In a double-displacement reaction, the ions in two compounds switch places.

14. D, Point D is located in the region of the graph that represents the vaporization of liquid water into gas.

15. B, Of the answer choices, ammonia has the highest pH.

UNIT 3 EARTH/SPACE SCIENCE

LESSON 1, *pp. 156–160*

1. C, If Wegener's hypothesis states that continents constantly move, in several million years they will be in different positions than they are today.

2. A, The "fit" of Africa and South America was one of the pieces of evidence Wegener used to support his hypothesis.

3. C, If the continents once had been joined, the same organisms would probably have lived on both continents. Finding fossils of the same organisms on both continents therefore would suggest that the continents once were joined.

4. A, Unlike a hypothesis, a theory explains a large number of observations.

5. B, The passage states that the theory explains the formation of volcanoes and mountains.

6. B, If *Mesosaurus* could swim well, it might have swum across the Atlantic Ocean from Africa to South America.

7. C, Remnants of a land bridge from the time when *Mesosaurus* lived would support the idea that the animals traveled over a land bridge.

UNIT 3 (continued)

8. D, According to the text, Wegener's hypothesis states that Africa and South America once were connected, so the same fossils would be expected to exist in both areas.

9. C, If the two continents once were joined, it was likely that the same animals lived on both continents.

10. D, The map shows that an ice sheet covered parts of Africa 300 million years ago.

11. C, The map shows that parts of South America and Africa were once covered by ice sheets, which indicates that they were much colder.

12. A, The age of the ocean floor and the correlation of volcanoes and earthquakes with plate boundaries were unknown when Wegener developed the continental drift hypothesis.

13. B, Observations regarding the age of the ocean floor and the distribution of volcanoes and earthquakes were gathered long after Wegener developed the continental drift hypothesis.

14. C, If new seafloor is produced at the ridge, then seafloor would be expected to get older as you move away from the ridge.

15. A, Seafloor spreading provides a mechanism for continents to move.

16. D, The map shows that most earthquakes occur along plate boundaries.

LESSON 2, pp. 161–165

1. A, The callout states that lithosphere consists of the crust and the upper mantle, so it must be thicker than the crust alone.

2. C, The diagram shows that melting happens in the mantle.

3. A, The text and diagram indicate that volcanoes are common at plate boundaries.

4. A, The text and diagram state that most erosion occurs where water flows fastest, and water flows fastest on the outside of a meander.

5. A, The diagram shows that rock and soil are deposited on the inside of a meander, and the text states that the water flows slowest on the inside of a meander.

6. D, The diagram shows that the epicenter is the point on the surface that is directly above the focus.

7. A, The diagram shows waves of earthquake energy radiating outward from the focus.

8. B, The text states that an earthquake happens when rock beneath Earth's surface moves.

9. B, Volcanoes erupt ash and lava, which build up in layers on the surface.

10. C, Volcanoes grow as the erupted ash and lava build up. From this information, a logical inference is that when they first form and have erupted very little material, they are small.

11. B, The diagram shows that Mount Saint Helens was shorter after the eruption than it was before.

12. A, The melted rock that erupted came from the magma chamber below the surface; the force of the eruption blew off large pieces of rock from the mountain.

13. A, The diagram shows that convection currents in the mantle can cause plates to move.

14. A, The diagram shows that tectonic plates are made of lithosphere.

15. C, Trenches occur where plates collide and one plate sinks beneath another.

16. D, As the ledges collapse, the waterfall moves upstream.

17. C, The diagram shows that the water in the stream wears away the softer rock under the waterfall.

18. D, Rising mantle rock melts to form the magma that forms the new ocean crust.

LESSON 3, pp. 166–170

1. C, The burial of plant matter by sediment is the second box in the flowchart.

2. C, The flowchart shows that heat and pressure can change igneous rock into metamorphic rock.

3. B, A cycle is, by definition, continuous.

4. D, The flowchart shows that any rock type can be changed to any other rock type given the right conditions.

5. B, The diagram shows that magma results from melting rock.

6. D, The diagram shows that heat and pressure produce metamorphic rocks.

7. C, The diagram shows that igneous rock can be coarse-grained, fine-grained, or glassy.

8. B, Lava that erupts at a volcano cools quickly, so it is likely to form glassy igneous rock and fine-grained rock.

9. B, The cooling rate of melted rock determines the size of the grains in the resulting igneous rock.

10. A, The diagram shows that slow-cooling magma forms coarse-grained rock.

11. D, Evaporation occurs when liquid water changes to water vapor.

12. A, Rain droplets form as cloud droplets grow larger.

13. B, Precipitation occurs due to condensation in clouds.

14. A, If any part of the water cycle stopped working, the cycle would stop.

15. B, Clouds form when water vapor condenses to form tiny droplets.

16. A, Increased evaporation would increase the concentration of salt in a body of water.

17. B, If the river water carries more sediment, then more sediment will be deposited on the delta, and it will grow larger.

18. A, If sediment could not flow downstream, it could not be deposited on the delta.

19. B, The weight of the rock causes the cliff to collapse, and weight is the force of gravity on an object.

20. B, Waves would continue to wear away the collapsed cliff.

LESSON 4, pp. 171–175

1. D, The stream is at the bottom of a canyon in the second diagram.

2. B, The two diagrams show that the spit became larger over time, so it is reasonable to assume that it did not exist prior to the first illustration.

3. A, Illustration B shows a baymouth bar in place of the spit in Illustration A. It also shows the longshore current flowing in the same direction in both illustrations. It's logical to assume that the current further built up the spit.

UNIT 3 (continued)

4. D, The higher runoff in Stream A suggests that the soil in its watershed did not absorb as much rainwater.

5. D, The graphs show that there was more water in Stream A than in Stream B.

6. D, The sea cut through the headland to form a cave and then a sea stack.

7. A, Over time, the water eroded the rock in the headland, making the cave deeper.

8. B, Mountain A's maximum elevation is lower than Mountain B's maximum elevation.

9. B, Steeper mountains generally experience more erosion.

10. D, The glacier eroded the rock in the valley, making it U-shaped instead of V-shaped.

11. A, The glacier probably pushed large amounts of rock and soil ahead of it as it moved through the valley, so that rock and soil is probably located at the end of the valley.

12. D, The diagrams show that Krakatoa was much smaller after the eruption than before it.

13. C, If Krakatoa had not erupted since 1883, erosion would have worn it down, making it even shorter.

14. D, Mount St. Helens has erupted more than twice as often as any of the other volcanoes.

15. A, The map shows that most of the volcanoes lie along a relatively straight line.

16. B, The diagram shows that Mount Hood erupted twice in the last 200 years.

17. C, The diagram shows that all of the Washington volcanoes have erupted in the last 200 years, but only one volcano in Oregon has erupted in the last 200 years.

LESSON 5, pp. 176–180

1. B, A passage written by experts and supported by valid data is a reliable source of information.

2. C, The passage is based on scientific research, so it is most likely fact.

3. A, Some people may believe that a different theory is the best explanation for how the solar system formed.

4. A, The timeline shows that galaxies began to form around 12 billion years ago, not long after the Big Bang.

5. C, Data based on scientific research would provide the most accurate information.

6. A, Because scientists have evidence that the Big Bang was the initial event in the formation of our universe, they would disagree with this statement.

7. B, Although scientists have learned much about stars in our universe, there likely is more discovery to come in the future.

8. A, The timeline shows that an average star will become a white dwarf star before it collapses.

9. C, People may have differing opinions as to the best method of determining fossil age.

10. D, Only the discovery of fossils that are more than 3.8 billion years old will support the hypothesis that life started earlier than is presently thought.

11. A, Various people may have differing opinions as to the importance of the telescope to astronomy.

12. A, The definition of astronomy and the areas that it covers are different now than they were in the early 1600s.

13. D, An essay published in a scholarly journal is likely to present the most accurate information of the sources listed.

14. B, The shuttle program continued for more than 20 years after the loss of the shuttle *Challenger* in 1986.

15. A, NASA announced the end of the shuttle program in 2004, about one year after the *Columbia* disaster.

16. D, The amount of energy required for spacecraft to escape Earth's gravity can be measured.

17. B, The significance to the United States space program of future trips to the moon is unknown.

18. D, NASA developed the plan for exploration of the moon, so its details are likely factual.

LESSON 6, pp. 181–185

1. D, Respected newspapers, such as *The New York Times,* are generally considered to be reliable sources of information.

2. C, The most reliable source of information about a decision is the organization that made it.

3. B, Planetariums are generally good sources of scientific information about astronomy.

4. B, A source that gives mainly opinions is not a reliable source.

5. C, More recent information is generally more reliable than older information.

6. D, Expertise in a subject area generally makes one a reliable source about information about that area.

7. B, Some people may disagree with the statement that Pluto is "puny."

8. C, NASA is responsible for space missions, so it is expected that it would include information on those missions in its article.

9. A, Both articles list the criteria identified by the IAU as requirements for planet status.

10. D, A Web site that can be updated by anyone with an Internet connection is probably reviewed frequently.

11. D, The people writing the information may not be experts or reliable sources.

12. B, The passage talks about wind and seasons, and the timeline indicates when scientists learned that Pluto has winds and seasons.

13. C, Objective information is more reliable than fiction.

14. C, Pluto is no longer classified as a planet.

15. A, References should include the most up-to-date information available.

16. A, The table gives quantitative data about the planets, so each planet's mass would be an appropriate addition to the table.

17. C, Average distance is a more accurate measure of the size of a planet's orbit than is absolute distance.

18. A, NASA is the most reliable source for information about our solar system and beyond.

LESSON 7, pp. 186–190

1. B, The paragraph describes problems caused by a lack of clean drinking water, which is exacerbated by lack of sanitation.

UNIT 3 (continued)

2. C, Improving sanitation will improve the health of people in sub-Saharan Africa.

3. D, The graph shows that only 1% of the water on Earth is fresh water.

4. B, Conserving fresh water is the best way to make sure everyone has enough.

5. A, The paragraph states that fresh water is scarce in some parts of the world.

6. C, An assessment of the effectiveness of desalination must include an analysis of its costs and efficiency.

7. B, The map shows the areas on Earth that do not have enough water.

8. C, Areas shown on the map with high water stress are not all desert areas.

9. C, Southern Africa does not have as much water stress as northern Africa does, and building a pipeline between them would be within the technological capabilities of our current society.

10. C, If an area has enough precipitation or groundwater, it will have enough fresh water for its residents.

11. C, Some areas are far from reaching their 2015 goals.

12. B, Increasing access to clean water will move the regions closer to their 2015 goals.

13. A, The passage lists several diseases spread by unclean water.

14. D, Most developing countries are poor.

15. B, The paragraph describes how modern agricultural practices can lead to water contamination.

16. D, The passage suggests that rotating crops will reduce the negative effects of agriculture on water supplies.

17. D, Much of the water pollution from farming comes from chemical fertilizers and pesticides.

18. B, One of the proposed solutions is allowing animals to graze over larger areas.

19. A, The passage states that any alternative farming methods must still produce enough food to feed everyone.

LESSON 8, pp. 191–195

1. C, An explosive Big Bang would have caused galaxies to fly apart, meaning that they are farther apart now than they were 50 years ago.

2. C, Dinosaurs became extinct about 65 million years ago.

3. B, Dinosaurs lived only during the Mesozoic era and were its dominant life form until becoming extinct.

4. D, The table shows that echinoderms evolved hundreds of millions of years before mammals did.

5. C, The earliest forms of life on Earth lived in the water.

6. C, The rows in the table are arranged with the oldest time periods at the bottom and the most recent at the top.

7. A, In the diagram, the jawed fish fossil is in the part of the rock layers labeled "Paleozoic Era." More precisely, it is shown at about halfway through the Paleozoic layer, indicating that the animal came into existence in the middle of the Paleozoic.

8. B, The passage explains that that the rate of decay for any given isotope is constant. Thus, the more decay product present, the older the rock.

9. A, The diagram indicates that dinosaurs lived during the Mesozoic Era.

10. C, Because jawless fish appear much lower in the rock column in the diagram than early mammals, it is safe to conclude that a rock column in which jawless fish appear above early mammals has been disturbed at some time in the past.

11. A, The passage implies that Americans use more water than they need.

12. A, Industry and agriculture are two of the largest consumers of fresh water.

13. B, For the test to be valid, all conditions except the condition being tested should be kept the same.

14. A, The hypothesis that areas without trees and foliage are generally warmer than areas with trees and foliage can be tested and disproved.

15. D, The flowchart indicates that water on the surface must be warmed by the sun in order to evaporate as water vapor.

16. C, The flowchart indicates that rain falls when drops grow large and heavy enough to be pulled to Earth by gravity.

17. C, The passage indicates that the pattern of visible constellations changes throughout the year as Earth revolves around the sun.

18. A, Because stars move over time, a constellation will not look exactly as it does now in the future.

UNIT 3 REVIEW, pp. 196–200

1. B, Most sinkholes form when acidic water dissolves rock below the ground.

2. D, Limestone bedrock is most susceptible to chemical weathering by rainwater.

3. A, Quotes from people involved in making a decision are generally good sources of information about the decision.

4. B, The person interviewed disagrees with the IAU's decision, and the article probably describes why.

5. B, The diagram shows vents on the side of the volcano, and lava comes out of vents.

6. B, The diagram shows that the volcano is made of layers of lava and ash.

7. B, The diagram shows that very large hail is carried downward by a downdraft.

8. C, The diagram shows that both small and large pieces of hail can fall to the ground.

9. D, The diagram shows that hailstones rise and sink in clouds due to rising and sinking air.

10. A, No evidence has been found for life on Mars and its presence there is speculative.

11. C, A diagram showing the locations and orbits of the planets would illustrate that the first group is closer to the sun and the second group is farther away.

12. A, If undrinkable water can safely be used to irrigate crops, then using drinkable water to irrigate them is a waste of drinkable water.

13. B, The graph shows that power plants are the second largest consumers of fresh water.

14. C, The graph shows that the largest percentage of freshwater use in the United States is to water crops, including feed crops.

UNIT 3 *(continued)*

15. D, The diagram shows that about 80% of the fresh water used in the United States is used for some form of power generation or agriculture.

16. B, The passage states that most of the energy we use is produced by the combustion of fossils fuels, which has been pouring carbon dioxide into the atmosphere for hundreds of years. Therefore, the problem identified is that an excess amount of carbon dioxide is entering the atmosphere.

17. C, The passage states that several alternative energy sources that are not widely used do not produce carbon dioxide as a waste gas. The passage is suggesting that using more of these alternative sources is a possible solution.

18. A, Development of cars, busses, and trucks that use alternative fuel methods would be necessary to reduce the amount of fossil fuels used to power motor vehicles.

19. C, The passage basically contrasts the negative effects on the natural environment of the river below the dam and the land that was flooded to create the reservoir behind it with the advantages of the dam for farmers and for electricity production.

Index

Note: Page numbers in **boldface** indicate definitions or main discussion with examples. Page numbers in *italic* indicate a visual representation. Page ranges indicate practice.

INDEX

INDEX

INDEX

INDEX

INDEX

X

Y

Z